"PROMISE ME YOU'LL SHOOT YOURSELF"

"PROMISE ME YOU'LL SHOOT YOURSELF"

THE MASS SUICIDE OF ORDINARY GERMANS IN 1945

FLORIAN HUBER

Translated by Imogen Taylor

Little, Brown Spark
New York Boston London

Little, Brown Spark
Hachette Book Group
1290 Avenue of the Americas, New York, NY 10104
littlebrownspark.com

First North American edition: March 2020
Originally published in Germany under the title *Kind, versprich mir, dass du dich erschießt* by Berlin Verlag, Piper Verlag GmbH, February 2015
First English edition published in Australia by The Text Publishing Company, June 2019

Little, Brown Spark is an imprint of Little, Brown and Company, a division of Hachette Book Group, Inc. The Little, Brown Spark name and logo are trademarks of Hachette Book Group, Inc.

The publisher is not responsible for websites (or their content) that are not owned by the publisher.

The Hachette Speakers Bureau provides a wide range of authors for speaking events. To find out more, go to hachettespeakersbureau.com or call (866) 376-6591.

ISBN 9780316534307
Library of Congress Control Number: 2019957422

10 9 8 7 6 5 4 3 2 1

LSC-C

Printed in the United States of America

Contents

Contents

Part IV
THE PULL OF SILENCE

Part I

FOUR DAYS IN DEMMIN

River Without Bridges

'We reached another town towards morning. Demmin.'

At the end of the dead-straight avenue, a massive church tower was silhouetted against the dim light of dawn. The rows of sycamores, receding into the distance, led the eye to the tip of the spire, which pointed, needle-like, into the soft pink sky—a tissue-paper cut-out scored with a razor blade, at once slender and powerful, filigree and solid. It was the first time that Irene Bröker had seen anything to break the monotony of the landscape. All she had to do now was to make straight for it.

Irene Bröker was a twenty-three-year-old woman who in late April 1945 was fleeing with her family—or what was left of it—from the north-eastern city of Stettin. Her husband, Werner-Walter, had been missing since the previous autumn, and she had been separated from her parents, father-in-law and sister-in-law during an air raid the day before as they passed through the town of Anklam. Her parents' carriage had been left behind with a broken wheel, while she was shunted out of town in her car, caught up in the dense flow of vehicles, people and horses. When she looked for her family later, she couldn't find them. Only little Holger, her two-year-old son, was still with her. She was careful not to let him stray from her side.

The two of them were not, however, entirely alone; in Löcknitz, a few miles west of Stettin, they had been joined by an elderly doctor and his wife. Like many women faced with hardship after a previously well-ordered life, Irene Bröker had developed remarkable coping skills—not only the ability to suppress all but her most vital emotions, but also the art of finding allies in strangers. Dr P., as Irene Bröker calls the doctor in her memoirs, was to be her greatest support in the days to come. She knew that difficulties lay ahead; she had even provided for a time when she might no longer want to live. On a string around her neck, Irene Bröker carried a small watertight pouch.

Towards morning, then, they arrived in Demmin. For Irene Bröker it was just another name on the escape route; the town surrounding the red-brick church tower that dominated the landscape for miles around held neither memories nor meaning for her. The end of her march lay much further west, beyond the reach of the Russian soldiers.

The horrors of the winter trek—frosty nights and snowstorms on icy roads—were a thing of the past. The second half of April was marked by beautiful spring weather; the countryside was burgeoning. A haze of young green covered the trees and fields; the days were warm, the nights mild. Apart from the occasional shower, there was no rain. But like so many others, Irene Bröker and the doctor and his wife had made only halting progress during the night. By the time they reached the eastern outskirts of Demmin that morning, they were worn out.

> We got bogged on a sandy track and had to abandon some
> luggage to get going again. Many, many valuables had already
> been left by the roadside and in the fields. We stopped on the
> outskirts of Demmin, at a big house next to the cemetery.
> The occupants had fled town that evening. Too exhausted to
> go any further, we treated ourselves to a night's rest.

After many sleepless nights, broken only by the occasional chilly
nap by the roadside when the trek came to a halt, Irene Bröker had
lost all sense of time and was longing for a rest. The stopover in
Demmin wasn't supposed to be more than a quick breather. But
the town was a bottleneck. There were three rivers to be crossed
on the road west.

• • •

A few hundred yards from the house where Irene Bröker slept,
a unit of Wehrmacht soldiers had taken up quarters at a former
Prussian cavalry barracks. Among them was Gustav Adolf Skibbe,
a fifty-three-year-old from the West Prussian city of Elbing. Skibbe
had entered the war late. If the Volkssturm—the old men and
Hitler Youth boys called up to serve as a national militia—were
the country's last reserves, Skibbe was among the second-to-last.
A few months earlier, he'd been hoping to survive the war at home
with his family, but since general mobilisation in January 1943,
the civilian population had been sifted with an ever finer sieve
until he, too, was caught in its mesh. Skibbe was conscripted in
December 1944. Scarcely two months later, his native Elbing
was lost in a fierce battle, and he spent the weeks that followed
far from the action, mainly around Berlin, nearly five hundred kilometres to the south-west. Then, on 14 March, he came to Demmin.
It was four weeks since he'd last seen his family. It was a trying
part of the war for him; there was a lot of waiting and toiling and

standing around on draughty railway stations. His bones ached; he felt his age. 'Wretched night, sore feet,' he writes in the slim note-book he used as a war journal. 'In Oranienburg, thank God, I was given insoles.'

In his journal, Skibbe kept a brief record of the places where he was billeted, his health and—on rare occasions—his emotions. He wasted hardly a word on the war itself, and less still on politics.

In Demmin, Skibbe's unit was billeted in the former Uhlan Barracks on Jarmener Strasse. He was kept busy there—mainly, his journal suggests, servicing and repairing machinery—but he noticed the mood of nervous apprehension that had taken hold of residents and refugees alike. He noticed, too, their growing distrust of the troops who were to defend them.

> Everything at sixes + sevens. Got hold of sawdust mattresses. 3 men, Möller, Schink and I, sleep in backroom. V. prim-itive. People v. subdued, almost desperate because of over-crowding in town.

Days passed 'without much of note'. There was a lot of work to be done. Skibbe concentrated on his machines and, in between times, made the most of the lovely spring weather. On the east side of town, women and schoolchildren dug miles of steep-sided anti-tank ditches and drove wooden stakes into the ground to make tank traps, while the never-ending flow of refugees surged between them into town in dense clutches. The Red Army, which had begun its advance on Western Pomerania, drove them along like water before the bow of a ship.

• • •

Demmin-born Marie Dabs, daughter of a sea captain and wife of the furrier and gentlemen's outfitter Walter Dabs, was familiar with the refugees. Wave after wave of them had passed through town since February, some staying with relatives, others in rooms or dormitories allocated by the billeting office. Most of them carried on westwards, but they were soon replaced by the next lot. Since her husband had been called up, Marie Dabs had been living alone with her children, Nanni, nineteen, and Otto, fifteen, in the flat behind their shop on Luisenstrasse. The billeting office had sent her an elderly refugee woman from Memel, who complained all the time and hogged the kitchen. 'She was forever frying,' Marie Dabs remembered later, 'especially in the evenings.' They had let her have Otto's bedroom, which was soon the worse for wear. When the woman moved on west with her daughter, two young sisters from another refugee family moved in, this time taking over Nanni's newly decorated room.

Forty-two years old, Marie Dabs had lived all her life in the bourgeois milieu of the small district town. An artfully composed photographer's portrait of her shows a woman with carefully pinned-up hair whose face speaks of pride at a prosperous life. Now she was having to share that life with complete strangers from the east, and, seeing the fate of the refugees, she often found herself worrying about her own future. Several times she got as far as deciding to leave town with the children. Her friends the Hansens, landowners who lived near Flensburg, in north-west Germany, had sent telegrams urging her to join them; the suitcases were packed and ready. But Marie Dabs let bureaucrats and military brass convince her to stay and keep the shop up and running; the authorised medal and military-decoration business that she ran alongside the furriery had seen a sudden surge in sales in the past weeks. A Wehrmacht general had bought up her entire stock of medals, explaining that, after so many battles, he'd run out. Marie Dabs could feel the front moving closer.

Once again, though, she let herself be reassured; this time, the local chief of police promised to vouch personally for her safety, if she had to flee with her family. In the meantime, he asked her to put up the wife and child of an SS officer friend of his. Marie Dabs clutched at this straw, trusting the authorities rather than her own inner voice. She would later write in her memoir:

> They joined us for every meal, but the high-ranking SS officer didn't see fit to give me any advice. We couldn't help but wonder, though, when we saw the crowds trekking west along our streets, and the ships of refugees in the harbour. I sincerely hoped that our police chief would keep his promise to bring us to safety along with his wife and daughter!

. . .

Until then, the people of Demmin had known the war only from the newspapers, radio and weekly newsreels. Sometimes, it is true, they were driven into their cellars by the air-raid sirens, but the bombers always flew on, to Stettin or Berlin. On some nights, residents had seen the glow of Anklam, burning on the eastern horizon, and on a few occasions the US bombers had attacked the air base at Tutow, only ten kilometres further east. But not a single bomb had fallen on Demmin. The town was an island in the middle of the war.

Ursula Strohschein, who lived with her parents not far from the Dabs' fur shop in the old town, in Luisenstrasse, had recently returned home from a visit to the ruined wastes of bombed-out Hamburg. After such a harrowing experience, the sight of the undamaged town gave her new hope. 'It wasn't just that I was glad to see it again,' she said. 'I felt blessed, too.' The burgher houses with their pediments and casement windows, the old half-timbered houses, the sixteenth-century tower still standing on Turmstrasse, the Luise Gate beyond, the gently flowing River Peene—all these things made it easy to feel that events might simply pass Demmin by.

Market square, town hall and the church of St Bartholomaeus
in pre-1945 Demmin

But Ursula wasn't stupid, and nor was she deaf or blind. She knew what she'd seen in Hamburg. She'd heard the reports from soldiers home on leave or billeted in Demmin. She knew what had happened to the refugees who had lost their towns and villages to the Russians and were now flooding west in even larger numbers than before—stubbly-whiskered old men in battered hats, stooped grannies, hollow-eyed young women in headscarves with harassed looks on their faces, snotty-nosed children in stinking pants. 'Crammed full of strangers' was Ursula Strohschein's description of Demmin at that time. The 'strangers' inched their way along the streets in halting convoys of carts and barrows and prams, all piled high with swaying towers of the possessions they'd managed to salvage: blankets and pillows, washing baskets, suitcases and rucksacks, wedged and lashed with string. They were a wretched procession, flushed out onto the streets and squares and fields by the ever-advancing front. By late April, the party quartermaster no longer knew what to do with them all. The houses and schools were full to bursting; so were the estates and farms in the surrounding countryside. Those without a roof over their head had to stay in their carts and spend the nights on the road. Even the people of Demmin, so far mere onlookers, had to ask themselves whether to stay or go.

Ursula Strohschein could feel fear and apprehension all through the town. A Hitler Youth banner leader was billeted in her aunt's beautiful burgher house near the marketplace. 'What will become of Demmin?' her aunt asked the young man. 'We'll defend Demmin!' he replied. *We*, Ursula observed drily, meant a handful of Hitler Youth boys and Volkssturm men. 'Herr Banner Leader' did not hang around to discuss the matter, but hurried upstairs to get changed and then made himself scarce.

. . .

On Saturday 28 April, Dr Wilhelm Damann took a walk through the boys' high school in Frauenstrasse, a dark-red building with a pointed ridge turret. Damann had been a teacher himself, but lost his job when the Nazis came to power. Now lessons had been suspended all over town, and the red-brick school had been converted into a military hospital, its corridors filled with wounded and dying soldiers. In the school hall, where leaving ceremonies had once been held in solemn formality, and half-grown men sent forth into the world with edifying words, doctors now cut bullets and shrapnel out of the half-grown men's flesh and sawed off their arms and legs. Today, though, Wilhelm Damann could see from the corridor that the hall was being cleared of wounded men. Those who didn't get a place in a truck or requisitioned removal van had to make do with a horse and cart. When Damann stepped out onto Frauenstrasse again, the street was full of German soldiers, all heading towards Peene Bridge. Fighting against this flow were people carrying boxes and bags crammed full of groceries. The army food stores and depots had been opened. That's when Damann knew it was the beginning of the end: 'Things were starting to fall apart.'

. . .

The Wehrmacht made no secret of their intention to surrender the town and blow up the bridges behind them as they moved west. It was the last chance of escape for any doubters and ditherers. Others had long been preparing for this moment. High-ranking Nazis, leaders of party organisations, the district administrator, the mayor, the head of the grammar school, local officials—such people set off west with few regrets.

From Marie Dab's fur shop, it was only a short walk to the wide market square, and she went to the town hall to talk to the chief of police, who had promised to vouch for her when the time came. What she saw in the square 'beggared belief':

> Our entire police force was sitting on the back of a truck, and the chief stood beside it, ready to join them. He called out to me: 'Do you want to come with us? Jump up!' I stood there, stunned, unable to say a word.

Without the children? Never! Marie Dabs could only stand and watch as the truck drove off—and with it, her last hope of getting out of Demmin in time. Two things struck her at this moment. The first was her betrayal by the chief of police, whose promises she had blindly trusted to the end—and he hadn't been alone in jumping on the truck; all the other policemen in town who'd talked her into staying were complicit in this betrayal. Marie Dabs thought, too, of the high-ranking SS officer whose wife and child had moved in with her. He'd blown in for dinner from time to time but had little to say for himself, although he must have been well informed—and then one day he'd been gone, and his wife with him. There was the Wehrmacht general, too, who'd bought up her entire supply of medals and sworn blithely: 'The Russians won't make it over the River Oder!' She'd never seen him again either. It was the same story with all the people from the party—Otto's Deutsches Jungvolk leader, for example, and the district group leader—they had all spread hope and refused to hear of escape, and now they'd gone and escaped themselves.

Worse, though, than these people's betrayal was that Marie Dabs had believed them rather than herself. 'How naive I was.' She was shocked by her own gullible stupidity, her feeble wait-and-see attitude. Despite having some idea of what was going on and sensing that their lives were at risk, she'd persisted in shutting out the truth and letting herself be hushed. Now it was too late. From this point in her memoirs, Marie Dabs' narrative is shot through with self-reproach, as she accuses herself of having failed herself and her children. 'Why didn't I do it? Why didn't I leave when the Hansens telegraphed me? I did all the wrong things, and cruel fate ran its course.'

Distraught, she returned to the fur shop and called the children. The three of them packed their bags—a small suitcase of groceries, cognac and cigarettes for bartering, and a larger suitcase containing good clothes, an eiderdown and the children's photo albums—and prepared to flee the town. They hid the valuables they couldn't carry in the cellar, along with the medals and military decorations from the shop. Then they tied everything to the luggage racks of their bicycles. Throughout all of this, Marie Dabs didn't for a moment forget that she was the furrier's wife: 'I had on my dark-grey tailor-made suit, a red-and-white blouse and a pair of stout shoes, and carried my two fur coats over my arm.' She cast a last look around the familiar rooms, taking in the white sales cabinets, the racks of shirts and ties and caps, and the fur room with its white wardrobe full of fur coats and muffs.

Just as they were about to set off, the youngest daughter of the local cinema operator, Herr Feindt, came running up and told them that her father had died of a heart attack. No one had been able to save him. Frau Feindt and her three daughters ended up leaving the dead man behind in their flat and fleeing towards Lake Kummerow. Meanwhile, Marie, Nanni and Otto Dabs pushed their bikes down to the harbour and over Kahlden Bridge in the flood of soldiers and fleeing people.

. . .

That same day, Gustav Skibbe noted in his war journal that his unit was to abandon its garrison. No final battle in Demmin. The Wehrmacht was clearing all its bases. To his delight, Skibbe received an extra vehicle 'for withdrawal purposes'. After a sleepless night, he drove to the army's food stores, where the liquidation of the base was well underway. Broken and emptied packing cases were strewn all over the place. Meat, cigars, schnapps. Soldiers and civilians were carting off sacks of potatoes and whole cartons of cigarettes, snapping and shouting at each other, tearing the loot out of each other's hands and laying into one another. 'Murder. Manslaughter,' Skibbe wrote. He packed what he could for himself and the men in his unit. It was a 'hasty retreat' rather than an orderly withdrawal. The first aircraft buzzing the town, the first dead. The war had finally reached Demmin. It was 29 April. 'Mum's birthday,' Skibbe wrote. 'What gloomy thoughts drift out to her.

Office cleared amid bombing, low-flying aircraft—several deaths among refugees. Rush hour—one unit came flooding back, a hideous to-do. Moved overnight to bridge by harbour. No one to be allowed out.'

Retreating without a fight had its price. Civilians were surrendered to the enemy with no means of defence. Residents and refugees alike were prevented from leaving town on the roads west so as not to hold up the withdrawing army. The soldiers began their retreat over the Peene. Once on the other side, they would blow up the bridges.

. . .

Irene Bröker and her companions had chosen the worst possible moment to break their journey. The day of respite in the abandoned house by the cemetery almost proved their undoing. The Waffen SS searched the house, looking for deserters and traitors; Dr P. managed to hide under the bed just in time. The military police—known derisively as the 'chained dogs' because they wore big metal gorgets round their necks—had only a cursory look round.

Bröker later remembered how strange the house felt after they'd left:

> The telephone in the house suddenly stopped working. It had gone eerily quiet. We wanted to go on our way and hoped no one else would show up now that the house had been searched. We didn't want to end up in the ditches that had been dug around the town.

As they were cramming their suitcases back in the car, some women passed and told them that the SS had blocked the bridges. Irene Bröker felt a sudden chill. She cursed the army for commandeering the main routes west for military vehicles. She and her family had been forced to make a detour north to the Baltic as they fled, travelling on congested back roads. If they'd headed straight for the west, she thought, they could be in Mecklenburg by now, which was presumably in British hands. They'd be safe. 'But there we were in late April, caught in Demmin as if in a trap.'

. . .

Demmin was known as *Dreistromland*—the land of three rivers. The River Peene rises in the hills of Mecklenburg, about forty kilometres south-west of Demmin, and winds its way down through the plains of Western Pomerania to the Baltic. The Peene is no wild torrent, its banks a bare two metres above sea level at Demmin, its gradient gentle and current sluggish. In a tenacious east wind, the river will give up and flow uphill. Demmin lies on a kind of peninsula in a westward loop of the Peene. Seen from the air, the river forms a blackish green semicircle around the slight hill on which Demmin's old town is situated—the market square, with the town hall standing solitary in the middle; the proud brick church of St Bartholomaeus; and Luise Gate, the town's only surviving gatehouse—and sometime prison—with its thick stone walls and gothic stepped gables. In the course of this semicircular loop, the Peene is joined by two tributaries—the Trebel from the west and the Tollense from the east, both sharply meandering little rivers, too. In and around Demmin, these three rivers form a complex network of branches and canals, basins and ditches, pools and marshland. The town's location at this junction of three rivers once gave it some standing as a seaport. Its red-brick warehouses are quite imposing enough to compete with the church tower.

Demmin seen from the Peene

In late April 1945, Demmin had fifteen thousand townspeople and a few thousand refugees. The bridges had been blocked by Wehrmacht soldiers, who were waiting for orders to dynamite them. From the air, the blackish-green ribbon of the Peene could be seen cutting off the escape routes to the west. From the air, it was obvious: they were all trapped.

. . .

Since 25 April 1945, a hundred thousand Red Army soldiers—the 65th Army of the 2nd Belorussian Front—had been on the final leg of their march from Stettin to the demarcation line between the Soviet and Western Allied occupation zones. Their current objective was to capture the German territory north of Berlin as far as the Demmin-Malchin-Waren line within a fortnight. As the troops advanced, they came across the dwindling remains of the XXXIInd Army Corps, a largely worn-down division of Flemish SS legionaries and a few bedraggled Volkssturm units. Although these soldiers were in no fit state to repel the Soviet tanks and troops, they fought on and inflicted appreciable losses; the Soviets had no reason to regard the fighting and killing as over. They even quickened the pace of their own advance to prevent the retreating Germans from drawing up a new defence line on the Baltic coast.

And so the heavy Soviet tanks and armoured personnel carriers rolled swiftly north-west, along country roads and over fields which the many streams and canals made hard to navigate. They passed through the small towns and tiny villages of Western Pomerania: Altentreptow, Letzin, Alt Teterin—and Hohenmocker, where the foremost brigade spent the night of 29 April. On the following day, the Red Army soldiers were to capture Demmin and then push on rapidly in pursuit of the enemy. Those were their orders.

War Without Limits

By this time, Soviet soldiers had been fighting for three years and ten months, or 1409 days, in a war foisted on them by Nazi Germany on 22 June 1941. Under the slogan 'Crusade against Bolshevism', the Germans' eastern campaign was, from the outset, planned as a war of extermination against an inferior race, the Soviet *Untermensch*. Even before the first shots were fired, the German command had issued to troops a series of orders in clear breach of international law—orders that not only encouraged but actually demanded that they commit crimes against enemy soldiers, prisoners and civilians. It was hardly surprising, then, that the battle was fought from the start with unprecedented ruthlessness and brutality on both sides. Behind the 1600 kilometres of front line, SS units were organising systematic murder operations and the industrial extermination of the so-called enemies of the people. And when the German retreat began in 1943, Wehrmacht soldiers set fire to thousands of towns and villages and fields in the east as part of the 'scorched earth' policy.

From day one, the eastern campaign claimed an exceptional number of losses. While an average of 2100 Germans died daily, the death toll on the Soviet side—slain soldiers, starved POWs, murdered civilians—reached more than 14,100 a day. By the end of April 1945, at least twenty million Soviet nationals had lost their lives—at the hands of the Germans whose towns and villages the Red Army soldiers were now rolling through with their tanks. It is unlikely that the Russian soldiers were aware of the precise figures, but they all knew that the Germans had set out to herd them into slave camps or throw their bodies into pits. Each one of them had cause for revenge and retribution, for feelings of hatred and triumph. Many had lost loved ones, and what's more, they had been fighting since 1941 without a single day's leave. Now, after 1409 days of exterminatory war, they were on the point of victory, declaring: 'The time has come to annihilate the fascist beast once and for all, so that it can never again threaten our homeland with a new war.'

• • •

Two hundred kilometres south of Demmin, the soldiers of the 1st Belorussian Front saw their goal near at hand when they stormed the Reichstag on the morning of 30 April. The Soviet commanders hoped to see the red hammer-and-sickle flag fluttering on the roof in time for the victory parade in Moscow on 1 May. Tanks, assault guns, howitzers and rocket launchers fired endless salvos at the Reichstag and into the government district, where about ten thousand people were congregated in small clusters. This motley crew at the heart of the Third Reich was all that remained of its former elite: grim defenders and despondent reservists, Waffen SS men, Hitler Youth boys and Volkssturm soldiers, government clerks and party representatives. Meanwhile, in a bunker deep down below the Reich Chancellery with his retinue, the Führer and Chancellor of the Reich, Adolf Hitler, was, in his own way, preparing for the final act.

The night before, mindful of posterity, he had dictated to his secretary a political and a private testament setting out his vision of the world—a vision he had repeatedly set out to his entourage over the years in endlessly circling monologues. The subjects are the same as ever: his struggle for peace, international Jewry's responsibility for war and destruction, his own people's betrayal. But the tone changes when he turns his attention to the imminent end of the Reich; suddenly his self-righteous litany is shot through with fear of the opponent's revenge:

> I do not, moreover, want to fall into the hands of enemies who are eager for a new Jewish-staged spectacle to amuse the hate-filled masses. For that reason, I have decided to remain in Berlin and to die by my own free will at such a time as I believe that the very position of Führer and Chancellor is no longer tenable.

Directly confronting the enemy, negotiating a ceasefire, perhaps even signing a capitulation—all that was inconceivable to Hitler. Surrendering himself to the victorious Soviets would have been at once the worst possible ignomiy and a terrible punishment. Leaving the burning capital to become a prisoner of whatever kind in southern or western Germany was equally out of the question. It would never have entered his mind to answer for his twelve years as the leader of the German Reich before a judge, before the Allies, the world or his own people. Even less did it occur to him to face his conscience.

That left suicide. After a life of such extremes—from deepest humiliation to supreme power—there could be no alternative.

A number of people had long predicted this move; in 1939, a German writer living in exile in London had called him 'the potential suicide par excellence'. No one knew this better than Hitler himself, who had prepared for the eventuality that his plans might fail by indulging in self-destructive fantasies and researching various suicide methods, some of which he discussed openly. If he failed, there could be no carrying on—not for him, and not for his people either. Downfall had to be total. His political testament ends with a call to fight on in the knowledge 'that the surrender of a territory or a city is impossible'. Hitler's own suicide presupposed the annihilation of Germany. The longer he put off the former, the closer he came to the latter.

Few farewell performances have been so minutely documented as that staged on 30 April 1945 in Hitler's bunker—those thirty rooms spread over two floors, five metres underground. We have the reminiscences of the telephone operator, the secretary, the adjutant, the chauffeur, the valet, the commander of the Berlin Defence Area, the captain lieutenant, the Reich youth leader, the staff sergeant—and each of these accounts points at a contradiction at the heart of this epochal event. In every one we see the Thousand Year Reich gutter out in a cramped, dank bunker—a setting vastly at odds with the bombastic nature of the regime. The rooms were crammed with an indiscriminate collection of occasional tables, armchairs and narrow sofas. The somewhat feeble attempt to liven up the cold grey of the bunker walls with rattan chairs and brightly coloured rugs only accentuated the atmosphere of gloom, and perhaps most oppressive of all was the oversized oil portrait of Frederick the Great, whose sad gaze dominated the Führer's tiny study.

By the end of April 1945, Adolf Hitler had given up. His back was hunched, his face sallow, his eyes lacklustre, his arms trembling, his whole body slumped. And yet he remained the fulcrum of the last few square feet of unoccupied German territory. In the early hours of 30 April, he embarked on an extended leave-taking ceremony, shaking the hands of dozens of servants and guards, doctors and nurses, to thank them for their service. Some replied with the oft-repeated slogans of *Treue, Endsieg*—loyalty, final victory—and *Heil*. At about seven o'clock, Hitler received the last update from the commander of Berlin, predicting that the city would fall within twenty-four hours. While Soviet artillery fire sent shock wave after shock wave through the bunker, he conferred with his personal adjutant, Otto Günsche.

> I don't want the Russians to display my corpse in a panopticon. Günsche, I expressly order you once again to ensure that nothing of the kind can happen under any circumstance.

. . .

In Demmin, a magnificent spring day was dawning, bright and fresh and sunny. The Wehrmacht men were interested only in their own retreat. The military hospitals had been evacuated, the depots and warehouses cleared or looted. Most of the remaining soldiers were on the far side of the old town, on the west bank of the Peene. 'Didn't sleep all night—how many does that make it?' Gustav Skibbe noted in his journal. He could feel the front closing in, like an immense force hurtling towards him, a dark wave of pressure and noise.

Two days before, after weeks of calm, his unit had been ordered to up sticks, and now the soldiers were in a frenzy of activity, coming and going, running and shouting. Skibbe was glad of any assignment that allowed him to use his new vehicle.

At daybreak, he was rolling along the country road. He

crossed Meyenkrebs Bridge over the Peene on the northern edge of town and drove a few miles through the marshland of the Trebel Valley, past farmsteads and squat houses and the village church of Wotenick to the town of Nossendorf. What a relief it was to feel the wind on his face after the atmosphere of panic and despair that had filled Demmin. In Nossendorf, he stocked up on fuel for the forthcoming retreat towards Dargun and Rostock. No one knew where they would end up. There were no longer clear destinations—only stops on the escape route. But the only way Skibbe could get onto the main road west was to drive all the way back and over the two bridges that had just been made ready to dynamite.

. . .

If the previous weeks had seen Demmin become ever more crowded, the old town was now emptying as if on command. Ursula Strohschein looked on with a sense of growing unease: 'Many, many people were leaving town on foot over Kahlden Bridge, with or without handcarts—or by car, though cars were a rare sight now.' In the depot, soldiers distributed the last of the tinned food to remaining residents before marching away over Kahlden Bridge. People were hurrying to get home, and the streets were soon deserted—no soldiers, and barely any locals, only a few refugees.

Ursula stood around in the yard with the other people from her building, at a loss and dully apprehensive, knowing that nobody was going to help them. It was not reassuring that the Russian and Polish women, forced labourers billeted across the road, were as frightened of the Soviet soldiers as they were. Out on the street, Ursula could see no one. She looked up at the buildings and wondered whether there was anyone left in them. Around the corner, on Baustrasse, the vicarage was the only house that was still inhabited. Over at one house, an elderly couple called the Kessels had hung a white sheet from the window. Not long after, Ursula said, a couple of her neighbours arrived:

> Herr Stoldt, a town councillor of many years' standing and latterly deputy mayor, came round with his wife to say goodbye. They were heading west on bicycles laden with suitcases. 'Please keep an eye on our flat,' he said before they left.

The sun shone in a clear, blue sky. The German troops, including the SS, had left the centre of town. The promised Volkssturm units were nowhere to be seen. The traffic had come to a halt. Only a grinding, clattering noise could be heard in the distance, accompanied by a low rumble. For those who had stayed behind, there was nothing to do but wait. When Adolf Hitler's twelve-year reign came to an end, the world stopped for a moment in Demmin. Those still in town had time to wonder whether they'd been wise to stay.

The furrier's and gentlemen's outfitter's was a hive of activity that morning. The day before, Marie Dabs had walked to a friend's estate in the district of Deven, on the west bank of the Peene, with her children and her servant Martha Schröder, then twenty-five years old. When they got there, the place was full of German soldiers, who offered to take the children along with them. Again, Marie Dabs passed up the opportunity. 'If only I'd said yes! But could I have let them go without knowing what the future held?' After a peaceful night on the straw of the farmhouse cellar, she and Nanni had fought their way back across the Peene against the flood of soldiers and refugees. On the other side, they were met by oppressive emptiness; the old town was deserted as they walked home over the cobbles. During the night, lying in her friend's cellar, Marie Dabs had decided to secure the flat against shelling. They took the big paintings down from the walls and put them behind the sofa. They rolled up the rugs. The water had already been turned off. In the distance they heard the thunder of heavy artillery. *That* scared them.

Nanni took her mother by the hand, saying, 'Come on, quick, quick!' All they wanted now, Marie Dabs says, was to get out:

> We managed to get across Kahlden Bridge just before it was blown up along with the other bridge over the Peene and the Tollense Bridge. What a terrible fate to befall our beautiful and beloved Demmin.

Three massive detonations broke the silence and put an end to the peace—explosions that could be heard far off in the surrounding villages. At the same time, the grinding and clattering of the Soviet tanks grew closer, as they approached the southern and eastern outskirts of the town. For the people of Demmin, these explosions were a signal to take refuge in their cellars. Some took a suitcase, packed with a change of clothes, identity papers, valuables and a few provisions, as if they could escape their fates by going underground. Everyone expected heavy fighting.

In the cellars, communities born of necessity gathered in the half-darkness—mothers and children, aunts and grandparents, young women and old men, thrown together by the war. Families were joined by friends and relations with no cellars of their own, and by refugees from the east who'd been billeted in Demmin homes by the party. The Strohscheins shared their cellar with some of the forced labourers from across the road. In some places, twenty or more people were squeezed in together, near strangers to one another. The young women wished they could disappear; their only hope was to smear their faces with soot, painting crow's feet and wrinkles around their eyes with charred matchsticks and wrapping their faces in torn headscarves to make themselves old and ugly—inconspicuous, if not invisible. They had heard of this ploy along with stories of the Soviet advance. Some held children on their laps.

. . .

But not everyone in Demmin took refuge underground. Some decided to anticipate the town's capture and the end of the world as they knew it. Twenty-seven-year-old Lothar Büchner of the National Labour Service was dead even before Russian soldiers reached his house in Jahnstrasse. He had hanged himself, as had his wife, her sister, and their mother and grandmother. Before that happened, though, one of them had first put a noose around the neck of three-year-old Georg-Peter. Something similar took place in the house of the seventy-one-year-old director of the General Local Health Insurance Fund Bewersdorff. Before he, his wife and their grown-up daughter hanged themselves, his two grandchildren, aged two and nine, had died in the same way. The young wife of a first lieutenant who lived alone with her three-year-old son somehow summoned the will to loop a noose around the boy's neck and hang him before doing the same to herself. Within these same few hours, an elderly policeman and his wife also hanged themselves. The wife of a chief police constable hanged herself. Her two grown daughters hanged themselves. Only three people—a forty-seven-year-old carpenter, and the wife and daughter of a landowner in Waldberg, west of the Peene—chose another way out: they shot themselves in the head.

These twenty-one suicides—classifying the deaths of the children as 'murder suicide', in line with common legal parlance—are recorded in the death register of Demmin Registry Office. Looking at the register and seeing the sudden spate of suicides in Demmin on 30 April 1945, even before the Soviet invasion, you have the sense that this was something unprecedented—but those twenty-one suicides were only a prelude.

The Eyes of the Enemy

On the same day, at around noon, Adolf Hitler announced in his bunker in Berlin that his time was up, and that he would commit suicide that afternoon with his wife, Eva, whom he had married the day before: 'I myself and my wife choose to die, rather than face the ignominy of deposition or capitulation.' Hitler had given a great deal of thought to his death and the surest method of killing himself; an SS doctor in the bunker kept a ready supply of brass capsules of prussic acid—the liquid form of hydrogen cyanide. The Führer had convinced himself of their efficacy by having his Alsatian poisoned in the Reich Chancellery garden. Nothing could go wrong at this final stage; he was determined not to fall into Soviet hands alive. He knew the fate of his old political role model Mussolini, executed only two days before and strung up by his legs, along with his mistress, in front of an angry crowd in the middle of Milan. Hitler was determined not to fall into his opponents' hands, alive or dead. Nothing was to remain of him: 'It is our will to be cremated immediately in the place where I have done most of my daily work during my twelve years' service to my people.'

Soviet grenades rained down without cease throughout the Reich Chancellery garden and the government district. The thunder of cannon fire grew ever fiercer. Walls and houses were collapsing on all sides. A thick haze of acrid smoke and dust smothered the entire area, and sand crunched between people's teeth. While Hitler's adjutant and chauffeur hurried to fetch the canisters of petrol they would need to carry out his final order, their Führer sat down to lunch with his cook and secretaries. After lunch, he said goodbye to them and his other trusted employees—among them his close confidant Martin Bormann, propaganda minister Joseph Goebbels and his wife, Magda, and a few high-ranking officers. A weary handshake, a few mumbled words. His wife stood beside him. He was wearing his habitual brown uniform jacket and a pair of black trousers.

. . .

As the soldiers of the 1st Belorussian Front pushed forward into the heart of Berlin, their comrades from the 2nd Belorussian Front were outside Demmin. Late on the morning of 30 April, the first troops of the 30th Tank Brigade reached the small southern district of Vorwerk, just across the River Tollense from the old town. They had seventeen IS-122 heavy tanks, a number of armoured personnel carriers and self-propelled guns, and about four hundred infantry soldiers. On the twenty-kilometre march to Demmin that morning they had captured 805 prisoners, 120 cars and ten motorbikes, and destroyed a battery of three flak guns that had been supposed to hold off their steel behemoths. There were still boy-faced soldiers lying dead by the roadside days later. Towards noon, the tanks got stuck at the Tollense, because the bridge had been blown up. Soviet pioneers set to work to build a temporary bridge over the not quite twenty-metre-wide river.

Before long, the Soviets were also making inroads from the east along Reich Road 110, heading for the tree-lined stretch known as Jarmener Chaussee, which led towards the town centre. Here on the edge of town, in the abandoned house by the cemetery, Irene Bröker and Dr P. and his wife had known since morning that their attempt to get away had failed, and that the advancing Soviets would overrun them. 'We heard desolate cries and shots in the distance,' she later remembered. In vain they searched the cellar and attic for somewhere to hide. Out in the garden, Irene came across a brick-lined shelter dug into the ground beneath a compost heap, its narrow entrance concealed by raspberry canes. They would soon need it:

> When we heard explosions and then gunfire, it was clear to us all that the Russian army had caught up with us. The four of us fled into the hole beneath the compost heap with a blanket. I saw soldiers' legs in the garden next door and heard my heart pounding in my ears.

She sat at the entrance to the passageway, the reek of slurry and the roar of the advancing army all around her. Alarmed by the noise and his mother's whispers, two-year-old Holger set up a wail. Irene saw a soldier's boot trampling twigs, inches from her face, and heard a shot whistle past her neck into the shelter. A solitary Soviet soldier, with an old, broad peasant's face, grey and fierce and furrowed, drove her out of the hole at gunpoint. Irene Bröker's flight from the Russians was over. The soldier took her back to the house and told her in stuttering German that he'd been taken prisoner by the Germans in the First World War. They saw him often after that; he'd drop in on them to make sure that the little boy was all right. The soldier warned Irene and her companions to be careful:

> He told us that not all soldiers were good—there were a lot more coming and we ought to hide. We saw Russian planes passing over town. The town centre was swathed in thick smoke. There were fires all over the place. When I looked out of the attic window, I could see flames blazing up into the sky.

· · ·

Driving back from Nossendorf with the petrol on board and his heart in his mouth, Gustav Skibbe only just made it to the west bank of the Peene before his comrades blew up the bridge. In his war journal, his usually neat handwriting becomes a nervous scrawl, as if he were reliving that drive back across the Peene with the hot breath of war on his neck:

> When we got back to the bridge by the harbour, the Russians were there, having come in over Tollense Bridge! Shelling in town from Tutow at the same time. Hasty retreat … as far as Gnoien.

That was Gustav Skibbe's last entry on Demmin. He never saw the town again.

· · ·

After the Wehrmacht and the SS had, for reasons of military strategy, spared Demmin a final battle, some of the townspeople found the courage to ignore the fanatics' threats. White flags, hastily cobbled together out of poles and sheets or towels, were hung out of windows. There was even one rigged up on the church tower, visible for miles. At the vicarage, a sheet was fixed in the dormer window. The vicar's wife, Maria Buske, and her father had spent the day before on their hands and knees, chiselling out the bars of their cellar windows with household tools. They had eventually managed to break open an escape route, but now that the bridges had been blown up, there was nowhere to escape to.

Maria Buske and her two small sons had been waiting for the boys' father to return since he'd been called up at the beginning of the war. She worked for the Red Cross and remained in the vicarage, a two-storey house marked out from the others on Baustrasse by its distinctive gable. Over the past days it had become something of a refuge: eighteen people, including a refugee family from Stettin with seven children, were crammed into the small house. The Buskes had abandoned their last-minute attempt to leave, because there was no longer any way out of town. Maria would later describe that night for her son:

> We young women sat in the cellar with the children. My parents went into the garage at the end of the garden to avoid the risk of shrapnel, and so as to be on hand in case we were buried under debris. We were the only people left on our block. The others had fled to the country to escape the shock of the first Russian attack.

In the cellar, they heard shots all the way from Treptower Strasse, as the first Russian tanks moved into Demmin. But the final battle wasn't fought by the Wehrmacht or the SS, by reservists or a trained guerrilla force; it was fought by a lone civilian, Gerhard Moldenhauer, a schoolmaster from Demmin. When fellow teacher Wilhelm Damann met him in the early 1930s—they had flats in the same building—Moldenhauer was an opponent of Hitler. As Damann later explained, this meant that his neighbour faced a dilemma when Hitler came to power:

He was too intelligent to be taken in by the hocus-pocus of the Third Reich, but at the same time too ambitious and too young to be willing or able to be relegated to the sidelines. Frau Moldenhauer and their three children were keen Hitler supporters, the girls in particular.

Like millions of other Germans, he'd had to make a choice: either he could toe the line and silence his inner voice, or he could stay true to his convictions and be ostracised. On this choice hung, on the one hand, his future and the unity of his family and, on the other, his peace of mind and self-respect. Unlike his colleague Damann, who was fired when the Nazis came to power, Moldenhauer decided to take a gamble on life in the 'new' Germany rather than resist the pressure of circumstances and the expectations of his family. He joined the Nazi Party, opening the door to a teaching career in the Third Reich.

At around noon on 30 April 1945, the entire Moldenhauer family was sitting in the cellar beneath the building at 6 Treptower Strasse. They heard the three bridges being blown up. They heard the rumble and roar of the approaching tanks. After a while, Gerhard Moldenhauer took out his gun and shot his wife and three children, one after the other. Then he made his way upstairs. Damann heard the details from a neighbour:

> Old Frau Rentner, who lived on our corridor and stayed in the same flat until the day she died, later told me that Herr Moldenhauer had come out of the cellar and said: 'I've just shot my wife and children. Now I'm going to do in a few Russians!'

From the window of his flat, Moldenhauer fired a few shots at the advance guard of Soviet soldiers who were moving in along Treptower Strasse. It was a short, violent skirmish. Before the soldiers could storm the house, Moldenhauer had shot himself in the head.

When Wilhelm Damann came to write his report on Demmin a decade after these events, he tried to make sense of this desperate act. But he cited neither Moldenhauer's hatred and fear of the Russians, nor his desire to defend Demmin at whatever cost. As Damann saw it, the root cause lay in Moldenhauer's past life and the betrayal of his principles—a betrayal which caught up with him in the moment of defeat. 'I see his act as that of a gambler who'd staked everything on one card and knew he'd lost. Presumably shame played a part too.'

. . .

Soon afterwards, there was another gunfight in the town centre. Some Hitler Youth boys apparently decided to do their bit for final victory by firing shots from the gatehouse windows in the thick walls of Luise Gate, and the Soviets responded by blasting anti-tank grenades into the facade of the ancient gatehouse—at the foot of which, beneath the ground, the Strohscheins were sheltering in their cellar. Ursula Strohschein later described what it was like:

> Gunshots cracked, shells roared against the east side of Luise Gate. We sat there, just on the other side of it, afraid it might collapse at any moment. But we didn't have to wait long. The shooting was soon over. All was quiet. Very cautiously, we ventured out of the cellar.

Out on the street, Ursula risked a glance through the gate and immediately shrank back. A young officer in an earth-brown uniform jumped off a cart and came hurtling towards her—but ran off again, after giving her a quick pat on the shoulder. She had seen her first Russian. It was the encounter they had all been dreading for months.

. . .

On 23 October 1944, the Germans had been confronted with a reality for which Nazi propaganda, with its terrifying slogans about 'Bolshevik Mongol hordes', had long prepared them. On this day, Wehrmacht soldiers reclaimed the East Prussian village of Nemmersdorf from the Red Army and found traces of a massacre. Soviet soldiers, setting foot on enemy soil for the first time after three and a half years of war, had killed a number of German civilians. The Wehrmacht soldiers' first reports spoke of about twenty deaths—women, children and elderly people. Other facts were harder to ascertain, not least because the propaganda machine in Berlin immediately sent in photographers and cameramen to mount a sensationalist campaign.

In the days and weeks that followed, party newspapers reported repeatedly on 'the horrors of Nemmersdorf'. Shocking photo spreads showed close-ups of murdered Germans, their heads punctured with shot wounds, their skulls crushed, their faces battered beyond recognition. They showed long rows of dead children and of women who had clearly been raped, their skirts pushed up and their underwear ripped away. Cinemas ran newsreels showing looted refugee carts, twisted children's bodies in muddy pits, horrified onlookers gawping at rows of corpses, and the ubiquitous shot of the village sign, so that it wasn't long before almost everyone had heard of Nemmersdorf. The aim was to show the Germans what to expect in the case of a Soviet invasion, and there is no doubt that the images left their mark. But rather than fuel a loathing of the 'Soviet beasts' and a fierce spirit of resistance, they terrified the civilian population. Although the Nazi leadership held out against evacuation to the end, there was soon a steady flow of people leaving East Prussia. Three months later, this flow had swelled to a mass exodus, with handcarts and horse-drawn wagons.

In January 1945, the Red Army launched its winter offensive against East Prussia as it pushed on towards Berlin. Those who didn't escape in time felt the full force of retribution for the crimes committed during the German war of extermination. Many refugees were trapped between the Allied and Soviet fronts or caught up with by Russian panzer spearheads. Hardened by the war, whipped up by Russian propaganda and stripped of their inhibitions by alcohol, the Red Army soldiers went on a massive crime spree. German women and girls, in particular, from the very young to the very old, were exposed to horrific violence. It is estimated that up to two million women were raped by Red Army soldiers in the final stages of the war. The frenzy of the troops was such that even their own leaders considered them a risk to military operations. The commander of the 2nd Belorussian Front called for severe punishment for looting, violence and wanton destruction, but to no real effect. As the Red Army advanced, the atrocities begun in East Prussia continued in West Prussia, Silesia and Pomerania: everywhere houses were burnt down, women raped, civilians murdered. As the columns of refugees moved westwards, fears spread that the hysterical Nazi propaganda might have been spot on for once. By the time the first real-life Red Army soldiers reached Western Pomerania, everyone had heard the stories.

. . .

Roaring diesel engines, the rattle of tank treads on cobblestones, the tramp of boots marching in double time. After two brief exchanges of fire in the early afternoon of 30 April, the fight for Demmin was over and the town occupied by Soviet troops. There was no doubt who had won control. Now the two armoured brigades that had captured Demmin were to continue their rapid pursuit of the German forces heading for Rostock, on the north coast. But when they reached the destroyed bridges at Meyenkrebs and by the harbour, they could advance no further. The quietly flowing Peene, forty metres across and five metres deep, was the most effective obstacle that the Red Army troops encountered that day. Desperate though they were to bring the campaign to an end at last, the soldiers had no choice but to park their tanks and other vehicles at the riverside. There were dozens of them; the line of armoured behemoths extended far into the old town, a herd of steel beasts, raring to go, but forced to inaction. More and more moved in from the east. A Soviet battle log records the time of Demmin's capture as 4.30 pm. The log was kept in Moscow time. In Berlin, it was an hour earlier—3.30 pm.

. . .

It was at half past three in the afternoon that Adolf Hitler committed suicide in his bunker in Berlin. After lunch, he had withdrawn to his study, followed by Eva Braun—or Eva Hitler, as she was now. No one in the bunker seems to have heard the shot to his temple. The two of them were found sitting side by side on a little sofa. His valet described the scene:

> His head was tilted slightly towards the wall; there was blood spattered on the rug next to the sofa. To his right sat his wife, her legs drawn up onto the sofa. A grimace betrayed the cause of her death: cyanide poisoning. Its 'bite' showed clearly on her face.

This prosaic and unglamorous death was followed by a brisk cremation. Hitler's corpse was carried out into the Reich Chancellery garden wrapped in a military blanket. The two bodies were laid side by side on a patch of sand next to the entrance to the bunker, doused with petrol and set alight. A tower sentry looking on pointed this scene out to the watch master. 'Look, that's Adolf Hitler there—he's on fire.' As the flames shot up in a ball of fire, a barrage of Soviet artillery grenades rained down. The small funeral gathering hastily returned to the bunker. None of Hitler's retinue cared to witness the burning of the Führer's body for any longer than was necessary. None of them looked back to make sure that his final instructions had been thoroughly carried out.

. . .

In Demmin, meanwhile, there were tanks backed all the way up Baustrasse. Four Soviet officers and twenty soldiers billeted themselves in the vicarage, which was now the only inhabited house on the block. They belonged to a pioneer squad that was putting up a temporary bridge over the Peene. 'Why they came to our house, when all the neighbouring houses were empty, I do not know. Nobody asked at the time,' Maria Buske said. The vicar's wife and her family had to clear the second floor, but were allowed to stay on in their house. Although the soldiers took Maria's watch and wedding ring when they first searched the house, they were to prove more friend than foe in the hours that followed. Thanks to them, the vicarage escaped the brunt of the first attack.

> A guard was posted in the hall to act as an intermediary. Fellow soldiers who came looking for women were sent packing with the words 'officers' quarters'. My father had a small quantity of tobacco over and gave him some in the long hours of his watch.

The battle noise had blown over like a minor storm front, rattling the windows of Demmin and smashing the occasional pane, but without bringing the devastation that people had feared. Many families emerged from their cellars and went back up to their flats. Some even dared hope that Demmin might, once again, escape unscathed. Ursula Strohschein had been scared rigid when she met the Russian soldier, but he had only given her a comforting pat and gone on his way. At the flat in Luisenstrasse, her family looked about in astonished disbelief, as if seeing the place for the first time.

> My mother was crying for joy: 'Thank the Lord! They've left us our flat…' She kept running her hand lovingly over the upholstery. Cautiously, we peered out of the paneless window. Glass all over Luisenstrasse.

A menacing face stared up at them from under a black leather cap. Ursula's mother shrank back from the window. The next thing they knew, the man was in their flat with two soldiers, charging around, shouting, looking for fascists. Over the desk hung a certificate belonging to Ursula's father, honouring him as a member of Demmin's historical marksmen's guild. *A militarist!* The Russian refused to be calmed. After he'd left, they noticed palm-sized black circles on the outside of the doors, front and back. They had no idea what they signified, Ursula said, 'but an uneasy sense of foreboding crept over us'.

• • •

Parallel to Luisenstrasse and connected to it by a series of alleyways was Frauenstrasse; here, next to the red-brick boys' school and up from Swan Pond, lived the Schlössers, an extended family comprising grandparents and great-grandparents as well as a mother and her two sons. The boys' father had gone off to fight at the beginning of the war; a few weeks before they had heard that he'd been killed in East Prussia in March. Ten-year-old Karl Schlösser was the elder son, and since his father had been away at war, more and more duties had fallen to him; he had been catapulted out of his sheltered, petty-bourgeois childhood into premature adulthood. He had to tend and slaughter the chickens, geese and rabbits in the garden. War had been part of everyday life for as long as he could remember. Now, though, that familiar world was falling apart: no father to come back to them, no lessons to attend. Karl had seen waves of refugees surging through Demmin and knew the Red Army soldiers were coming. He had grown up on Nazi propaganda—'The Russians cut off children's tongues!'— and was afraid. When the air-raid siren sounded that morning, he'd run down to the cellar. But the people around him spoke only of 'collapse', not of defeat—as if the ground had been pulled from under their feet, not as if they'd lost the war.

Once the gunfire was over, the Schlössers went back upstairs. From the window, Karl watched Soviet soldiers creeping along the walls of the houses, stooped, cautious and silent. As in every German town, the Russians anticipated ambush—a Hitler Youth boy with a bazooka, taking aim at them from a coalhole, or an SS squad hiding behind a window. There had been two gun battles. Now the Red Army's advance troops were combing the houses one by one in search of any remaining German soldiers, kicking down door after door with their heavy boots.

No one had prepared Karl Schlösser for this moment. None of the grown-ups had any idea what was going to happen or what to do. The family took refuge in Karl's parents' bedroom at the back of the house, overlooking the garden. They sat there and waited—great-grandparents, grandparents, the two boys, their mother, an aunt. It was a bright afternoon and the overcrowded room was stuffy. When the Russians arrived, Karl was surprised. The two men who came into the bedroom where the family was gathered were ridiculously young. They looked nothing like the Bolshevik soldiers he'd imagined—the murderous arsonists, child abusers and rapists whose pictures he'd pieced together in his head from posters, newspapers and overheard conversations. In their mud-coloured uniforms, they looked more like schoolboys playing dressing-up. They stood there, clutching their weapons, at as much of a loss as the Schlössers. Nobody spoke; there was nothing to say and no common language to say it in. Those awkward moments of silence would stay with Karl Schlösser for the rest of his life.

This was partly because of what happened next: 'One of them grabbed Mother and disappeared with her, while the other guarded the door with his rifle.' The family sat there, powerless to move, while, in another room, the Soviet soldier threw himself on Magdalena Schlösser and raped her.

• • •

At Deven Farm, Marie Dabs stood at the attic window with a whole crowd of other refugees, watching Soviet soldiers storming towards them. They belonged to advance divisions that had crossed the Peene that afternoon without tanks or heavy guns, and were pushing ahead into the parts of Demmin that lay to the west of the river. Among them was a young man with a camouflage tarpaulin draped around his shoulders like a cape, and white ladies' gloves on his hands. He explained to them in German that they needn't be afraid of the Russian soldiers.

But come evening, they were ordered to evacuate. 'The lovely big farm was empty,' Marie Dabs said. 'Not a cart in sight, no animals, no horses, no cows, no pigs, not so much as a chicken. Everything had been driven out or carried off by the Russians and

Poles.' Carrying their remaining belongings, Marie Dabs and her children set off, accompanied by Martha, their maid, but soldiers stopped them and ordered nineteen-year-old Nanni back into the farmhouse. Another soldier was waiting for her in the smoking room and locked the door on the inside, leaving Marie Dabs pleading and crying in the hall. Some high-ranking Soviet officers turned up and released the girl. Mother, daughter, son and maid ran off towards Deven Wood, but were caught by more soldiers before they got there.

> Several Russians charged at us, grabbed Martha and disappeared with her behind a barn. They took my handbag and rummaged through it. They drank a big bottle of eau de Cologne, every last drop, and tossed Otto's little medal, which I was keeping safe for him in my bag, over the field in a high arc.

The family broke away, Martha with them, and tore off into the thick of the woods, deeper and deeper into the dense undergrowth, until they were out of sight of the soldiers.

. . .

At the house of veterinary surgeon Dr Erich Kuhlmann, in Bahnhofstrasse, the morning of 30 April had begun much as usual. The fifty-two-year-old vet and his wife, Maria, had waited for the arrival of the Soviet soldiers along with their fifteen-year-old daughter, Ilse, their maid, Else, and some other residents of the building. Werner, Ilse's older brother, was not with them. He was at the front and wouldn't find out about what happened in his parents' house that day until six months later, when the maid wrote to him in British captivity. In her letter, Else told him of their original plan to flee the Soviets and go to Hamburg, more than two hundred kilometres to the west. 'But in the end your parents decided we should stay. They said things couldn't possibly be as bad as people were saying.'

The Kuhlmanns, Else and several others, among them Else's future husband, spent the hours leading up to the invasion in the cellar, taking with them food, bedclothes and their valuables. In the early afternoon, Erich Kuhlmann saw the first Russian soldier and hoisted a white flag. In this part of Demmin, tucked away on a wooded hillside next to the cemetery, a little way from the old town, the invasion went off peacefully. A few Russians demanded their watches and schnapps. One or two wanted medical treatment and had Dr Kuhlmann minister to them. In the cellar, Else laid the table for dinner. It looked as if Werner and Ilse's parents might be right after all. The doctor and his wife took their bedclothes and carried them back up to their room. Their daughter and the maid thought about sleeping in the attic, but couldn't find a good place to hide and decided to remain in the cellar.

That night they heard strangers' voices overhead and the tramp of boots. Their faint hope was dashed in a moment. Else described for Werner how they had squeezed themselves into the darkest corners of the cellar, terrified:

> We immediately started shaking and trembling again from head to foot. Upstairs we heard several heavy footsteps— they even came as far as the cellar stairs, but no further. By the time things went quiet up there, we'd been trembling for a good hour.

When the soldiers had gone, Erich and Maria Kuhlmann joined the girls in the cellar. They explained that under the soldiers' insistent questioning, another tenant, Frau Lorenz, had claimed to be the Kuhlmanns' daughter, and been raped four times in a row. The doctor and his wife had abandoned all hope of escaping their fate.

> Ilse was quite desperate and said to me: 'It would be best if Daddy just shot us. What's the point in carrying on playing hide-and-seek like this?' Then your mother said to me: 'Else, brace yourself—we're going to take our lives.' I didn't think she was serious and only replied unsuspectingly: 'You can't do that! It's not possible!'

Else failed to hear the note of determination in their words, evidence of a long-hatched plan. Shortly before midnight, Dr Kuhlmann returned to the cellar, two Soviet officers on his heels. The soldiers didn't stay long. They took two women back upstairs with them—other tenants who had also been hiding in the communal cellar. Everyone knew what was in store for them.

· · ·

Since the October Revolution of 1917, Labour Day, held annually on 1 May, had been one of the most important public holidays in the Soviet Union. The Russian soldiers in Demmin knew that on this day all eyes were turned to Berlin, where their comrades from the 1st Belorussian Front were going to destroy the fascist beast in its lair. That year, the May Day celebrations in Moscow, the greatest victory celebrations in the history of Russia, were held to honour the heroes who had taken Berlin. No one was interested in Demmin. But the soldiers wanted a May Day of their own all the same.

The officers sat in the vicarage's easy chairs by candlelight, drinking wine from the vicar's cellar out of large preserving jars. The delicate wineglasses Maria Buske had offered them were too small for the Russians. They knocked back jar after jar. On the other side of the room, as far away from the easy chairs as they could get, the family lay huddled up against the wall. 'We cowered there on the rug,' Maria Buske said, 'a big bundle of fear.'

The officers asked them—the vicar's wife and children, the grandparents and other relatives—to join in their celebrations. They wanted the grandfather to make music, to play their Russian songs on the piano for them to sing along to, in celebration of their victory over Germany, the end of the war, their liberation from the Nazis, the big May Day holiday. But the family lay there, clinging to each other, too tense to move or speak. The grandfather didn't know any of the songs the officers wanted to hear. Maria's son, Norbert Buske, never forgot that night: the victors by candlelight with their preserving jars full of wine, the family on the floor in front of them, and his own flickering fear.

Tower of Darkness

On the night of 30 April, Demmin's fate was sealed. Apart from a handful of advance troops, no Soviet unit had managed to make it across the Peene. The tanks, armoured personnel carriers, anti-aircraft gun carriages, trucks and vast quantities of military equipment transformed the town into a seething army camp. Hundreds of soldiers, checked in their march of victory, swarmed out in search of watches and jewellery, schnapps and women, fun and lust and violence.

They found the ammunition depots; they found the schnapps distillery. Some of them swallowed anything that burnt their gullets and smelt of rotgut. Their feeling of triumph at the imminent victory over the Nazis was heightened by the general May Day merriment. That night, the first houses in Demmin went up in flames.

Deep in the undergrowth of Deven Wood, in among the firs and bushes, Marie Dabs spent the night out in the open with her children, Otto and Nanni, and a few other displaced people. She remembered the happy Sundays of her childhood, when she had strolled through Deven Wood with her parents in a white knitted dress and floppy hat. Now all they had were the clothes on their backs. Even the big suitcase containing the children's photo albums had been left somewhere along the way. Only that morning she'd been in her fur shop on Demmin's main shopping street; right up to the end she'd refused to believe that all that was in jeopardy, already as good as lost. She hadn't realised that she'd swallowed the lies fed to her by party, government and army officials—swallowed their words and made them her own. Now here she was with what little was left to her, on a dank bed of moss in a dark wood.

> It was a cold and dreadful night that we spent on the bare forest floor…I had one of my fur coats with me, and my eiderdown, so I was able to cover up the children. In the distance we heard the screams of women being tortured and raped, and saw the first glow of fire above the burning town.

The fires spread until morning, destroying large swathes of the old town. The closely built half-timbered houses with their wooden window frames, rafters, workshops and sheds fed the flames all through the night, and the fire ate its way from house to house and street to street. There was no water in the pipes. People with a few buckets of water to hand tried to protect their houses by laying wet towels on the windowsills and roof beams—damp cloths to hold back a sea of flames.

The fire brigade didn't turn out, because it couldn't, or because it wasn't allowed to. Afterwards there was much dispute over what or who had started the inferno that was to scar the old provincial town forever. Some suspected that arson—even medieval-style torching and pillaging—had been carried out at the behest of

Soviet military leadership as punishment for the brief skirmishes when the town was captured. Others believed that isolated fires had been started by the Soviets in the houses of well-known local Nazis and got out of control. Others again wondered whether it had actually been the Soviets at all, given that burning down the town served no military purpose.

Luisenstrasse and Luise Gate after the fire

When Ursula Strohschein and her mother stepped out of the cellar into their yard outside Luise Gate in the morning, after a night broken by screams, they sensed that a few smashed windowpanes would not be the last of it. They thought of the angry commissar who had searched their house—and of the strange black circles the Russians had painted on the doors.

> Peering apprehensively onto the street, we saw Red Army soldiers engaged in a curious exercise. They were plunging long-handled brooms wrapped in rags into enormous pails and hastily daubing the walls of the houses. To our astonishment we saw a red sky over the market square. Fire!

Soon their house, too, was on fire. Soldiers armed with carbines looked on as Ursula and her mother carted blankets, clothes and food out of the house, through acrid, billowing smoke. In the yard, they loaded everything onto a wheelbarrow. They found a loose, shapeless tracksuit for Ursula, and a peaked cap, which she pulled down over her ears.

The blazing heat propelled them along. They ran through the Luise Gate into Turmstrasse and away, leaving behind them the fire, their house and their past life. They slid and stumbled over the cobbles, pushing their swaying wheelbarrow. Flames leapt out of the houses, licking at their skin and hair. The fire hadn't yet got past the town wall and into the alleyways where the houses were smaller and built in brick. Ursula and her mother knocked at the door of their old washerwoman, who gave them the key to her summerhouse. There they hunkered down. Russian soldiers came by and rummaged through their suitcases. Ursula hid at the bottom of a mound of bedclothes.

'Day and night we saw fire and thick clouds of smoke,' she would remember in years to come. The fire raged for days. In the old town it claimed whole streets, including the main thoroughfares. In the smaller, connecting streets, most of the half-timbered houses with wooden roof trusses went up in flames. Further out of town, towards the station, the River Tollense and the town common, some buildings were hit by the fire while others escaped—but half if not three-quarters of the houses in Demmin were completely destroyed.

Most of those who had decided to stay in town and make it through the Russian invasion as best they could now had to flee the fire. There was no time to pack. People took refuge in the surrounding woods or escaped to the meadows by the rivers, to fields and pastures. Many sought shelter in nearby villages:

Eugenieberg, Lindenfelde, Pensin. The more fortunate found a place to sleep in a barn or hayloft. Others spent the nights in the half-finished anti-tank ditches they had dug themselves only a few days before. Yet others slept by the canals, between bales of straw, or on the bare earth of the oilseed fields.

. . .

Those who fled the town saw a devastating sight when they turned to look back. Beneath a sky reddened by flames—and behind columns of smoke and dense grey-black mountains of clouds—the church tower of Demmin had vanished. The hundred-metre-high red-brick tower, with its windowed turrets and filigree spire—once a reassuring symbol of home for everyone who lived there and a prominent local landmark—had disappeared, shrouded in smoke. Marie Dabs, who had lived all her life within sight of the tower, wrote in her memoirs: 'Our beautiful tall church tower—all our childhood, the first thing we saw when we returned home from a journey—was no longer to be seen.' Although it was hidden, she still felt its power. But the comforting pull of home and familiarity had given way to the dark pull of impending disaster.

The first of May had started like any other bright spring day. But Karl Schlösser, who was at home with his family, saw nothing of the sun. Night had descended on them in broad daylight. Dense smoke billowed from the burning houses in Frauenstrasse, darkening the sky. Karl's grandfather came down the stairs. 'We must all get out of here,' he said. The roof beams and rafters had caught fire. Together with their grandparents and great-grandparents, Karl and his younger brother fled the house with nothing but the clothes on their backs. Only his mother, Magdalena Schlösser, packed some provisions—and a handful of razor blades. The night the Soviet soldier had assaulted her, she had formed a resolve.

They set off at a run, past the red-brick school building that hadn't yet caught fire, down the dirt path to Swan Pond, and along the bank between the willows. The streets were full of people fleeing the flames. They crossed the railway lines at the station and slipped through a small wooded thicket surrounding the Uhlan memorial. On the other side was the town boundary, and beyond that the open fields, where they stopped to rest amid the furrows and clumps of grass. For the moment they felt little more than relief at having made it out of town—away from the burning houses, the looting soldiers and the panic-stricken people, away from all the screaming and raging and groaning. All they could see when they looked back was a column of smoke rising above the fir trees.

Then Karl saw his mother standing before him. In her hand she held one of the razor blades she had packed before they took flight. 'We're going to heaven now, to join your father!' Magdalena Schlösser was planning to kill them—Karl, his brother, their grandparents and great-grandparents—and then herself. There, in the middle of the field, she wanted to put an end to their nightmare. Karl's grandfather shouted at her, grabbing her arms and wresting the razor blade from her hand. He saved the family's lives. None of them ever mentioned the incident afterwards. But they had escaped a fate that was hurtling towards the people of Demmin with terrific force.

· · ·

In a letter to Werner Kuhlmann written in December 1945, his parents' former maid, Else, informs him of the events that took place in their house on 1 May. Her letter is vivid and detailed. Werner Kuhlmann had clearly been without news of his parents since being taken prisoner by the British. 'I am afraid that a cruel fate has befallen you since then,' Else wrote. 'I am afraid the time has come to tell you the sad and awful truth.'

At seven o'clock in the morning, Dr Erich Kuhlmann had come to her in the cellar and told her what had gone on in town since the previous evening. He placed a small parcel on the table. 'For you, Else.' Then he said a brief goodbye and went back upstairs. Else picked up the parcel and put it to one side. It was poison—she was sure of it. Herr Kuhlmann had often intimated that if the worst should come to the worst, this would always be a possible way out for them. After she'd washed in the laundry room, one of the other tenants came downstairs with his suitcases and told her that Erich Kuhlmann had shot himself, and that his wife Maria and their daughter Ilse were lying dead in one of the bedrooms. By then the roof was on fire, too.

> I was all confused. I ran upstairs [...] but was met by such thick smoke that I couldn't see a thing. Why I didn't go in the bedroom is a mystery to me. Herr Jeschke told me that your mother and Ilse were lying dead in bed, hand in hand.

Else packed a few things and rushed out of the burning house. Later, when she came to open the small parcel Erich Kuhlmann had given her in farewell, she found that it contained not poison, but the couple's wedding rings and a few parting words from her now deceased employers. Their son was lucky to hear from Else; if it hadn't been for the dissuasive powers of her future husband, she, too, would have poisoned herself soon afterwards.

• • •

Since struggling up at dawn, frozen stiff after their night in the undergrowth of Deven Wood, Marie Dabs, her children and the three others accompanying her had been wandering aimlessly about the outskirts of town. They tried their luck at the house of Dr Emil Melzer, an old acquaintance who had taken in a number of refugees and whom they'd bumped into on their way to take shelter at Deven Farm. In the garden of his house they came across a refugee woman, shovelling earth. It seemed to them a strange time to be doing that kind of garden work. Marie recognised her as one of the women who'd waited for the Russian invasion with them in the farmhouse attic. Unsuspecting, Marie asked the woman why she was so grimly intent on her work. The answer was so horrific that she would never forget it:

> 'This is the last of the three graves I have dug for my children! I shall be going soon too. We've had a dreadful night. There are many more women and children in the house, lying in their own blood!'

They went in and found the doctor and his wife about to leave. The couple seemed close to madness. They had a packet of poison with them; they too had made up their minds to put an end to it all. Marie Dabs began to realise something of what had gone on in town that night while she'd been shivering in Deven Wood. It stirred a deep dread in her, but at the same time she felt a strange pull. Suddenly she, too, found herself able to imagine the previously unimaginable. 'I asked them to give us some poison as well, but there was only enough for the two of them, and they went on their way.' The corpses of Dr Melzer and his wife lay on the edge of Deven Wood for days.

Marie Dabs and her small party kept going, leaving the outskirts of Demmin for the open countryside, until they arrived at the nearby village of Eichholz, where her father owned a plot of meadowland and a poultry farm on the Trebel. She had previously arranged to meet him here in the event of a Russian invasion, and found when she arrived that he had already taken in several other refugees. He put his daughter and her party up in a hut made of bundles of thatch, together with the Wockersins and their twelve-year-old son. Like the Dabs, Herr Wockersin ran a fur business in Demmin. He had always been a man of few words and rather aloof, seeing them as competitors; now, in extreme plight, he remained reserved and silent. After one night with Marie Dabs and the others, the Wockersins strapped three bulging rucksacks on their backs without a word of explanation and went off in silence. 'When my father brought us a small pail of milk early the next morning, he told us that the Wockersins had walked into the Trebel.'

In the space of only a few hours, Marie Dabs had encountered several people about to commit one of the most extreme acts a human can. Even she, inveterate optimist that she was, came close to succumbing. The dark mood that was dragging so many into the abyss had taken hold of her, too.

. . .

In the days between 30 April and 3 May 1945, Demmin became the scene of an unprecedented wave of suicides. People went to their deaths in droves: young men and women, staid married couples, people in the prime of life, the retired and the elderly. Many took their children with them: infants and toddlers, schoolchildren and adolescents. The victims could not be easily categorised. Hundreds were refugees from Pomerania, East and West Prussia and elsewhere, but there were also hundreds from Demmin and the surrounding area. Blue- and white-collar workers died, clerks and tradesmen, doctors and pharmacists, housewives and war widows, shopkeepers and policemen, managers and accountants, pensioners and teachers. Among the dead were a butcher, a carpenter, a cartwright, a charwoman, a tax clerk, a mechanic, a manager, a chef, a hotelier, a joiner, a chemist, a postman, a post office assistant, a retired postal inspector, a well-digger, a turner, a dentist, a seamstress, a tax inspector, a cattle dealer, a midwife, a retired customs clerk, a notary, a forester, a roadmender, a prison warden, a farmer, a smith, a former headmaster, a paver, a barber and a mayor. Dozens of unidentified bodies were also buried in the mass graves dug in Demmin's cemetery in early May—people whose names and backgrounds remain unknown. Those who went to their deaths were of all ages, classes and professions. The suicides of Demmin represented a cross-section of small-town German society. It was as if the death urge had suddenly gripped them all.

. . .

Some people decided to go this way alone. Elise Ramm, an elderly widow, hanged herself in her flat. Former chief post office clerk Albert Wollbrecht drowned in the River Tollense, aged almost eighty. Charlotte Höffler, an accountant, died in a summerhouse on 1 May.

Many married couples and families, though, committed joint suicide. Elderly couples killed themselves together, like sixty-four-year-old cartwright Franz Höffler and his wife, Gertrud, who hanged themselves in their flat in Mühlenstrasse, or master barber Ernst Hoffmann and his wife, Hertha, both seventy-four, who drowned themselves in a canal by the gasworks. Some killed themselves along with their parents or grown-up children: mechanic Ernst Hirrick died with his wife, Käte, and their twenty-year-old daughter, Gerda, in a canal by the sewage works; chemist's wife Käte Müller was found dead in her flat in Anklamer Strasse together with her seventeen-year-old daughter and seventy-year-old mother. Even large families were wiped out at a single blow. In Bahnhofstrasse, on 1 May, forty-eight-year-old teacher

Paul Heinrich Behnke killed his entire family—his fifteen-year-old daughter, Irmgard Johanna, his two-year-old son, Hans, his wife, Irmgard Gertrud, and himself. That same day, another entire family gave up the struggle only a few streets away: young cook Hermann Halmich and his wife, their year-old child and its grandmother.

A particularly unusual case of collective suicide took place in the house of sixty-six-year-old furniture manufacturer Oskar Günther. On the morning of 30 April, about twenty people were gathered in his house in Baustrasse—his sister, his daughter, his daughter-in-law and a host of other friends and relations, including a forester called Gustav Sembach. The Soviet soldiers came, the looting and rape began, and the sea of flames crept steadily closer. After two days, Oskar Günther, his wife, Elsa, and her sister Hedwig poisoned themselves. Neighbours reported that the Günthers' daughter had hastened their deaths by slitting their wrists with razor blades. Their bodies were burnt along with the house, but not before their friends and family had fled from Baustrasse, some of them making for a couple of summerhouses north of the old town. Here, another bloodbath ensued. Sembach the forester took his rifle and shot Günther's daughter-in-law Gertrud and her four-year-old daughter. He then shot his wife, Paula, and elderly merchant's wife Charlotte Richter and *her* daughter. When he was the only one left, Gustav Sembach put a bullet in his own head, but it did not immediately prove fatal. He was to live almost two months more before succumbing to his injuries.

. . .

Considerable numbers of women and children died in Demmin. At the time of the Soviet conquest, most young and middle-aged men were at the front, in POW camps or buried in soldiers' graves. The women had been left behind in Demmin with their children or stranded there while fleeing westwards. For days, they were at the mercy of the conquering soldiers' frenzied violence. Almost all reports describe the rape and abuse that were a constant and ever-present threat to women of all ages: soldiers who broke into flats and cellars in the middle of the night and shone torches into women's faces; soldiers who raped a young girl several times on an asparagus patch; soldiers who assaulted a sixty-four-year-old woman on the street, in front of her daughter and grandson.

A young medical student, Lotte-Lore Martens, who was evacuated from Demmin's eastern outskirts by Soviet soldiers on 1 May, describes in her memoirs the moment when horror gave way to a feeling of doom. After asking relatives in Campstrasse to look after her father, who'd been an invalid since the First World War, she set off with her mother in search of new lodgings for the family. But the way into town was blocked. 'My mother and I had just reached the corner of Augustastrasse when we saw a huge crowd rushing towards us like an avalanche.' They had come up against the mass of people fleeing eastwards—away from the prowling Soviet soldiers and the flames of the old town. Swept along by the crowd, they headed the same way, up the hill past the cemetery to a rise outside town, above the Tollense valley. From this vantage point, Lotte-Lore Martens saw clouds of smoke rising from the old town, and was reminded of Rome burning under Nero. But it was another sight that left her reeling: a never-ending line of women, running not so much from the fire as from their own fate. A desperate procession in broad daylight.

> With the smoke came hosts of raped women, some of them
> still heavily bleeding, staggering up Jarmener Chaussee in
> a trance, trailing a child—or two or three or sometimes

four—by the hand. Sooner or later, they all turned off right, towards the Tollense. There was no stopping them. Mass psychosis. They went to their deaths in the water.

Of all the different ways of committing suicide, drowning was the most common in Demmin. Because the town was on a peninsula, at the intersection of three rivers, no one in Demmin was ever more than ten minutes' walk from a waterway. The marshland and reed beds along the rivers began just behind the houses; muddy paths led through the waist-high reeds to the willows and birches at the water's edge. The current was weak, sometimes barely noticeable, and the river was shallow. You had to be determined to drown in those waters. Some people carried rucksacks so full of stones that they could barely be tied shut, and the straps cut deep into their shoulders. Others bound themselves together. Children were pulled along by strings and ropes, knotted around their wrists. Small babies clung to their mothers as they waded into the water.

As well as the three rivers, there are dozens of canals, ditches, pools and reservoirs scattered about the countryside. These, too, were sought out by the suicidal. People drowned themselves in the straight, narrow canals alongside the Peene or by the commons— or in the canals by the sewage works and the gasworks and the public baths. On 2 May, a middle-aged woman was found lying in Swan Pond. By the afternoon, a mother with her three-year-old son had been discovered there too. In a number of cases, the survival instinct prevailed despite desperate attempts to die. This led to scenes such as those observed by Lotte-Lore Martens from her lookout point on the hill above the Tollense: 'Some women could swim, though their children couldn't, so the women ended up surviving. Can they ever have got over what happened, I wonder?' On 1 May, a three-month-old boy died in a canal by the gasworks.

It was his mother who reported his death to the authorities. Seven-year-old Dieter Zorr, who drowned in the Peene by the sewage works, was likewise survived by his mother.

Anyone with a rifle or pistol was better off. Like the teacher Gerhard Moldenhauer, Paul Behnke, another teacher, shot first his family and then himself. But only very few civilians had thought to prepare for the Soviet invasion by providing themselves with firearms. Some got hold of poison—prussic acid or Veronal. This was an obvious choice for the Österlins, who kept a chemist's shop on Bergstrasse and died on 30 April, and for veterinary surgeon Dr Melzer and his wife. In some cases, however, the poison—depending on the dosage, and the individual's constitution—proved insufficiently effective. This was particularly tragic in attempted family suicides where only the weakest—the children, that is—were killed by the poison, as in the case of the fifteen-year-old daughter of a ship-broker and his wife, or the four-year-old daughter of a pastor. An even more uncertain way to die, especially when it was done carelessly or in panic, was to slit one's wrists. From the very first day, people came to Demmin Hospital with severed tendons and veins, their arteries still intact. They were left with withered hands and telltale scars on their wrists.

Many had no choice but to hang themselves. Single people did it alone; others went to their deaths together—married couples, elderly mothers with grown-up daughters, even entire families, like that of a Reich Labour Service leader named Büchner. A master blacksmith's widow who lived at 1 Schwedenwallweg hanged herself on 1 May, along with her two daughters and grandson. Only a day later, a turner and his wife and the forty-three-year-old wife of a labourer hanged themselves in the same building; within twenty-four hours, almost all the occupants had died by hanging. One woman who tried to hang herself in a tree after poisoning her three children and burying them in the countryside was cut down three times by Soviet soldiers. Elsewhere, the enemy soldiers rescued people from rivers or bandaged bleeding wrists.

Deven Wood

There were scenes of desperation and despair throughout the town and the surrounding area. There were dead bodies all over the place—hanging in houses and streets and green spaces and floating wherever there was water. The oaks and copper beeches of Deven Wood, on the western edge of town, had always made it a popular destination for families and walkers. Now people were going there to poison themselves in the shade of the trees. It was the same at the other end of town, in the sparsely wooded slopes that bordered the cemetery. One man even went to the cemetery to shoot himself, while his wife and mother-in-law poisoned them-selves in the same spot. A woman was found poisoned on the grass in a meadow. An elderly man was found dead on a motorboat by Drönnewitz Field. There were corpses drifting in the Tollense and the Peene, among the debris from the dynamited railway bridges;

there were corpses in the tributaries, canals and ponds. Some people sought out the seclusion of their summerhouses outside the northern wall of the town, and hanged or shot themselves there. But those who didn't throw themselves in the rivers mostly died in the familiar surroundings of their own homes.

A particularly striking aspect of the reports is the number of suicides involving children. Like the adults, these children were shot or drowned, hanged or poisoned, or bled to death from slit wrists—but with the exception of a few who were old enough to kill themselves, it was their mothers and fathers or sometimes their grandparents or other family members who slipped the noose round their necks, put the poison in their mouths or slashed their wrists. For those who died by drowning it must have taken enormous strength to drag their babies and children along with them and press them down under the water until they no longer felt any resistance. A six-week-old baby boy and three little girls, aged five, three and three months, died in the Peene, by the railway bridge. A young mother killed herself and her two children, aged three and four, in a canal. A woman from Tilsit killed her three sons in her flat before going on to kill herself.

Of almost two hundred nameless dead buried in Demmin's cemetery, more than a third are young boys and girls and babies. There were, though, rare cases of survival. A mother who died after slitting her wrists was survived by her daughter. Another who was planning to drown herself and her four children was dragged away from the banks of the Tollense by her fifteen-year-old son.

• • •

Trapped in Demmin at the worst possible moment, Irene Bröker survived the first wave of Soviet troops on 30 April unharmed, but had no idea of the horrors she was yet to witness. There was no escape from the disaster that had befallen Demmin. When the fires and lootings and rapes began in the old town, women and girls came flocking to the house by the cemetery, but Soviet soldiers soon drove up in trucks, looking for them. Bröker had several lucky escapes from rape, saved by ruse, or the intervention of her companion Dr P. It was an uncertain time, she said.

> Nobody knew what would happen next. We had no rights and nothing to bargain with. We heard no news. I slept in a different place every night.

Irene Bröker spent the nights in constantly changing hiding places to avoid assault. She slept in hedges of brambles and behind rabbit hutches, in a concrete trough in the attic, and in the shelter beneath the compost heap. During the day, she had two-year-old Holger to look after, so she never had the opportunity—or the courage—to leave the house by the cemetery, and saw nothing of what was going on in the streets and parks and rivers of Demmin. Then one day they were visited by the old Soviet soldier who had discovered them in their makeshift shelter. He took Dr P. with him, saying that he was needed for a special task. The doctor returned that evening with grim news:

> Dr P. told us that about 600 people, many of them children, had walked into the Peene. He'd had to help fish them from the water and lay them out in long rows. All day long, bodies had kept washing ashore.

It took days to pile up all the bodies and take them to the cemetery to be buried. Once it was done, Dr P. had to help clean up the river-banks and streets. Every evening he returned with the same bleak look on his face. Irene Bröker, meanwhile, spent the days searching the garden and fields for things dropped by looters: things they needed, like forks and spoons. One morning she went out into the garden and froze, seeing the horror with her own eyes for the first time. Beside the garden fence lay the body of a woman who had killed herself and her two small children. Irene Bröker saw only the children's shoes and stockings. She didn't dare go nearer, or touch them. 'No one will ever know exactly what happened,' she wrote later. 'The three dead bodies lay there till evening. Then somebody must have given them a makeshift burial under cover of darkness.'

But the three nameless bodies didn't rest for long. The next day, Russian soldiers came into the garden to root around in the ground with long, sharp-ended sticks, knowing that many Germans had buried their valuables in their gardens before taking flight. The earth over the dead woman and her two children had been churned up, exposing the bodies. Irene Bröker saw their pale faces, streaked with dirt, and painstakingly covered them with earth again. It was the same story the next day.

> At last I came up with the rather horrible idea of leaving the children's legs sticking up out of the earth. That way, there were always four little legs in shoes and brown stockings, peeping out as a 'warning' to foragers. We were very much upset by this macabre sight, but there were no more soldiers digging there after that.

Irene's head was spinning. She had lost all sense of time. Her husband was missing, her parents lost along the way. A strange town was smouldering in the distance, and all around her was violence and looting. She heard Dr P.'s muted reports of what he had seen, saw those little legs sticking out of the earth, felt helpless and uncertain. She had no idea what was going on or how it would turn out. There was just her and little Holger—no hope for the future. Irene Bröker was physically and mentally robust, but she felt herself losing her grip. She, too, began to think it might be better to kill herself. The tablets were still there, in the watertight pouch around her neck. Her fingers rose to her throat when she thought of them.

Once she had made up her mind, Irene waited. When no one was about, she went into the kitchen and dissolved the tablets in two cups. Then she took a spoon and tried to feed a little of the liquid to her son. 'He pulled a terrible face,' she said, 'but it was time for his meal so he gulped at it bravely.' She felt a quiet desperation. A woman came into the kitchen unexpectedly, grabbed the cups and tipped the poison down the drain. But Irene Bröker stuck to her resolve to die and take Holger with her. 'When the woman was gone, I decided to hang myself in the attic. But the thought of seeing my little boy dangling there, struggling, held me back.'

In the end, then, her suicide attempt failed, not because of her fear of death or her respect for life, but because of her vivid imagination. Without it, she might have shared the fate of many others in Demmin.

The next morning, little Holger slept late. At this point in the narrative, Irene's tone changes: she sounds more grounded again. The days of numb desperation were over. The Soviets set up a provisional administration department, and the Germans in Demmin reconciled themselves to living alongside the enemy soldiers who stayed on. Before long, Irene Bröker was making plans to return to her hometown—although she did sometimes wonder whether she wouldn't have been better off buried in the cemetery in Demmin. Writing about her experiences, she said: 'All this sounds very far-fetched! But anyone who lived through that time in Demmin will understand.'

The Ghosts of Demmin

By Friday 4 May, most of the fires had been put out. Thin columns of smoke still rose from the charred heaps of rubble, but behind them the silhouette of the church tower could be seen again and was surprisingly unscathed. Many townspeople who had spent the last few days sheltering in barns, or in the fields or the woods outside Demmin, took this as a sign to venture back to their houses. The combat troops had moved on with their tanks over the temporary bridges, and the triumphant fury of those who remained behind had blown over.

Ursula Strohschein walked through the streets of the old town with her father, stumbling over smouldering piles of debris. Smoke-blackened holes where windows had been gaped out of the facades. At 16 Luisenstrasse, they stood before the mountain of rubble that had been Ursula's father's mineral-water factory. Here and there, machine parts and iron girders jutted into the air, looking strangely defiant. Nothing was left of what had once been Ursula's childhood home—no house, no garage, no stables, no sheds. Her father managed to get hold of an undamaged flat in Anklamer Strasse, but only, as Ursula soon realised, because the people who had lived there had died:

> The deserted dental practice had belonged to Dr Enders, who'd been found with his wife in Sandbergtannen Wood, half buried…shot dead. Only now did we discover the extent of the horror.

The dead bodies in the rivers and woods and houses hadn't yet been retrieved and buried. Returning from the fields outside town, having narrowly escaped death at the hands of his own mother, ten-year-old Karl Schlösser saw corpses lying in the water, swollen to shapeless masses in the warm spring weather, some of them tied to one another with ropes. He saw hanged bodies swaying in the wind. Decades later, Karl Schlösser could still see those people hanging in the apple trees when he shut his eyes. 'A heavy blanket of smog lay over the town for days, partly from the smoke and fire, and partly from the sickly sweet smell of all those dead bodies.'

In some of the burnt-out houses, people returning home found the charred remains of those who had hanged or shot themselves. Many only discovered now that their relatives, neighbours or friends had taken their lives. On Soviet orders, the bodies were hastily buried in gardens and yards. Orders were also given for corpses to be retrieved from the rivers and canals before they became a source of disease and a threat to the living. There were still horses pulling covered carts up the hill to the cemetery weeks later. Drowned bodies continued to wash up on the shallow, reedy banks, and with each day that passed they became harder to identify.

Medical student Lotte-Lore Martens spent days looking for her invalid father. He was no longer in the flat in Campstrasse where she'd left him with relatives; he'd gone off, saying that he was going to kill himself. The bank of the Tollense was only a few yards from Campstrasse. As Lotte-Lore and her uncle paced up and down beneath the blossoming willows of the winding flood plains, she shuddered at the spring countryside's indifference to the disaster.

> The sight of the riverbank moved me more each day. The meadows by the river, resplendent in their spring finery, were edged, like the border of a dress, with about 1.5–2 metres of baby's clothes and other garments—expensive frocks and furs in particular—and identity papers and passports. Money, too—a lot of money—but nobody stooped to pick it up; it seemed to us worthless.

Lotte-Lore Martens never found her father, but she did find his military ID and his fur coat, on the bank opposite the waterworks. She also found coats belonging to her aunt and grandmother.

• • •

On 6 May, Marga Behnke, the daughter of the cemetery gardener, began to keep a record of the suicides in Demmin. On this day alone, the first day of mass burials, she made thirty-four entries, and for more than nine weeks afterwards she kept daily records. Here and there a name or date has been added in her mother's handwriting. Rather than use the official register, they recorded everything in the cemetery nursery's slim black receipt book. The names and origins of the dead (insofar as they were identifiable) were entered in the column headed *Lieferer* or 'supplier'. The next two columns were reserved for as precise a record as possible of the day and the manner of death. When this information could not be established, as was often the case with the drowned bodies,

Marga Behnke had to make do with registering an unknown woman, man, boy or girl. Refusing to consign hundreds of people to anonymity and oblivion, she noted even the slightest clue to a person's identity: the initials on a handkerchief, a red blouse, a missing index finger.

Cemetery nursery receipt book

On the twenty-eight pages of this improvised death register, which they kept until 15 July, Marga and her mother recorded the deaths of more than six hundred people, most of whom had either committed suicide or, in the case of children, died along with their parents. More than half, many of them refugees or unidentified, were buried in a mass grave, including the family of schoolteacher Gerhard Moldenhauer, who had shot at the Soviets from his window after killing his wife and children. Many other residents of Demmin, though, were buried in individual graves—the furrier Herr Wockersin and his family, for example, who had drowned themselves in the Trebel; Gustav Sembach, the forester, who had shot himself in the head and died of the wound some time later; and military vet Dr Melzer and his wife, who had poisoned themselves in Deven Wood. Often it was dependants of the deceased who arranged for them to have graves of their own. The Kuhlmanns' family maid, Else, ends her account of the family's demise as follows:

> Another thing I should like to tell you, my dear Werner, is that your mother and Ilse were buried in a grave in the cemetery. Your father couldn't be recovered from the rubble, because there was too big a fire in the dispensary. Your mother and Ilse were found in the ruins of the dining room, their bodies charred. I have put a cross on their grave. I'm afraid it's only a wooden one, but it can always be replaced at a later date.

In the black receipt book, Marga Behnke had at first listed Werner's father, Dr Kuhlmann, under grave no. 240, after his wife (grave no. 238) and daughter (grave no. 239). Eventually, though, when his body wasn't found, she had to strike 'veterinary surgeon' off the list.

· · ·

Official record keeping of the recent events in Demmin also began at about this time. On 19 May, Sorge, the registrar, opened a makeshift office, because the old town hall had been reduced to a gaping facade. As the death records from 1945 had burnt along with everything else in the registry office, Sorge had to begin at the beginning and start his records at number one. He received long lines of husbands and wives, mothers and fathers, sons and daughters, uncles, nieces, mothers-in-law and grandmothers who had survived, and came to Sorge to register their relatives' deaths. Sometimes it was neighbours or friends who came to him; sometimes people whose connection to the dead was in no way obvious. Within two weeks, Sorge's figures had soared into the hundreds, though some deaths weren't reported until weeks or even months after the event.

All through that summer and far on into the autumn, Sorge the registrar listened to the grim stories of death in Demmin. In many cases, the misery of the survivors overshadowed even the horrors suffered by the dead. On 25 May, Elfriede Schultz, whose son-in-law had already been missing for some time, came to report the suicide of her daughter and grandchild. The death of three-year-old Gerd Wedhorn in a canal was registered by his mother, whose own suicide attempt had evidently failed. A musician reported that his wife had drowned herself and their child in Swan Pond. On 12 June, Marie Büchner told Herr Sorge of the deaths of her son, daughter-in-law, grandchild and three other members of her family, who had all been found together, hanged.

On the one-page death certificates on which the registrar set his seal, he recorded, sometimes in the spiky Sütterlin script then common in Germany, the dead person's age, denomination, place of residence and birth, and marital status. He recorded the place and time of death and noted down the personal details of the individual reporting the case. There was no space on the form, however, for the circumstances of death, let alone the cause or motives. Herr Sorge seemed to regard this as unsatisfactory, and began to add postscripts such as 'Death by suicide (hanging)' to the final time-of-death section. Before long, he had switched to inserting footnotes at the bottom left-hand side of the page. If, at first, Sorge restricted himself to the single word 'suicide', he was soon elaborating on this: 'suicide by hanging', 'suicide by poison', 'suicide by slit wrists', 'suicide by shooting', 'killed by mother', 'killed by parents with poison'. Sometimes he intimated the nature of an individual's death by replacing the word 'deceased' with the expression 'found dead'. Such minor tweaks allowed the registrar to pull aside the curtain of bureaucratic formalism and give a glimpse of the events of those days.

On 19 October, he signed the last two suicides reported to him: numbers 926 and 927, the wife and youngest son of senior medical officer Dr Herbst. By this point Sorge had heard, recorded and certified almost two hundred deaths. The few that followed bear the signature of a different clerk.

Part II

DEMMIN IS EVERYWHERE

A Voice from the Bombed-out Temple

The vicar of Kaiser Wilhelm Memorial Church on Berlin's Kurfürstendamm was an unassuming-looking man, with his narrow shoulders, narrow face and receding chin. His shy-looking eyes peered out through round glasses, and his moustache was as sparse as the hair on his head—a pale parody of the Führer's famous toothbrush. But Gerhard Jacobi was by no means as timid and cautious as he appeared. As head of the oppositional Confessing Church, he had been taking a stand against the regime for twelve years, and had often been mocked, arrested or beaten up for his convictions. He himself was merciless with his congregation, insisting that they face up to the many contemporary horrors challenging them as Christians.

One Sunday in early March 1945, Jacobi preached against one of the archenemies of life and soul—suicide. In the congregation was Danish newspaper correspondent Jacob Kronika, who regularly combed Berlin's churches in search of dissenting voices that spoke out above the drone of official rhetoric. He felt strangely moved by the powerful sermon Jacobi gave that morning. It seemed to him somehow out of place in that particular parish.

The Kaiser Wilhelm Memorial Church, a many-towered monument to empire in the western centre of the capital, had suffered repeated bombings. The roof over the nave had fallen in and the tip of the spire snapped off. It stood there, gutted, like a pile of gnawed and broken bones, a boarded-up, bombed-out temple—but a considerable crowd had gathered for the service nevertheless, in draughty makeshift premises. 'The parish hall was bursting,' Kronika said. He saw a flock of believers undeterred by air raids and winter weather, and observed: 'Something of a sense of their fighting spirit can be felt in the way they sing.'

These were the people whom the Reverend Jacobi lectured sternly on the subject of suicide, making it quite clear that under no circumstances did Christians have the option of killing themselves. No matter how bleak or miserable life on earth, particularly in times such as these, the prohibition against suicide was incontrovertible. To Kronika it seemed he was preaching directly to each and every person present:

> We have no right to it, the preacher said. As Christians, we must be prepared to endure yet greater woes than those inflicted on us thus far. It was a profoundly earnest congregation that left this strange service.

Two things in particular struck the Danish journalist as odd. First of all, the people spilling wordlessly out of the parish hall had already been through quite a bit. They had been bombed out of their homes—or if not, they lived in fear of it. They had lost sons, husbands and other loved ones. Some had lost their livelihood. And now they were expected to endure even worse. But—and this was the second strange thing—Kronika saw no surprise in their grey, tight-lipped faces at the accusations of suicidal intent levelled at them by their vicar. Kronika decided to investigate. He waylaid the Reverend Jacobi at the door and asked him the reason for his sermon. Jacobi led him into his office and closed the door behind him. 'There is risk of a suicide epidemic,' the vicar said. 'I have regular visits from parishioners who confide in me that they have procured ampoules of cyanide. They see no way out.'

Suicide epidemic—the Reverend Gerhard Jacobi was the first to use this term, evoking thoughts of an infectious disease lurking in large numbers of people, ready to break out at any time and spread like wildfire. Jacobi feared that such a disease was on the point of taking hold. Nazi propaganda had drummed it into the Germans that the Soviets brought hell on earth wherever they went. It was almost impossible to escape the horror stories, and, confronted with them day after day, many people saw no alternative but to equip themselves with poison.

. . .

The visit made a lasting impression on Jacob Kronika; in subsequent diary entries from a foundering Berlin, he would often return to that late-winter sermon and its prophecy of the rising wave of suicide across the German Reich. He saw it as a troubling echo of his own sense of foreboding a few days before, when he had come across a German colleague, a loyal Nazi journalist, on the verge of giving up. 'I can't carry on,' the man had sighed. 'Everything I believed in is turning out to be madness and crime.' When Kronika bumped into him on Wilhelmplatz, in the government district, he was still wearing his swastika badge, still attending the press conferences at the Propaganda Ministry, like a good Nazi, still taking the mandatory tone in his writing, urging the people to carry on. And yet he could see that it was over. He was desperate, Kronika wrote.

> But the tyranny forces him to keep going, the same as always,
> the same as since 1933 ... That is, in effect, the terrible tragedy
> of the German people: they can't muster the strength or see
> their way to freeing themselves from the rule of evil.

This tragedy, a leitmotiv of Kronika's diary, was also his own personal tragedy, at least on paper. As a member of the Danish minority in the German Reich, he held German citizenship as well as Danish and wrote not only for Danish and Swedish newspapers but also in the German press. He had initially welcomed the Nazi takeover, but soon distanced himself from 'war's rebellion against peace'.

You could tell just by looking at him. He was a civilian through and through. Although he'd been living in Berlin for thirteen years—he was in his late forties at the end of the war—he strolled the streets of the Nazi capital like a tourist, with his carefully coiffed salt-and-pepper hair, and a handkerchief in the pocket of his well-kept suit, like in peacetime. He had made it his mission to record Germany's downfall to the end, so he spent his days wandering the city—pounding the pavements with their gritty covering of air-raid debris, or tramping through weed-choked parks. He passed scorched houses, bathtubs rusting on piles of rubble, twisted copper pipes and gaping rooms in which tiled stoves clung to the walls with a kind of vicious defiance.

He saw and analysed the symptoms of collapse and self-destruction, but above all he listened, and people seemed happy to open up to the friendly foreigner and tell him their stories. A favourite place for such conversations was the air-raid shelter, where Kronika sat out many hours with people from all walks of life. On 6 March 1945, the day of the Reverend Jacobi's stern sermon, he noted in his diary:

Wilhelm II promised us glorious times, but they didn't come. Hitler and Goebbels promise us large numbers of suicides and it's exactly what we get! That's what people were saying loud and clear in the air-raid shelter yesterday.

Kronika had noticed that suicide came up frequently now—in newspapers, on state radio, and even in the Nazi leadership's rhetoric. 'Goebbels has changed his tune: he is talking of suicide as a last resort.' In a radio broadcast dripping with pathos, Goebbels had invoked the example of Frederick II, who had believed only in death or victory. Goebbels offered up the Prussian king as a heroic martyr because he had once, at a time of military crisis, toyed with the idea of taking poison. Rarely had the propaganda machine appealed so heavy-handedly to the self-sacrificing spirit of the German people.

At the end of his diary entry for 6 March, Jacob Kronika quotes the Reverend Jacobi: 'The brunt of responsibility for this growing tendency to suicide falls on Dr Goebbels.' But even the vicar failed to realise how serious the situation had become: in early March 1945, the suicide epidemic he feared was no longer a mere danger; it had already broken out and was spreading rapidly.

A Wave Rolling over the Reich

The thought of living on is unbearable, and it is equally unthinkable that I could now live a happy life with you, darling Inge, and our dear little girl, because the war—which seems to me as good as lost, what with the indestructible Bolsheviks on one side and the Americans joining on the other—will leave me unable to earn sufficient money, either now or in the future. The first and last cause of my despair is the hopelessness of victory.

This very thorough suicide note was found by the Berlin police on the body of a fifty-six-year-old teacher from Weissensee. It was addressed to his wife and dated 21 August 1943. The defeat of the German army at Stalingrad six months before had triggered a first spate of suicides throughout the Reich—suicides that had their root in the specific fear of Bolshevism and the more general fear of Germany's bleak future.

This phenomenon was not restricted to civilians. After the

debacle of Stalingrad, more than two thousand cases of suicide among Wehrmacht soldiers were reported in a few months— twice as many as in the first three *years* of the war. After the D-day landings in 1944, the Luftwaffe recorded another significant rise in suicides and suicide attempts. At this stage, however, incidents were still isolated, often planned long in advance, the decisions explained in suicide notes. Suicide in Germany still followed the classic pattern it had known in times of peace.

. . .

The military setbacks and blows to morale suffered at Stalingrad and on D-day, as well as the demoralising air raids on German cities, had cast a dark shadow, and not only over the prospect of victory. They also added a new—and quite unforeseen—dimension to the gruesome imagery used in anti-Allied propaganda. Portraying the enemy as barbarous murderers had been useful in rousing the German people to support the war effort, but there was nothing rousing in the thought that those same barbarous murderers were about to take Berlin and sweep triumphant across Germany. Rather than being bolstered by hate and pride, the German psyche was consumed by existential fear. The fear of invasion, of losing honour, homeland, family. The fear of losing life and its meaning.

In autumn 1944, this fear was fanned into panic in Germany's eastern territories by the media's widespread and sensationalist coverage of the Nemmersdorf massacre. Although German troops had managed to halt the Soviets' advance at Nemmersdorf and even push them back across the border, the terror of what had happened there—and what was yet to come—had the nation firmly in its grip.

'It was still hard to understand what was going on,' Hans von Lehndorff wrote in his diary, 'and no one dared voice secret fears in public.' In those last weeks of the year, von Lehndorff, a thirty-five-year-old doctor from the East Prussian town of Insterburg, spotted many villagers staring dreamily into the sky, watching the birds head south for the winter. 'They must all have felt the same when they saw them: "You're all right, you're flying away! But what about us? What's to become of us and our country?"'

At night, the villagers had seen the eastern border towns under shellfire, bright pulsing points in the distance. It was fewer than thirty kilometres from Insterburg to Nemmersdorf. Even without the constant, hysterical propaganda, the fate of the neighbouring town made their blood run cold. They knew that just across the border were millions of Soviet soldiers who'd waited four years for the moment when they could finally set foot on German soil and overrun the enemy towns. They knew that when the huge wave of rage and hatred broke they would be the first to be hit.

When the Soviet attack on East Prussia began on 13 January 1945, Hans von Lehndorff took charge of a military hospital in Königsberg. People in the 'fortress of Königsberg', which was soon surrounded by Soviets, seemed to him detached from reality. In his diary, he describes being visited on 23 January by an elderly lady, who asked for long-deferred surgery on her varicose veins, even as the cannons were thundering outside. She wouldn't hear of fleeing the city. Von Lehndorff couldn't believe his ears when he heard her say: 'The Führer won't let us fall to the Russians; he'd sooner gas us.' The doctor glanced furtively about him, but no one, he said, seemed to think anything of this remark.

It wasn't long before he himself had started to feel a vague sense of doom. 'It doesn't really matter what happens to us now,' he wrote. Only a few days later, the Russian artillery was shelling Königsberg. Hans von Lehndorff went with his assistant, a young doctor, to visit her parents in the suburb of Juditten and help them prepare to flee westwards. This young woman, whom he respectfully calls 'Doktora' in his diary, was to become his closest companion in the months that followed. Even the worst times are easier to bear when there's someone to share them.

In Juditten, the young woman's parents told them that they had abandoned their plans to flee. Instead, after thirty years of happy marriage, they were thinking of putting an end to their lives. Neither their daughter nor her colleague could talk them out of it. They clearly didn't even try. The brief notes in von Lehndorff's diary betray neither surprise nor outrage, nor even resistance to the idea, which had by now become commonplace.

> They are not the only ones faced with this decision. Wherever you go these days, people are talking about cyanide, which seems to be available in any quantity. The question of whether to resort to it is not even debated. Only the requisite quantity is discussed—in an easy, offhand manner, the way people usually talk about, say, food.

These few lines succinctly describe the symptoms of the epidemic that began in East Prussia and would soon sweep the country. Against the backdrop of the physical, emotional and mental horrors of Germany's downfall, social conventions classifying suicide as an extreme, almost incomprehensible act no longer seemed to apply. Condemned by the church over the centuries, it had, until now, been considered immoral, and forbidden as a sin. The subject of a potent taboo, it provoked a profound horror, and had been spoken of only in hushed tones behind closed doors, prompting feelings of shock, shame and guilt. The act itself was regarded as unnatural; by committing suicide, victims positioned themselves outside or even against the accepted social order.

The power of this taboo quietly faded away as Germany began

to fall to the Soviets in the east and to Allied forces in the west. The well-ordered society that had once upheld it was now in the process of destroying itself; people were coming to expect chaos and anarchy, terror, oppression, violence and humiliation. They felt a nameless fear of the future. Suicide was no longer a sin; it was now seen as a last resort before total surrender. It was a consolation to the desperate to know that they could cut short their suffering on earth. Soon, people all over Germany were talking openly about putting an end to it all—about ways and means and the right place and appropriate time. The taboo was broken.

This became plain to Hans von Lehndorff on the night of 28 January 1945, when he and his young colleague returned once more to Juditten to check on her parents, and found that the elderly couple had already put their plan into action. Von Lehndorff notes their suicide in his diary without a flicker of surprise, as if her parents had simply been out when they arrived:

> We return to Juditten that night and find the dead couple in their beds, carefully laid out by the elder daughter, who's already left the house. The windows are open. It's icy in the room. For a while we stand there in silence. Out on the stairs we say the Lord's Prayer.

But the night wasn't over yet:

> As we're coming out of the front door, a woman rushes towards us from across the road. 'Frau Doktor, is that you? Come quickly, my husband has poisoned himself with gas.'

The epidemic had begun. In the weeks leading up to and beyond the surrender of Königsberg on 9 April, von Lehndorff recorded more and more incidents confirming his diagnosis. He and his assistant treated people who'd been in a deep sleep for days after taking large quantities of tablets. They noticed the envy with which the living eyed the dead. Von Lehndorff struggled for days to dissuade his theatre nurse from killing herself. He gave speeches in the operating theatre of the military hospital, 'to fight the risk of contagion posed by suicide'. He found one of his colleagues dead, his wrists slit; others he was able to save from bleeding to death.

Von Lehndorff and his assistant's deep faith saved them from being sucked into this maelstrom. The words of the gospel helped them hold firm. But even this source of strength was not inexhaustible. A few days after Königsberg was taken, von Lehndorff was unable to stop a Soviet soldier raping his young assistant. After this, he broke down and retreated inside himself. He, too, was ready to burn his bridges behind him. 'A thorn is piercing what is left of my soul. I creep away and let myself fall on an iron bedstead. Now to sleep and sleep and see nothing more. It is enough.' It was Doktora who fetched him back and reminded him of their shared faith. She begged him to leave, to make his way west alone, even though she no longer saw this as a possibility for herself. 'There's nothing more you can do here,' she told him. 'I have my tablets, and besides, I know that God demands nothing impossible.'

One morning in July 1945, two months after the end of the war, Doktora didn't wake up. On her table lay a note, saying that she had taken some sleeping pills and wasn't to be woken. 'All feeling has died in me. I go about my day's work as if it were no concern of mine. Am I perhaps already dead inside?' The next day, her heart stopped.

. . .

Hans von Lehndorff wouldn't set off for the west until two years later. His Königsberg diaries were published some years after that as part of the series *Dokumentation der Vertreibung der Deutschen aus Ost-Mitteleuropa* (*Documents on the Expulsion of Germans from Eastern Central Europe*). This sprawling collection of primary sources, selected from a fund of material ten times the size, made more than a thousand eyewitness accounts available to the public soon after the end of the war. Reading them, you can trace the wave of suicide as if on a map, from East Prussia to the Oder-Neisse line and into the smallest villages. Like mass exodus, looting and rape, suicide inevitably accompanied the final battles for the Third Reich. This first wave of suicides in the eastern Reich followed close behind the advancing Red Army, sometimes even preceding it.

Few of the accounts in the collection are as extensive or detailed as von Lehndorff's journal, but they nevertheless confirm his experiences in Königsberg. All along the roads leading west, men and children and women and soldiers hanged or drowned or poisoned or shot themselves or each other, together or alone.

In the town of Liebemühl, for example, a family was found united in death: 'Dead bodies sitting on the sofa, draped over chairs, lying in the beds.'

In the district of Osterode: 'Shudder after shudder ran down our spines. If I had any poison, one man said, I'd poison myself and all the family.'

In the West Prussian city of Elbing: 'The most senior constable said absently that Herr Hauptmann had shot himself at the command post last night.'

In the town of Tempelburg: 'In the course of the morning, the landlord came back inside from his garden and said that there were four corpses (men and women) under a tree in the garden and three corpses hanging in the tree.'

In Treptow, near the Baltic: 'When I said goodbye, he said: "This is the last time we'll see each other." He seemed to have made

86

up his mind. He didn't leave his place of work and I later heard that he'd ended his life that very day.'

In Belgard in Middle Pomerania: 'Mass graves had been dug in the cemetery because there was no other way of burying the corpses. A lot of people had taken their own lives.'

In Lauenberg: 'It's hardly surprising that about 600 inhabitants chose to die on that terrible night.'

In Occalitz in Pomerania: 'In the forest alone, 62 people from Occalitz went to their deaths—they drowned in the lake, were shot by Täger the forester, took poison or hanged themselves.'

In Labischin: 'Several Germans, especially Baltic Germans, committed suicide on the very first day, some together with their entire families—taking poison or slitting their wrists.'

In Kurzig in East Brandenburg: 'Young Frau Lemke shot herself and her two children. Her husband was a soldier. He'd left her his pistol.'

In Lossen in Lower Silesia: 'In her despair, the master tailor's wife Frau Pfeifer hanged her three children, aged between eight and thirteen, and then herself.'

Near Breslau: 'In the night, I poisoned myself with Quadronox (approx. 10 pills), but unfortunately came round again three days later.'

In the Silesian city of Liegnitz: 'Countless suicides were committed over the course of those days. My daughter and a woman with two little girls wanted to do it too. The desperation was indescribable.'

In Possen in Lower Silesia: 'My uncle, mother and younger brother committed suicide by shutting the coal-fired stove too soon. They wanted me to go with them, but after a while I could bear it no longer and ran away.'

In Sternberg in the Sudetenland: 'The list of people who have committed suicide out of fear of the Russians is growing longer and longer.'

In Mährisch Schönberg: 'On the evening of 8 May our land-lady hugged my wife and said: "Now we've put the worst behind us." Later she and her husband chose to commit suicide.'

. . .

Only a few years separate such accounts from the experiences they describe. When people came to record their memories, they were still reeling from what they'd been through, and the suicides' person-alities, motives and past histories merge into a blur, subsumed by the chaotic end of the war and the arrival of the Soviet army. Occasionally, though, an eyewitness account gives you a sense of the state of mind of these people on the edge of the abyss. One such account is the story of Johannes and Hildegard Theinert.

The Teacher and His Wife

Johannes Theinert was a Latin teacher in Glatz, an elegant baroque and Renaissance town in south-west Lower Silesia, tucked away in the Neisse basin, not a hundred kilometres from the city of Breslau. His house was by the river, and he would sit on his balcony and look down at the gentle eddies of the water. Popular with his pupils, he had a plump, open, kindly face, somewhat at odds with his neatly trimmed Hitler moustache, and he invariably wore an old-fashioned suit with a spotted tie. In 1936, aged fifty-three, he had married Hildegard Linke. A year later he began a diary, which he kept until the end of the Second World War—and not a day longer.

The last entry is in his wife's handwriting. On 9 May 1945, the day the Germans capitulated, Hildegard Theinert took up her pen and wrote: 'The war is over. The guns are silent.' She had seen the German soldiers flooding back, singly or in groups, as they headed for the mountains in the west; she had seen the straggling refugees, following one route or another, and often getting held up along the way. Otherwise, the people of Glatz had remained untouched by the war. No bombs, no fighting, not a single shot fired. No foreign soldier had yet set foot in the town. And yet the Theinerts found it hard to rejoice in the end of the war, or their escape. 'The rumours are coming thick and fast,' Hildegard Theinert wrote. 'Everywhere the same anxious question: "What next? What will become of us?"'

It wasn't anti-Bolshevik propaganda that had them frightened of the advancing Russians; the two of them had seen through that from the start. It was, instead, something the propaganda had kept from them. A few weeks before, Hildegard and Johannes Theinert had learnt that the Russian soldiers had every reason to feel hatred and anger towards the Germans; they now had no choice but to believe the horror stories circulating in town.

Three weeks earlier, a former pupil on leave in Glatz had paid a visit to his beloved Latin teacher. He had come straight from the Eastern front, where, during his long years as a soldier, he had witnessed atrocities committed by both sides. The teacher and his wife listened in silence to his stories of Soviet villages burnt down by the Germans, scorched fields, hanged 'partisans' who were little more than children, wounded men shot in the neck to put them out of their misery, starving prisoners and the Soviets' acts of retribution. They remained silent when he began to report on events behind the front lines. A lot of what the soldiers had seen and been through behind the front, in German territory, had so far only been hinted at back at home, but now that the end was in sight, they were done with being cautious and no longer inclined to spare their audience. The onetime pupil now assumed the role of teacher and taught his former schoolmaster the whole horrifying truth. He told him of the foul pits, the piles of clothes, the long queues of desperate people, the watchtowers behind barbed-wire fences, the murderous soldiers in German uniform.

Although many of the places the former pupil mentioned were only names to them, the Theinerts understood how closely they were implicated—how much this was their own story. 'SS, field gendarmerie, special units, the execution of countless Jews, the treatment of Russian POWs, what went on in the concentration camps—hatred will soon be upon us,' Hildegard would later write. The young man had brought the war into their peaceful living room overlooking the river, and with it crimes and guilt. There might have been an element of reproach in his tale: many of Herr Theinert's pupils had found it hard to understand that such an esteemed and respected master had gone to teach at an Adolf Hitler school, an establishment catering to the Nazi elite.

When the pupil left at last, there was little need for discussion. The couple knew that their world would never be the same again. In her diary entry of 9 May, Hildegard Theinert wrote:

> Johannes had listened to it all in silence. All evening and into the night he sat pale and slumped at the window, staring down into the Neisse, like a man turned to stone. We exchanged only a few words that evening.

The river was no comfort. Complicity, culpability, guilt—the Theinerts had no need to say the words aloud as they reached their unanimous verdict. If the war was lost, they would suffer the victors' revenge. Johannes Theinert was a teacher in a Nazi establishment; he knew they'd come for him. But the couple ruled out leaving their town by the river, their home. 'Life would have no meaning for us if we did that,' Hildegard explained. They took a silent decision to which they saw no alternative. 'We would go to our deaths together.'

They began to take leave of all that was dear to them—the town and its inhabitants, their house, the river. It was a long farewell that went on for three weeks. Then, on 9 May 1945, after six years of war, they heard news of the capitulation. It was a beautiful, balmy day; a soft breeze seemed to be coaxing people out into the fresh air.

For the first time, it is the teacher's wife, Hildegard, who sits down at the desk to write the diary. 'Glittering and colourful, the Neisse flows past our hometown, serene and so familiar. The rays of the afternoon sun reflect in its rippling waters.' She tries to capture the mood in their house—and her own mood. She knows it will be the final entry. 'I have said a last farewell to our flat. It has given us so many hours of happiness.' For almost the entire war, they had thought it impossible that things should end this way. They had kept on hoping, believing, dreaming. 'How lovely the future could be, if only—yes, if only—grim reality hadn't destroyed all our dreams of life after the war. One last long look across at the town, up at the fortress.'

Their dreams were the dreams of many millions of Germans. They had all preferred to ignore grim reality, but it could no longer be denied—it was upon them now, harsh and noisy and triumphant. The time had come, Frau Theinert wrote:

> The Russians are in town. We have just heard that Dr Nebler killed his wife and daughters and then himself. A local landlord has hanged his young wife. This kind of thing is happening more and more.

Fear, contagion, a sense of urgency. The Theinerts were not the only ones who had given up hope. Suicide was suddenly rife in the streets and houses of the small town. During these moments of drama, the teacher's wife withdrew to her desk and wrote these final lines in her diary—as if to pause time, to stop it moving forwards. 'Only a little while longer, then it will all be over, forever!'

They must have agreed on a time. When it came, Johannes Theinert took his gun and shot Hildegard and then himself. Their diary was found in the house, beside their dead bodies. The last entry was complete, right up to the moment of their deaths. 'Who will think of us, who will know how we ended? Do my words have any meaning?'

Hell Machine

In January 1945, the 1st Belorussian Front had advanced to the west bank of the Oder at Küstrin and Frankfurt and established two bridgeheads. Nazi authorities declared Frankfurt an der Oder a stronghold, and the commanding officer evacuated parts of the town and prepared it for defence. Another two months would elapse, however, before the Soviets attacked. During this time, between late January and early April 1945, the German police investigated more than sixty suicides. In early February, a retired major general had turned a gun on himself after leaving a tersely worded suicide note: 'I have shot myself so as not to be a burden to my household.' Other cases included joint or group suicides involving everyone within a household; in early March, for instance, a widow and her companion poisoned themselves in their kitchen with coal gas in anticipation of the forced evacuation of their flat.

These deaths were a prelude to the second big wave of suicides that would spread across the German territories west of the

Oder-Neisse line at the beginning of the Red Army's Berlin offensive. Nowhere do the later accounts reach such a pitch of intensity as in Western Pomerania and Mecklenburg, where events were often reconstructed by survivors, partly from their own memories, partly from the gradually emerging stories of their friends and relations.

Norbert Buske, the vicar's son from Demmin, witnessed the Soviet invasion with his mother and brother; he saw the destruction of the town and the mass suicide of its inhabitants, and watched the people with bandaged wrists queuing outside the makeshift doctor's surgery in the room where confirmation classes were held. Week after week, he heard the names of the dead being read out in church, a list that seemed to go on for longer than the service itself. Decades later, he would compile the reports of the deaths of his friends and family and other townspeople as a way of taking stock of those dreadful days. The contours of the disaster were finally becoming clear, and it emerged that the pattern of events had, with slight variations, been repeated many times throughout the region. What went on between 28 April and 3 May 1945 in Demmin, where there were an estimated seven hundred to a thousand suicides, had also happened in countless other places, from Stettin to Rostock.

Take, for instance, the small town of Friedland on the Mecklenburg Lake Plateau, a stop on the westward route of the 2nd Belorussian Front. On 27 April, the Wehrmacht began to evacuate the military hospitals there. The Volkssturm soldiers who were charged with defending the town were caught up in the general panic of retreat, along with many townspeople and refugees. When the first Soviet soldiers reconnoitred on foot the next evening, a police superintendent shot two of them before going on to kill himself. He had already killed his family. The German troops retreated from Friedland before further fighting could break out. After the Soviet invasion, most of the town burnt down. Various sources indicate that more than five hundred people killed themselves, including several families.

In the former duchy capital of Neustrelitz, a medium-sized town in southern Mecklenburg, the parish registers and cemetery records document the suicides of just under three hundred adults at the time of the Red Army invasion—by hanging, poisoning, shooting, drowning, wrist-slashing. At least eighty children and adolescents died with them. In one building, ten people hanged themselves: a locksmith and his wife, the three members of a barber's family, a cobbler together with his son and mother, and a teacher and his wife. For days, the living had to heave the dead up cellar stairs, drag them down from attics, or fish them out of lakes and other bodies of water.

Neubrandenburg hardly put up a fight when it was captured on 29 April, and soon the town was on fire. Hundreds of people chose to die. 'I remember opening a door and finding a large family seated around a table,' one woman said many years later. 'They had clearly celebrated the last day of their lives and then poisoned themselves. They were all dead.'

Even in the more remote villages and hamlets, there was no escape from the shock waves caused by Germany's downfall. A few days after the war ended, a vicar's wife from the parish of Ducherow, near Anklam, described the events of that time in a kind of journal. Maria Meinhof addressed her 'diary of tough times' to her eight children, without knowing how many of them were still alive. All six of her sons were away at the front, and she wanted those who returned to be able to read about what had happened in their absence. 'As I record these events, I think of each one of you, as if I were writing you a letter. I wonder whether you'll ever hold this little book in your hands?' Writing the diary made her feel closer to her children.

Maria Meinhof's seventy-five-page account of the end of the war is written in a neat hand. She begins by describing the flood of refugees and how, for months, the vicarage had been transformed into an emergency shelter, housing up to forty people—but she soon moves on, anxious to write about the days when the world as she knew it came to an end. The first bombs fell on 28 April. There were dead German soldiers, Soviet panzer spearheads. That night, the suffering that had already been visited on so many other places reached Ducherow. Women in headscarves forced into corners. Probing torchlight, threats made at gunpoint. The tramp of soldiers' boots. Young women dragged into empty rooms. Sixty-year-old Maria Meinhof managed to fight off a soldier who tried to thrust himself on her. It was the most awful night of her life. The next day, the world seemed in disarray: 'Sunday dawned, but we didn't notice it was Sunday. There was no question of going to church.'

All day long, soldiers came to the house in twos and threes, wanting schnapps and watches. They opened all the chests and trunks, and kept threatening to shoot—though one soldier sat down to play with the children. A Russian officer came into the vicarage living room and designated one of the villagers mayor by acclamation. When night came, the 'Russian terror' set in again as the soldiers went out with their torches in pursuit of women.

> Then the grandmothers took a child each and the young mothers took their youngest from their prams, and they plunged out into the night, frightened and desperate, and drowned themselves in Farmer's Pond. A young woman, a young girl and a little boy of five were pulled out alive. But fourteen unfortunate people died that night—eight drowned themselves and six put an end to their lives by hanging.

Maria Meinhof writes about the funeral service and the burials in two mass graves. She writes about other suicides in Ducherow and the surrounding region. In Anklam alone, there were three hundred. She describes the desperation of a Frau Schöttler, who waded into the village pond and called to the people on the banks: 'Throw my children in after me.'

Losing and mourning loved ones was nothing new to Maria Meinhof; she had seen something of life. Yet even with her faith to shore her up, she could make no sense of what was happening. Her language is plain and sober; she never resorts to talk of divine providence or the mysterious ways in which God moves. In places, though, she goes no further than hints and roundabout descriptions; she keeps back a lot, because she has no comfort to offer her readers. 'I could describe many, many more such sad fates,' she said.

. . .

A particularly bizarre fate was suffered by the neighbouring parish of Alt Teterin, a tiny, remote speck on the map. The tanks of the 65th Soviet Army rolled down the main street early on the morning of 29 April, on their way to Demmin. Some families hid in the woods or in a ditch just outside the village; others stayed in their houses. That night, groups of soldiers went on the prowl, raping women and rounding up men. They took the men to the neighbouring village of Stretense.

As the people of Alt Teterin waited, tense and frightened, they heard a strange, menacing noise coming from the direction of Stretense—a hideous, nerve-shattering drone, like nothing they had ever heard before. It was to become the soundtrack to the horrors of that night; in the minds of some, the grinding, pounding sound became linked to the propaganda they had heard about the Soviet steamroller. Among the women, the rumour soon spread that the

Hell Machine

Red Army soldiers in Stretense had started up a 'hell machine'—a gigantic mincer, like a huge motorised human press, which they were feeding with the men they'd rounded up and led away.

Now Alt Teterin, too, was hit by a wave of suicides. The first to take their lives were three housefuls of women who had been raped. Then an elderly man went from house to house, collecting women and children; soon neighbours and relatives joined him and went with him from door to door. Scared and distraught, people made for the woods or the drainage ditch outside the village. Mothers drowned their children and hanged themselves in trees. The elderly man hanged himself last of all. By the end, thirty-two people had died in the tiny village of Alt Teterin. Urgency, contagion, fear. Demmin was everywhere.

Death in the West

Nowhere in the western territories of the German Reich was mass suicide as rife as in East and West Prussia, Silesia, Pomerania, Mecklenburg, Brandenburg or Berlin. Fear of the Red Army was so firmly rooted in people's minds that the Soviets' approach often triggered deadly panic. As Soviet troops marched into the towns and villages of the east, the rumours and propaganda were transformed again and again into dire reality. Women in particular saw no other way out than to kill themselves, and often their children too. There was a general feeling of desperation.

But this feeling wasn't limited to the east. In western Germany, too, many people no longer saw a future for themselves. All over the country, people felt frightened and helpless as they found themselves confronted with imminent defeat and the collapse of the social order. They sensed guilt closing in on them and feared that revenge and retribution were inevitable.

. . .

Herr Reidel from Rüsselsheim, in the Rhine-Main region, was a good-looking and imposing young man. He had left Rüsselsheim—a city important to the German arms industry because of its automobile factories—after the 1944 air raids and moved with his family to Siefersheim, fifty kilometres away. In this tight-knit village, Reidel was surrounded by an aura of rumour and secrecy. He and his family—his strikingly dressed wife and smart little girls—held a strange fascination for the local children. They presented an idyllic family picture such as most people in Germany hadn't seen since before the war. Johann Radein, who was just a boy at the time, devotes an entire chapter of his childhood memoirs to the Reidel family, who intrigued him. 'Aged twelve, I always wonder why Herr Reidel isn't a soldier at the front. I get no answer from the grown-ups.'

But Johann felt drawn to Herr Reidel. The boy often found him outside the Reidels' house, staring up at the sky through his binoculars, on the lookout for enemy aircraft. Herr Reidel would explain to Johann in expert detail all about the different kinds of planes circling overhead and occasionally looping down, trailing a wisp of smoke. At other times, Johann found him in his garden, sowing or weeding; he sometimes invited Johann to help him pick cherries. But Johann never solved the mystery of Herr Reidel—never worked out who or what he was, or how he'd managed to escape active service.

I don't dare ask him any questions, this fair, good-looking man with his flashing eyes, lively manner and brisk gestures. But when his charmingly dressed, curly blond daughter comes hand-in-hand with her friends to visit her father, the happy man devotes himself so intently and lovingly to them that he forgets I'm there, and I slip away from the intimate scene.

The village of Siefersheim made it through to the end of the war without bloody battles or losses, and in March 1945 it was occupied by US soldiers. The villagers took down their pictures of the Führer, burnt their brown shirts and tried to look ahead. But Siefersheim was not to escape altogether, and the horrors of defeat were finally visited on the village one day in June, when Herr Reidel, friendly neighbour and loving father, dispatched his entire family. Six-year-old Sigrid, baby Else, his wife and himself—he shot them all with his pistol. Johann Radein heard the news at the house of a friend, the son of the village mayor, who immediately rushed to Reidel's house:

> My friend and I follow. At the scene of the crime, we wait
> at the gate with two grown-ups. When Mayor Espenschied
> re-emerges from the Reidel family's house, he looks very
> pale and sounds agitated as he says: 'I told them so.'

The mayor had known that Reidel had two pistols in his possession, and had urged him to get rid of them or hand them in. Since the war had ended, he'd often tried to talk him out of his Nazi beliefs and suicidal plans, too. 'It's over. You have to resign yourself to that.' But Reidel didn't want to resign himself to the loss of his world and a life among enemies. In the note addressed to the parish of Siefersheim found in his house, he said he had chosen to commit suicide with his family so as not to burden anyone.

Now the rumours about Reidel ran riot. The villagers, seeking to explain the inexplicable, searched for motives in his past. One man suspected that he'd been involved in the Rüsselsheim massacre. In August 1944, after an air raid on Reidel's hometown, American airmen from a plane shot down by the Luftwaffe had been marched through the town, and members of the public had pelted them with stones and roof tiles, and hit them with hammers and spades. Six of the airmen died, and it was rumoured that Reidel was on the US military's wanted list. But the rumours were never confirmed. Even in later years, Johann Radein was unable to solve the mystery of Herr Reidel's guilt and desperation. 'I'll never forget the sight of those two horse-drawn carts carrying the children and their parents round the edge of the village to the cemetery,' he wrote.

· · ·

An hour further south is Neustadt an der Weinstrasse, where elementary school teacher and regional poet Leopold Reitz was a member of the Nazi Party and local group leader. Reitz came from a family of vintners, and most of his poems are devoted to the topic of winegrowing; they celebrate, in bucolic tones, the vineyards of his home soil and the charms of the Palatinate countryside. When war broke out, he began to keep a diary, which shows his struggle to define his own position. He is often vague and elusive, taking refuge in longwinded descriptions of nature. Leopold Reitz shrank from self-examination, unable to judge or justify himself or his involvement in the party.

He was, though, perceptive enough to have noticed a change among his fellow townspeople since war first broke out on the Eastern front in 1941—known in Germany as the 'year of the great murder', or the 'year of widows and orphans'. As the casualty rate soared, soldiers' death notices in the newspapers were no longer displayed as prominently; they literally shrank in size, so numerous now that they had lost their earlier shock value. People waited daily for telegrams bearing news of loved ones' deaths. 'Death is no longer sublime,' Reitz wrote. 'Dying has become more of a matter of course.' As the end of the war drew near, he noted, people were responding to the Nazis' jingoistic propaganda with increasingly fatalistic slogans of their own. 'The motto of the day is: make the most of the war, because peace is going to be dire.'

When his son-in-law pays an unexpected visit from the front, having survived the retreat from France, Reitz finds him neither glad to be home, nor relieved to have escaped death. Instead, he is demoralised, apparently done with life, unable to imagine a future for himself and his family. Reitz observes:

> Not only before battle—at home, too, a soldier has to come to terms with himself. Or as people say here: 'Anyone still alive in 1945 has only himself to blame.'

Meanwhile, he said, the wireless blared out heroic folk songs about the sweetness of dying for one's country.

In late March, American troops captured Neustadt. A few days later Leopold Reitz heard that the head of a local viticulture school had hanged himself. This was the first in a series of suicides to be mentioned by Reitz. 'Hanged, shot and arrested are now words as common as eat and drink.' He continued to record such cases until May 1946, a year after the war ended. The last, Frau R. from Gommersheim, hanged herself—from a sense of guilt, Reitz guessed, and out of despair at the death of her fallen son. 'The list of dead friends and acquaintances grows longer and longer,' he wrote. 'Dr Müller and his housekeeper had already written suicide notes, but let themselves be talked out of it.'

The suicidal mood was widespread elsewhere in western Germany too. Mathilde Wolff-Mönckeberg, a well-off middle-class woman from Hamburg who kept a kind of journal in the form of unsent letters to her children, observed it in her own family, even before the war had really got going. Anticipating the destruction to come, her daughter, Jacoba, thought of taking her life together with her husband and their five-year-old son. 'I could see the idea taking root in her,' Wolff-Mönckeberg writes. 'I could see the despair in Jacoba's usually clear eyes.' In Hamburg, as in other parts of the country, the news of Germany's defeat in the Battle of Stalingrad in February 1943 prompted many people to speculate out loud about the end of the war and the arrival of the Allies. Mathilde Wolff-Mönckeberg reports that a Frau Schlensog told her there would be nothing left but to take poison. She said it quite calmly, apparently, 'as if she were suggesting pancakes for dinner tomorrow'. Wolff-Mönckeberg's ex-husband did indeed go on to commit suicide a few months after British troops marched into Hamburg, one of many in that city who chose to end their lives at this time.

In Giessen, in Hesse, a fifteen-year-old schoolboy records in his memoirs how his teacher, the irritable Herr Frank, poisoned himself along with his wife when the Americans entered the town. In the small village of Södel, an elderly businessman hanged himself in his garden after writing a suicide note: 'I am awfully sorry to leave you, but you mustn't hold it against me; the war compels me.' In the neighbouring town of Friedberg, a thirty-five-year-old man hanged himself on 4 February 1945. His wife then killed their two small children and slit her own wrists.

In February 1945, a young woman from Ostwestfalen heard from a fellow student about the many crimes committed over the course of the war in the name of the German people. 'A friend of mine killed herself when she heard the truth,' the young woman said, 'and she wasn't the only one.'

In Upper Bavaria, the authorities registered ten times as many suicides in April and May as in the same months in previous years. Two German psychiatrists investigating suicidal behaviour in northern Baden and Bremen established that there had been a steep rise in numbers in both places in 1945.

From the front, too, soldiers sent news of the deaths of many comrades who were unable to cope with defeat and loss of faith. An officer in Norway reports in his war journal on 4 May 1945: 'A wave of suicides is beginning. Officers ring up to say goodbye before they die.' In Rotterdam, a sailor in the German navy heard bells ringing during his watch on 8 May and realised that the war was over. He decided to shoot himself when his watch came to an end. 'Given my conduct throughout the war, I had no hope of survival, and felt that only death could mask my shame.'

The Waxworks of Leipzig

Of the many thousands of scenes from the German suicide epidemic, only a handful were photographed. This was partly because of the chaotic circumstances, the official ban on photography and a lack of resources. It was also because nobody—neither friends and relations, nor the authorities, the military or anyone else dealing with the dead—felt inclined to capture the macabre sights on film.

Among the few exceptions, a series of photographs taken in Leipzig's new town hall in April 1945 stands out as remarkable. A heavily furnished office with dark wooden panelling and damask wallpaper is side-lit through tall casement windows. A wooden desk faces a massive upholstered sofa, a matching armchair and a large gilt-framed landscape. The floor is covered by a Persian carpet. The furniture and office paraphernalia—telephone, inkpad, inkwell—are covered in a layer of dust. Everything about this room is sombre and ponderous—everything except the three delicate human figures that inhabit it. With their neat clothes and hair, these figures look like a small party of travellers, about to set off on a journey. But they are all dead. The man sits in a chair, his head slumped on the desk, between his hands. He is wearing a discreetly patterned civilian suit and a shirt with cufflinks. The older woman is about his age. Dressed in a skirt and winter jacket, she sits opposite him, draped across a leather armchair, her left arm hanging over the armrest, her outstretched index finger hovering above the pattern of arabesques on the carpet. Behind her, a young woman in a long coat lies on the leather sofa, her legs stretched out in front of her, feet crossed at the ankle.

As the US Army's first female war correspondent, thirty-nine-year-old photojournalist Margaret Bourke-White had followed American troops to England, North Africa and Italy; now, in the spring of 1945, she was accompanying General Patton's Third Army through Germany as it captured large swathes of territory. She saw the thwarted Germans through a victor's eyes: in their grim hysteria, fighting for mere inches of ground as their entire nation was torn to shreds, they seemed to her like beings from another planet. 'What kind of people were these,' she asked, 'whose acquiescence, either passive or criminal, had made it possible for such evil forces to grow? How deeply had the ferment in the secret depths of Hitler's country eaten into the soul of the average man?'

As a reporter she was interested in the present moment, not the past—the how, not the why—and so she retained her outsider's eye, an eye as sharp and cool and ruthless as her camera lens. She clung to her camera, as if it could shield her against the bewildering human chaos confronting the American troops in Germany—a chaos which seemed to her to defy understanding.

I know of no way to convey the feeling of rising violence that we witnessed as we drove deeper into Germany: the waves of suicides, the women throwing themselves after their loved dead into newly dug graves, the passionate denunciations of friends and neighbors, the general lawlessness. Each street corner had its open tragedy; every life seemed shot through with its own individual terror.

It was the violence that the Germans turned against themselves, the widespread tendency towards self-destruction that Bourke-White found most disconcerting. She saw public outbreaks of fury and desperation, emotions that in everyday life would have been vented behind closed doors. 'Death seemed the only escape,' she writes, a little helplessly, in her report. As she drove through the villages and towns of the Rhineland, Hesse, Bavaria, Thuringia and Saxony in her army jeep, German life seemed to her like a chapter from a melodramatic novel. Yet the many suicides held a peculiar fascination for her that she struggled to understand.

During the retreat, German propaganda, with its tales of American soldiers who sucked the blood out of little children and raped all women in their path, had such a profound effect on the people that many families were sitting around with guns, ready to annihilate themselves when the Americans came.

When Margaret Bourke-White and a US sergeant tried to requisition a house for the press camp in the Lower Frankish town of Schweinfurt in April 1945, they discovered that a mother had killed herself and her two little boys only minutes before. She had given them poison, laid out their bodies in the living room, and then gone down to the coal cellar and shot herself. In

Bourke-White's photograph, the boys are lying on their backs, their hands folded on their tummies. White cloths are wrapped around their little heads like turbans; white scraps of cloth or paper cover their eyes. An elderly woman stands beside them with bowed head, about to spread a sheet over them. Bourke-White's professional detachment was momentarily pierced by the tragedy of these innocent children. 'Making myself photograph those tiny pathetic bodies, victims of forces which should be utterly remote from the life of a child, was one of the most difficult jobs I have ever had,' she said. After taking the photo, she groped her way down into the darkness of the cellar, where she set up her tripod and triggered the flash, on spec.

> In its brief flare, the picture was indelibly printed on my mind. On a mattress between the furnace and the coal pile lay the mother; she had dressed herself entirely in black, perhaps with the idea of mourning, but apparently she had few black garments to choose from. She was clothed in black underwear, complete with long black stockings. The sight was so fantastic and so dreadful that I could hardly get up the cellar stairs and into the open air fast enough.

A few days later, Bourke-White documented the liberation of Buchenwald concentration camp in Thuringia. Here, for the first time, she heard the refrain 'We didn't know! We didn't know!' from German citizens who were shown around the camp. Not long afterwards, she chanced on a recently cleared sub-camp in Leipzig-Thekla. By the time she reached the centre of Leipzig, her head was buzzing with the things she'd seen and photographed. On the evening of 18 April, American tanks were parked outside the town hall, where the mayor had barricaded himself in with his treasurer and their families and a few other loyal souls.

Early on the morning of 20 April, a colleague of Margaret Bourke-White tipped her off. 'Hurry to the Rathaus before they clean it out,' he said. 'The whole inside of it is like Madame Tussaud's waxworks!' The two of them jumped in the jeep and rushed to the town hall, which had been ravaged by artillery fire, damaging its ornate Gothic Revival facade. They ran up stone stairs and over toppled marble busts into an oppressively furnished office. What they saw took their breath away:

> Reclining on the ponderous leather furniture was a family group, so intimate, so lifelike, that it was hard to realize that these people were no longer living. Seated at the desk, head bowed on his hands as though he were resting, was Dr. Kurt Lisso. On the sofa was his daughter, and in the overstuffed armchair sat his wife. The documents for the whole family were laid out neatly on the desk.

Posioned—city treasurer Dr Kurt Lisso, his wife, Renate, and daughter, Regina, photographed by Margaret Bourke-White in Leipzig on 20 April 1945

Beside them stood a bottle—they had presumably poisoned themselves with cyanide as the enemy approached. From the high windows, they would have had an unimpeded view of the American tanks and infantry fighting their way closer. Ernst Kurt Lisso had been the city treasurer and an early Nazi Party member. He was not alone in choosing to end his life in his office.

> In a nearby room, seated in an equally lifelike circle, was Mayor Alfred Freiberg, Ober-burgermeister, with his wife, and pretty daughter, Magdalena. Adjoining rooms held similarly peaceful and silent characters, of whom the most striking was the Commander of the Volkssturm in his fine uniform, with a portrait of Hitler beside him.

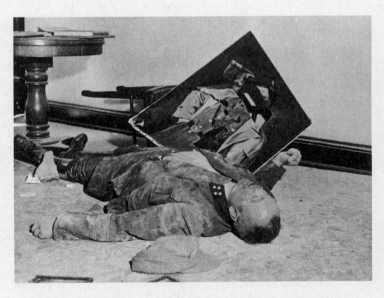

Poisoned—Volkssturm commander Walter Dönicke
next to a torn portrait of the Führer

• • •

Margaret Bourke-White wasn't the first to see this tableau as a symbol of the German catastrophe and to photograph it. Only the day before, on 19 April, another war reporter had found her way to the town hall. Elizabeth 'Lee' Miller, three years younger than Bourke-White, had been a model and a portrait photographer in New York before joining the US Army as a war correspondent in 1944. The former cover girl brought the war onto the glossy pages of *Vogue* with her harsh, gritty images. She wrote harshly, too; her journalism is steeped in disgust and contempt. Germany's 'beautiful landscape, dotted with jewel-like villages' was marred, she said, by its ruined cities and 'inhabited by schizophrenics'. She had seen the front and heard the roar of battle. She had taken photographs in Dachau and Buchenwald concentration camps soon after liberation. Her portraits of concentration camp guards are icily direct; she shows them front-lit, cowering on their knees, beaten to a pulp, hanged, drowned. When she stepped into the tableau at Leipzig's town hall, she immediately recognised an inner logic to what had happened:

> The love of death which is the under-pattern of the German living caught up with the high officials of the regime, and they gave a great party, toasted death and Hitler and poisoned themselves.

But both Lee Miller and Margaret Bourke-White were a long way from the Germans' indifference and inurement to suicide. For them, as for most people, regardless of nationality, suicide was a profoundly personal act, as intimate as it was bewildering, a disruption to the rhythm of everyday life. The scenes in the town hall impressed them both, each in her own way.

And so it happened that two iconic series of photographs of the same scene were produced by two great war correspondents, only twenty-four hours apart. The highly observant documentarian

Bourke-White kept her distance. Anxious not to leave out any detail, she climbed up to a gallery to photograph the dead family from as high a vantage point as possible, and although she didn't feel the same shocked sympathy that the family in Schweinfurt had stirred in her, she kept her camera at a respectful distance from the dead faces. Trained fashion photographer Lee Miller, on the other hand, went up close to the dead. In the surreal chiaroscuro of her close-up, the treasurer's daughter Regina Lisso looks like a model posing for a photo shoot. She wears a pristine white blouse under her dark coat and a Red Cross armband on her left arm. A later commentator said that, with her half-open lips, the dead woman looked as if she were waiting for a lover's kiss to bring her back to life. Miller's own description was cool and succinct: 'A girl with extraordinarily pretty teeth, waxen and dusty.'

The late Regina Lisso, photographed by Lee Miller
on 19 April 1945 in Leipzig

Alfred Freyberg, Kurt Lisso and Walter Dönicke—Leipzig's mayor, treasurer and Volkssturm commander—were all party members and high-ranking functionaries. When the regime collapsed and the Allies assumed power, they turned their attention to their own deaths. Following the example of their leader, party members all over the Reich were doing the same. Droves of Nazis of all ranks and ages took matters into their own hands, unwilling to face a tribunal of their victims and enemies.

Hitler's devoted propaganda minister, Joseph Goebbels, remained by his side to the end. Like Hitler, he had declared his intention to sacrifice his life for Germany many years earlier. The day after Hitler's death, Goebbels and his wife killed their six children with cyanide before poisoning themselves. Magda Goebbels left a letter for her son from her first marriage, in which she set out the Nazis' suicidal credo:

> Our glorious idea is ruined, and with it everything beautiful, admirable, noble and good that I have known in my life. The world that will come after the Führer and National Socialism won't be worth living in, so I have taken the children with me. They are too good for the life that will come after us, and a merciful God will understand my intentions in delivering them myself.

Countless stalwarts of the regime followed the Führer to their deaths. Martin Bormann, Hitler's most important confidant in his last days, died on the night of 1 May, on a Berlin railway bridge. Forensic pathologists later found remnants of an ampoule of prussic acid between his teeth. Reichsführer SS, Heinrich Himmler, bit into a cyanide capsule on 23 May 1945 after being arrested by the British military police. Hermann Göring, a key defendant at the Nuremberg war crimes trial, also swallowed cyanide; he poisoned himself in his prison cell on 15 October 1946 to escape the death by hanging to which he had been sentenced. Dozens of high-ranking political office bearers took their lives before and after capitulation—among them the Reich's minister for food, its ministers for justice, science and education, its chief physician, the head of the Führer's chancellery, the leader of the Nazis in Sudetenland, and the leader of the German Workers' Front. A dozen of the forty-three *Gauleiter*—regional party leaders—killed themselves too, some of them with their families. For those among the next ranks down, from mayors to Nazi Reichstag deputies, exact numbers are incalculable.

Representatives of the Nazis' security and terror apparatus had no less to lose than the party leadership. Many in the SS and the Gestapo, the police and the judiciary were unable to contemplate life after the death of the Nazi ideal, and chose to die by their own hand—SS generals, *Brigadeführer*, *Gruppenführer*, *Obergruppenführer*, *Standartenführer*, several concentration camp doctors, clerks at the Reich's security headquarters, the police president of Potsdam, the head of the Reich's genealogy office, the head of the Gestapo in Dresden, the special commissary of the Reichsführer SS for the deployment of foreign labour. Some waited longer than others. It wasn't until September 1949 that former SS group leader and supreme magistrate of the Nazi Party Walter Buch slit his wrists and threw himself into a lake in Bavaria.

There were also several high-ranking Wehrmacht officers for whom the end of the war brought the end of an illusion. They had gone to war with Hitler; they had carried out his orders all over Europe and in Africa, doing everything he told them to, right up to the last days, even when it effectively prolonged the suffering of millions and resulted in further needless deaths. Most Wehrmacht commanders were also accessories, if not accomplices, to crimes against civilians within German territory. They alone could have put an end to a war that had clearly been lost since before the defeat in Stalingrad, before D-day—an act that would have saved millions of lives and preserved their country from total destruction. But few had enough strength or conscience. Many saw Germany's defeat as a personal failure. Of 554 army generals, 53 killed themselves, as did 14 out of 98 Luftwaffe generals, and 11 out of 53 admirals.

City Without Hope

Potassium cyanide, commonly known as cyanide, is the potassium salt of hydrocyanic or prussic acid, a colourless crystal that resembles coarse table salt and, like salt, dissolves easily in water. If swallowed, it is converted into hydrocyanic acid in the stomach and becomes highly toxic. This causes painful corrosion of the stomach lining, but the way the poison kills is to attack the human respiratory system by preventing the cells from using oxygen. Internal suffocation follows, during which the body spasms as it struggles for air until, eventually, circulation shuts down altogether.

Cyanide or prussic acid poisoning is a very effective way of ending a human life. It is also an extremely agonising one. In a worst-case scenario, the fully conscious victim has to endure several minutes of violent death throes. A pinch is enough to kill. A lethal dose of cyanide fits into a tiny glass ampoule that can be carried everywhere—in a handbag, a small pouch around the neck, a gap left by a tooth, or simply in the mouth. For chemists, pharmacists or doctors, the poison, whose few basic components are widely used in industry and agriculture, is relatively easy to produce.

In the spring of 1945, large quantities of cyanide and prussic acid were circulating in Germany, in response to an explosion in demand. An SS report published at the end of March found that more and more Germans were contemplating suicide. All over the country, people were trying to get hold of poison or other means of ending their lives.

In Berlin, this was nothing new; forty-three-year-old journalist Margret Boveri noted that poison had already been a common topic of conversation in the German capital when she came back to live there in March 1944, after some years as a foreign correspondent in Stockholm, New York, Lisbon and Madrid. Her voluntary return coincided with the Battle of Berlin. RAF Bomber Command destroyed large areas of the city, killing thousands of people and leaving several hundred thousand homeless. Reports from the front told only of disaster, and the government spouted nothing but stale propaganda. Margret Boveri found her fellow Germans scared, apathetic and in a very divided state of mind:

> They should have been mutually exclusive, yet how closely linked they were, those two responses: on the one hand, conforming to the status quo, and on the other, mistrusting everything the powers that be said and did. Everyone knew defeat was imminent, and yet they lived as if the existing state of affairs would continue indefinitely.

The proximity of death and its insinuation into their daily lives was more than most people could stand. Unbearable scenarios threatened at every turn: being buried under debris or lying burnt in a cellar—while beyond lay the no-less-terrifying prospect of Allied capture and all it entailed: imprisonment, ill-treatment, retaliatory violence. After a few months in Berlin, Margret Boveri, too, had succumbed to the general mood. Her May 1945 musings on poison are as methodical as an instruction manual. She informed herself by talking to people and reading up on the subject in her encyclopaedia.

> I'd had a small tin of strychnine since last July, but was always on the lookout for cyanide and eventually managed to get hold of some this February (brave men do still exist). I'd meant to get in touch with pharmacist friends while there was still time and find out how it is transformed into prussic acid, which kills painlessly when inhaled.

Boveri wore her cork-stoppered glass ampoule on a string around her neck, but she began to have her doubts about its effectiveness, and these doubts were fed daily by conflicting rumours. One woman, for example, told Boveri about her failed attempt to kill herself with cyanide. Like Boveri, she had worn the poison next to her body, and someone had suggested that the powder might have lost its effect after being chemically altered by her body heat. The closer the end came, Boveri said, the more absurd the rumours became: 'In the last days before capitulation there was said to be widespread bartering: poison in exchange for bazookas.'

Nowhere was demand as high as in Berlin. Nowhere was it as easy to get hold of the deadly ampoules. Various sources suggest that the party was not only aware of this, but actively involved in distribution. The local health authorities themselves were said to have dispensed cyanide to the public. Rumour had it that on 12 April, after the last performance of the Berlin Philharmonic (Beethoven's *Violin Concerto*, Bruckner's *Romantic Symphony* and the finale from Wagner's *Götterdämmerung*), uniformed Hitler Youth boys stood at the exit with baskets of cyanide capsules.

According to the logic of the regime, the German people would inevitably be brought down as the regime itself collapsed. All those unable to make the ultimate sacrifice at the front were to take their fate in their own hands.

In the last weeks of the war, Berlin became the centre of the suicide epidemic. Once the Red Army had reached the Oder, it was clear that Berlin would be attacked by the Soviets from the east, and not, as many would have preferred, by Allied forces from the west. On the eve of the battle, there were nearly three million civilians still in the city. Some were Berliners; others were refugees from the eastern territories. Two-thirds of them were women; the remaining third were those too young or too old for military service. In their neighbourhoods, streets, flats and houses, these people waited for the war to come—waited for the onslaught of two and a half million Soviet soldiers. Last-minute radio broadcasts and propaganda articles in the Nazi newspaper *Der Panzerbär* painted a terrifying picture of Soviet conquest, but it was already clear in any case that the Soviets would mobilise all their destructive power in the final battle for the capital—the enemy's den. The official rhetoric of fear and sacrifice was accompanied by talk of poison and guns and putting an end to it all—talk that had been bubbling beneath the surface for months. The epidemic hit Berlin at full force, and thousands were driven to suicide.

• • •

The Danish-German journalist Jacob Kronika stayed in Berlin to the bitter end, observing people's changing attitudes to death. In his diary he tells the story of a dying man trapped between two walls in an air raid. When a doctor arrives to administer a lethal injection to spare him hours of agony, the man only asks for a cigarette and then looks on, unperturbed, as she does the deed. 'Can we really have reached the point where a cigarette means more to us than life and death?' Kronika asked. In the next day's entry, he describes receiving a phone call from an old acquaintance. The man says goodbye to him in a businesslike manner and explains that he's decided to shoot himself and his wife with his revolver.

Kronika regarded such submission to fate as peculiarly German. The tremendous fighting power that had sustained the Germans through a six-year war against half the world waned when the people were faced with the challenge of taking control. 'This paralysed nation no longer has the courage, will or power to act. It continues to let itself be maltreated, though the maltreatment costs it life and future.' While Kronika waited in vain for some sign of rebellion against the senseless mania for sacrifice, the Germans became more and more withdrawn. What energy they could muster they put into killing themselves.

On 7 April, on his way to a press conference at the Propaganda Ministry on Wilhelmplatz, Jacob Kronika found himself on one of his many rambles through the bombed-out wastes of Berlin. Heading north through the pleasure grounds of the Tiergarten—now a ghost park, after being battered by bombs, its woods chopped down for fuel—he came upon a small crowd of people on Siegesallee. A man had hanged himself from a tree, in public and in broad daylight. Kronika watched as his corpse was taken down without a word and loaded into a car. He called his account of this incident 'An Everyday Event in Berlin'.

Not many people watch the spectacle, and the few who do watch in silence. The event leaves no particularly deep impression on them. Day by day, night by night, so many suicides take place in this falling city that one more or less makes no difference.

Later that day, not far from the Tiergarten, Kronika was stopped by uniformed men on Hercules Bridge as he made his way over the Landwehr Canal to the Swedish embassy. The bodies of a woman and two small children had been pulled out of the cold canal water onto the bank, the children tied together with a length of coarse rope. 'Presumably a mother who had put an end to her life and that of her children,' Kronika mused. 'Why? We shall never know.' He was reminded of the portentous words that the vicar of Kaiser Wilhelm Memorial Church had addressed to his congregation a few weeks before. As the Battle of Berlin drew nearer, the vicar's warning of an epidemic was proving true. 'Death will catch up with all of us one way or another! But many people can't wait! The suicide epidemic is sweeping the country!'.

Even the top echelons of the state were not immune to the devaluation of human life or the indifference to the rising number of suicides. A few days later, Jacob Kronika heard that General Field Marshal Walter Model had taken his life after the defeat of his army in the Ruhr. Model, one of the most highly decorated commanders of the Wehrmacht and a devoted servant of the regime, was a key figure in the final battle on the Western front. His death must have had a considerable impact on frontline leadership. But when Kronika went to the Propaganda Ministry in the hope of finding out more, no one could give him any information. Instead, a ministerial spokesman told him that he saw no reason to waste time on a single suicide, when there were more than enough every day. 'There are droves of potential suicides around,' the spokesman said, 'all waiting for the right moment.' His words left no doubt about the German people's ultimate duty towards their leaders:

We see something heroic in the various forms of hara-kiri committed by mayors, district councillors and chief

administrative officers, often together with their entire families. It would no doubt be for the best if the only Germans
found by the advancing enemies were dead Germans.

One of the sources of this overt nihilism was the notion of lost
honour. The concept of honour, whether racial, military, familial or
feminine, occupied an important place in Nazi ideology, so its loss
was regarded as a threat to the very foundations of life. 'If you are
dishonoured,' a teacher in Berlin told a class of girls when collapse
was imminent, 'you have no choice but to die.'

In many German families, honour came before life. On
20 April, the Führer's birthday, twenty-one-year-old Friederike
Grensemann said goodbye to her father, who had been called up
to the Volkssturm to defend the city. They said little. Friederike's
father was already wearing his uniform and armband and went to
fetch his leather coat. Then he pressed his pistol into his daughter's hand. 'It's over, my child,' he said. 'Promise me you'll shoot
yourself when the Russians come, otherwise I won't have another
moment's peace.'

'He also instructed me to put the barrel in my mouth,'
Friederike would later remember. 'Then another hug, a kiss! All in
silence. He went.'

The young woman felt bound by her father's wish. When she
saw Soviet troops approaching the family home on Kurfürstendamm ten days later, she remembered her promise. The moment
had come to honour it. She felt for the pistol in her coat pocket and
was choked by fear.

It was so hard to decide! I hesitated. The pistol in my hand
was threatening and tempting at the same time. I crept into
a corner, took the pistol out of my pocket, with the safety
catch still on, and pointed the barrel down my throat!

She never forgot the life-or-death minutes that followed. Staring out into the backyard, she saw a rubbish bin full of guns. A thought darted into her mind: maybe the Russians wouldn't even get her? Maybe they weren't such awful *Untermenschen* as people said? Friederike chose to live. She ran down to the yard and threw her gun into the rubbish bin. She never saw her father again.

. . .

Around 170,000 soldiers and tens of thousands of civilians had lost their lives in the Battle of Berlin by the time the fighting ended on 2 May 1945, but it wasn't until much later that the wave of suicides receded from the city. Even during battle, large numbers of Nazi officials, Wehrmacht officers and soldiers shot themselves or deliberately exposed themselves to enemy fire. Many estimates suggest that about ten thousand women in Berlin committed suicide after being raped. On the first day of Soviet occupation, there were reportedly a hundred suicides in the suburb of Friedrichshagen alone, and the stories persisted through the summer and into autumn—stories of married couples shooting themselves amid the rubble, of women jumping out of windows, of poison victims lying wrapped in blackout paper at the side of the road, of families hanging from windows, of dead party functionaries and Nazi Women's League leaders. There was talk of a bank manager who had killed himself along with his wife and daughter, and of an actor who had taken poison together with twenty others in the leafy suburb of Bestensee.

. . .

On 6 May 1945, Jacob Kronika writes about the death of an acquaintance, Marie von Gerstorff, opposed to Hitler and his policies, who took cyanide a few hours after her home was seized by the

Soviets. The other residents of her villa buried her in the garden. Before bringing his diary of the German suicide epidemic to a close, Kronika comes full circle: he has recently spoken with another member of the Protestant clergy about how such desperate acts should be judged. Theologian Otto Dibelius prefers not to condemn those who have fled the horrors of life. But he does condemn their actions: 'It is up to us, as Christians, to judge and condemn the act of flight itself. It is a sin.'

They were almost the same words that Kronika had heard in Kaiser Wilhelm Memorial Church two months before. Since then, thousands had fallen prey to the epidemic. The vicar's prophecy had come to pass. But the fearless Danish journalist who had chronicled the epidemic ends his journal by confessing that even he couldn't remain immune to that black maelstrom. 'Who are we to judge?' he writes. 'I myself was among those who secured the necessary dose of poison before the Battle of Berlin, so as to be able to "escape", should things become unbearable.'

The Dark Figure

From tsunami to genocide, often all that survives of a human disaster in social memory is the number of deaths. If an event is large-scale and tragic enough, it will progress from news to history; the apparent objectivity of the death toll allows it to act as an official confirmation of the catastrophe. If, on the other hand, there is no verifiable figure—because it can't be established or doesn't arouse enough interest—the event fails to capture the public's attention and doesn't pass into collective memory.

In 1949, the Central Statistics Office of Greater Berlin published a compendium called *Berlin in Numbers*, concerned, among other things, with the rise of suicide in and around Berlin in 1945. The statisticians report a total of 7057 reported cases, more than half of which (3881) fall in the month of April; the suicide rate in the German capital had quintupled compared with that of previous years. This figure is one of the few statistics available on the topic of suicide in Germany in 1945. It gives only a minimum estimate and casts a long and incalculable shadow that criminologists refer to as 'the dark figure'.

To arrive at their estimate, the Berlin statisticians had no choice but to fall back on standard sources such as death registries and death certificates, as they would in peacetime. They must have been aware, though, that 1945 was no average year, and that the official figures available to them could provide only a glimpse of the full picture. The defeats inflicted that year led not only to the breakdown of local administration in Berlin and elsewhere, but eventually to the collapse of the entire state. Police, doctors, cemetery attendants and registrars were in many places unable to cope with the chaos caused by the destruction and mass death of those final months; they had to abandon their work temporarily or for good—if, that is, they didn't leave altogether, like those who fled Germany's eastern territories to move west. Shifting frontlines, long lists of missing soldiers, chaotic exodus in the face of the enemy, devastation of towns and villages and the need for anonymous mass graves meant that any estimate of the number of deaths in Germany in the last year of the war could only be rough. Often it was difficult to tell whether someone was a victim of military action, accident, natural causes or suicide.

The Nazi authorities stopped publishing suicide statistics when the war broke out, to avoid supplying the enemy with propaganda material. In 1939, the total number of suicides had been 22,273, as reported in the *Statistical Yearbook for the Territory of the German Reich*. For 1940, a year which saw the Wehrmacht storm from victory to victory, there was only internal party information, according to which the suicide rate in the Reich had fallen. But there is nothing to suggest how the numbers developed after defeats on all fronts and attacks on German territory. Nor are there figures for the suicide rate in the Wehrmacht during the last two years of the war, although the army had previously kept statistics. It was hard to tell, of course, whether a soldier killed at the front hadn't, perhaps, actually committed suicide or deliberately sought death. And not all soldiers or officers wanted to report the suicides of their comrades or subordinates as suicide.

. . .

Demmin, the site of probably the largest mass suicide in Germany, is a good illustration of the difficulties involved in counting the dead. On 19 May 1945, Sorge, the registrar, embarked on the task of recording the previous weeks' deaths. By then the fires in Demmin had been put out and the new Soviet town commandant, Major Petrov, had taken office, but horses were still pulling covered carts up to the cemetery. Even the first death Sorge registered raises questions. Certificate no. 1 tells us that West Prussian refugee and retired postal inspector Wilhelm Schwarzrock died at 35 Frauenstrasse at 4 am on 1 May, the first night after the Soviet conquest of Demmin. But there is no mention of the cause of death. Nor is this an isolated case: hundreds of the deaths registered by Sorge between May and November 1945 had not been confirmed by a doctor. The seventy-four-year-old Schwarzrock could, of course, have died of an illness or a heart attack, but this is barely plausible in the case of thirty-nine-year-old Margarete Butz and her three small children—or that of forty-nine-year-old notary Georg Bader, who was found dead in Deven Wood on 15 May, together with his wife, forty-three, and their daughter, eleven. Perhaps Herr Sorge failed to add his usual footnote in these cases because the people who reported the deaths preferred not to identify them as suicides. In certain circumstances, relatives of suicides could expect to lose financial entitlements. Suicide, moreover, did not always appear as such to an outsider. The dark figure looms even over the meticulously kept death registers of Demmin.

The figures in the improvised death register kept by the cemetery gardener's daughter, Marga Behnke, between 6 May and 4 July 1945 are even more imprecise. Behnke listed 612 dead altogether, 196 of whom were unidentified. In the column 'Cause of death', she recorded more than four hundred suicides by hanging, drowning and shooting, as well as isolated deaths due to illness, bullet wounds, shrapnel or simply old age. But in dozens of cases she was unable to give the cause of death, and instead put a question mark in the box or left it blank.

The first total figure appeared in a report published by Demmin's district councillor in November 1945: seven hundred deaths by suicide. Subsequent accounts provided their own estimations, based on personal impressions or hearsay. Irene Bröker, the woman from Stettin who narrowly survived those critical days in Demmin with her son, speaks of six hundred corpses being pulled out of the Peene alone. A landowner from outside the town writes of 1200 registered suicides, though without explaining how he arrived at the figure. Marie Dabs, the furrier's wife from Luisenstrasse, puts the number at over two thousand, Ursula Strohschein at several thousand. Norbert Buske, the eyewitness who, not long after the fall of the Berlin Wall, compiled some of these reports in his book about the end of the war in Demmin, speaks of more than a thousand. Almost twenty years later, Demmin's regional museum carried out meticulous checks, comparing the suicide figures in the death registers with those in the cemetery nursery records. The end result was a cautious estimate of about five hundred certain suicides (men and women, and the children they took with them) and a note indicating the existence of a considerable dark figure.

If Demmin, the best-documented case so far, yields no more precise figure than between five hundred and more than a thousand, many scenes of suicide in eastern Germany resist even such a vague estimate. Our only sources are lone voices such as that of a municipal employee in Schönlanke, who wrote a retrospective account of the Red Army's February 1945 invasion of the town: 'In their fear of the brutes from the East, many people in Schönlanke (ca. 500!) took their lives. Entire families were wiped out.' The town was a similar size to Demmin and suffered a similar fate, but it is now almost impossible to prove the accuracy or otherwise of the number of suicides cited in this report.

The total number of deaths claimed by the German suicide epidemic at the end of the Second World War eludes calculation, but whether we are talking about a low five-figure number or a high one, the suicides were a mass phenomenon of alarming scale, and for that reason they are significant. The causes go deeper than is suggested by the formulaic explanations of contemporary witnesses. It wasn't only fear of the Russians and of the victors' retaliation that inspired such a sense of doom and despair in the population. The example of Demmin shows that the wave of suicides cut across all professions and classes, affecting both sexes and all age groups. Even a person's closeness to or distance from the Nazi regime made no difference. What can the inner world of these Germans have looked like if the coming defeat made them see death as the only way out?

. . .

On the south-eastern edge of the old cemetery in Demmin, hundreds of dead from the suicide wave of 1945 lie buried, individually or in mass graves, marked or unmarked. A plain lawn with a few bare patches is dotted here and there with trees and memorial stones. At the edge of the grass, a heavy boulder is inscribed with words from the diary of a Demmin schoolteacher, written on 1 May 1945: *Suicides, overwhelmed by doubts about the meaning of life.* If ordinary people found it so hard to imagine living on after the collapse of the regime that they condemned themselves and their loved ones to death, it is important to find out what life meant to them. It is important to find out what was going on in their minds during those twelve years from 1933 to 1945—what buoyed them up, what they believed in. How did they feel about the Third Reich and its extremes—how did they experience them? And what did they feel when everything came to an end?

Part III

TUMULTUOUS EMOTIONS

The Wound That Was Germany

One Sunday in January 1926, Melita Maschmann and her brother were shaken awake by their parents at midnight and carried into the dining room to the wireless set, a wooden box with headphones. Their parents sat them down in front of it, stroked Melita's tousled hair out of her face and put the headphones over her ears. Through the atmospheric crackle, she heard a distant but carrying sound. Bells tolling, heavy, deep, admonishing. 'The din from the headphones was terrifying,' she said. 'My parents had tears in their eyes and we children felt in our hearts that this Germany must be a dreadful and glorious mystery.'

Melita was just eight years old, and her parents were anxious for her to hear the bells of Cologne Cathedral, ringing for Germany because the last British soldiers had left the Rhineland, which had been occupied by the victorious Allies since the end of the First World War. Even after this partial withdrawal, much of the Rhine country remained in French hands. For many Germans, the occupation was symbolic of the fate suffered by their home-land since defeat in 1918—humiliating and arbitrary. In the Maschmanns' conservative household, it was even considered a personal disgrace, because Frau Maschmann came from Darmstadt in Hesse, just outside the occupation zone.

The first time Melita and her brother had visited Darmstadt with their mother, they were still small children, not yet at school. On the train through the Rhineland they had encountered black soldiers and fled the compartment. Their mother had impressed it upon them that the ignominious Treaty of Versailles had destroyed Germany's border regions, plundered its economy and sullied its culture with their foreign ways. 'She loved Germany as unques-tioningly as she loved her hometown or her parents. But there was no joy in her love,' Melita observed. Her mother knew no peace. Political discussion at that time, no matter what one's social class, was always grounded in the same wrenching anger at the Treaty of Versailles. Indignation at the 'Diktat' forced on Germany at the end of the First World War is a dominant motif in the memoirs and diaries of the time.

For the young Melita Maschmann, Germany was, more than anything, a feeling—a dark, tragic feeling for her homeland, instilled in her by her parents. 'Even before I knew the meaning of the word "Germany", I loved it as something mysteriously over-shadowed by grief, something infinitely dear and vulnerable.'

The bleeding wound that was Germany shaped the childhood and youth of an entire generation.

• • •

When Gerhard Starcke went to university in Berlin at the end of the 1920s, he too had already been shaped by the political atmos-phere at home and in school. Like Melita, he had travelled to the occupied Rhineland with his parents as a teenager. On the Rhine Bridge at Mannheim they'd had to submit to inspections by soldiers from the French colonies and walk on the road, because Germans were forbidden from using the footpath on the bridge. Gerhard had never forgotten it. The situation seemed to him symbolic of the humiliation of Versailles. At university, he came into contact with alumni of his fraternity, veterans who spent their evenings extolling reactionary ideas over beer and dreaming of revenge. The occupation of the Rhineland had been forced on them by the 'Diktat', along with reparations, and, worst of all, unmitigated responsibility for the war. The veterans blamed not only the victorious powers, but also the politicians who had signed the treaty in Germany's name.

At the opposite end of the political spectrum were the radical left, who threw stones at Gerhard if he wore his fraternity armband and cap in public. 'That's how wide the gulf was in German society,' Gerhard said. And yet the left, too, deeply resented the imposition of the treaty on their country—perhaps the only thing uniting the two sides at a time of rampant extremism. More than forty years later, Gerhard Starcke would write in his memoirs:

> One belief was widespread in Germany on both the right and the left: that the injustice of Versailles was to blame for EVERYTHING.

· · ·

The German Revolution of 1918 started in early November, when sailors began to mutiny against naval command in the last days of the war, rapidly leading to civil unrest across Germany. A republic was proclaimed on 9 November, and Wilhelm II fled to the Netherlands the next day. Germany's new status as a parliamentary democracy was confirmed in February 1919, when, after a national assembly held in the town of Weimar in central Germany, Friedrich Ebert was elected president.

But the new 'Weimar Republic', as it was known, was controversial. Born of defeat, it was fiercely opposed by millions of soldiers who felt Germany had surrendered needlessly, and that they had been betrayed by 'enemies of the homeland'. At school, Gerhard Starcke had imbibed a contempt of the republic from his German teacher, a reserve officer. The new democracy was also opposed by those on the left who had hoped to see power vested in Soviet-style workers' councils. While communists advocated revolution, conservatives longed for a return to empire—but both sides agreed that the Weimar Republic was fatally compromised by the Treaty of Versailles, signed only a few months later, in June 1919.

· · ·

The age into which he is born is defined by the madness of Versailles, a treaty predestined, through its stipulations and consequences—unemployment, the enslavement of the German people and shortage of land—to start a new world war.

With these words Ilse Cordes begins her account of the life of her only child, Hermann-Friedrich Cordes, born in 1921. She has a curious style of writing, alternating between maternal devotion and political pathos as she traces the life of her son and all the highs and lows of the age that he has had to contend with—the flames of hate and the keenness of hope. Ilse Cordes writes of herself in the third person as 'the mother', and the text reveals more about her than about her son. Hers is the voice of a generation of disappointed parents who foisted their own desires for a better future onto their children. But here and there, when she recalls happy times spent with her little boy, a tenderness pervades the writing.

> The pair of them are almost inseparable. Until he's old enough to start school, they go for a walk every morning and every afternoon, chattering away to one another like two little friends. And woe betide anyone who hurts his darling mother!

Hermann-Friedrich Cordes grew up in the intensely military atmosphere fostered by his father, a publisher's salesman who had trouble settling down to civilian life when he returned home from the war. Sometimes he earned a lot and sometimes nothing at all, and he was almost always drunk. Members of the volunteer corps came and went like conspirators, but little Hermann-Friedrich was never sent out of the room; his parents preferred him to stay and listen to the men who'd been cheated of the rewards they believed were their due. Two million dead comrades—their deaths mustn't be in vain! Before Hermann-Friedrich had learnt to recite his times tables, he knew all about German discontent—and what was to be done about it.

> And so, from an early age, through the things he sees and hears in his parents' house, there grows silently and unawares in the boy the will to devote himself to the duty whose fulfilment shall be the crowning of his life.

At the elementary school that he attended from 1927, Hermann-Friedrich got into fights with the children of communists. On holiday at the seaside, much to his parents' delight, he decorated his sandcastle with the black, white and red imperial battle flag. But his parents were growing further and further apart. His father was drunk or away from home; his mother spent days on end in bed. Sometimes the bailiff would knock at the door and carry off a piece of furniture, and soon their voices were bouncing off the bare walls. Hermann-Friedrich learnt to go without. He became quiet and withdrawn. 'Day after day, mother and son return from their walks to the dark, empty flat. Only the comfort of her untiring little companion kept his mother from despair.'

. . .

Despite the frequent crises of the early years and the trauma suffered in 1923 due to disastrous hyperinflation, the Weimar Republic managed to attain economic and political stability by the mid-1920s, and important steps were taken to lead the country out of political isolation. But after the stock market crash of 1929, the nation was hit by the most severe shock wave the global economy had ever known.

At the Maschmanns', Melita's father screwed a sign to the front door that read 'No Beggars, No Hawkers!' but beggars rang the bell anyway, and the tunes of careworn buskers drifted up from the street. 'It wasn't possible to forget, even for a moment, that we'd been born into a poor country,' Melita said. Sometimes the neighbours' son lay drunk in the backyard. He was unemployed and spent his dole money on booze. One day, Melita met him on the street, dressed in his shabby military coat, barefoot and blank-faced. In his arms, he carried a small dog. A few hours later, she heard a scream. His mother had found him in the yard, his wrists slashed.

Gerhard Starcke's father, who ran a handicraft business and was saving for the petty-bourgeois dream of a house of his own, was terrified of losing everything. 'It was an awful time in Germany— a time when many people, some of them by no means unaccomplished, were so desperate that they saw the gas tap and the rope as the last, bitter resort.' Little by little, all prospects vanished. Gerhard, who was studying German and history, watched radical nation-alism gain a foothold among students. He developed views of his own on the best way out of the predicament. Like many others, he had a romanticised notion of life in the trenches, with its promise of heroic togetherness: 'One for all and all for one!'

Renate Finkh from Ulm was the youngest of three children. In the early 1930s, she was still too young to grasp that the war had driven a wedge between her parents—too young to understand why her father inspired more fear in her than trust, or why her darling mother was in such poor health. Nobody ever had time for Renate. That was her first conscious feeling, when she was only four: 'I know I'm lonely.' She was always hearing that there was no money left. No money for school, no money for tram tickets or butter. It was a relief to see that there were others who were even worse off. Sometimes there were poor children in the hall at the Finkhs', clinging to the skirts of their mothers—grey, skinny, ugly women, foul-smelling, too. Renate watched the maid put leftovers into the pots and pans they'd brought with them. 'But there was something threatening about the poor,' she said. 'Even when they'd been given food. I felt that more and more keenly.'

When Renate saw them from her window, marching in long rows down the street, she shuddered at the sight of them. 'The men wore peaked caps and had wild looks on their faces. Some of the women pushed black, high-wheeled prams. They had straggly hair and curiously large eyes.' One evening they came from all sides and gathered on Lindenhof. Communists, Renate's sister told her. Then their mother burst into the nursery and turned out the lights. Strangely stirring music rose from outside. There was a rattling noise; somebody screamed. Renate hid under the covers.

• • •

Any foreigner coming to Germany at this time was overwhelmed by the contradictions and high emotion of public life—and nowhere more than in Berlin. Sefton Delmer came to the city in September 1928, aged twenty-five. He wasn't exactly a foreigner. Although a British citizen, the son of Australian parents, he had been born and schooled in Berlin, where his father was a professor of English literature. This meant that he learnt German before he learnt English, and even after he and his family were sent to England in a prisoner exchange during the First World War, Germany never lost its fascination for him. When Delmer eventually returned to Berlin as a reporter for an English newspaper, he found all that a journalist could wish for: 'Sex, murder, political intrigue, money, mystery and bloodshed. Particularly bloodshed.' The rivalry between left and right had escalated into deadly enmity, with noisy, bloody clashes between their militants. Ten years on, Germany's nationalists still didn't regard the war as over. They saw the Treaty of Versailles as a mere ceasefire, an opportunity to fight the enemy within.

Recalling the heady mix of hedonism and lusty youthfulness of those years, Delmer writes: 'Looking back on it now, I see the mad whirl of this Berlin of 1928 and 1929 as a kind of Pompeian revel on the eve of the Vesuvius eruption.'

Two years later, Stéphane Roussel came to Berlin as a foreign correspondent for the French newspaper *Le Matin*. She had got the job by chance, through an acquaintance, and knew nothing of Germany when she arrived in the city; the torrent of confused impressions and the mix of different doctrines was almost more than she could cope with. Everything seemed politically charged and Roussel had trouble making sense of it all.

On the one hand there was Berlin's hedonistic high life, with a niche for every kind of pleasure, every vice: 'Complete liberty reigned, but so, too, did the German obsession with compartmentalising.' And then, on the other hand, there was the sweaty male fug of the city's backrooms and beer cellars, where the legend of an undefeated Germany rumbled on. By day, the men from the beer cellars were to be seen in Berlin's offices, where the same clerks who'd conducted business before the war did so still, mourning the old times and wishing democracy to hell. What struck Roussel most was that nothing was hidden: high life and low life alike were played out in full public view.

Raimund Pretzel—a writer who would later publish under the pseudonym Sebastian Haffner, and would famously describe Hitler as 'the potential suicide par excellence'—was still in Berlin at that time. He had observed over the years that beggars were as much a part of the city's street life as passers-by, and he read in the newspapers of suicides and desperate dramas. On one occasion he saw an old woman sitting on a park bench, strangely stiff. A small knot of people had gathered in front of her and he heard the words 'dead' and 'starved' detach themselves from the general murmur. After a quick glance, he turned away. 'It did not surprise me particularly,' he said. 'At home, we often went hungry too.'

Pretzel didn't live in one of the city's poorer districts. His father, Carl Louis Albert Pretzel, was a headmaster who also held a post at the Ministry of Culture. Carl saw himself as a dyed-in-the-wool Prussian official, didn't understand his son's enthusiasm for the campaigns of the Great War, never speculated on the stock market, and unfailingly fulfilled his professional duties. He shook his head at the noise and impetuousness of left and right alike. 'Indeed,' Raimund Pretzel wrote, 'my father was one of those who did not, or did not wish to, understand the times.'

The young man understood them better. He had acute judgment and a sharp eye for the suggestive detail, the telltale nuance. Perhaps that was the reason he decided to study law. As a schoolboy in the grip of war euphoria, he had seen the Germans' tendency to mass hysteria—'the uncurbed, cynical imagination, the nihilistic pleasure in the impossible for its own sake, and the energy that has become an end in itself'. He didn't exclude his younger self from this characterisation. Now he was a twenty-year-old law student and it struck him that, like the rest of his generation, he had got used to a public life punctuated by eruptions.

> A generation of young Germans had become accustomed to having their entire lives delivered gratis, so to speak, by the public sphere, all the raw material for their deeper emotions, for love and hate, joy and sorrow, but also all their sensations and thrills—accompanied though they might be by poverty, hunger, death, chaos and peril.

When the Great Depression hit, civil unrest broke out again, worse than before. Hardship robbed people of their dignity and self-respect. Men and women stood on street corners with signs around their necks: 'Seeking Any Kind of Work'. Blank-faced people queued outside the soup kitchens—family men, grandmothers, schoolchildren. Gangs of youths loitered in the city's squares; parents sent their children begging. The state might collapse at any time, and people waited almost indifferently for it to happen.

Hungry and Fanatical

Out of this festering morass of apathy and despair, some strange figures emerged, similar to those observed by Raimund Pretzel in the surreal climate of hyperinflation.

> Indeed, the mood had gradually become apocalyptic. Saviours appeared everywhere, people with flowing locks and hair shirts, declaring that they had been sent by God to save the world.

When British correspondent Sefton Delmer stepped out of his office onto the streets of Berlin, he saw miracle men proselytising in an atmosphere of unreality—revivalists, charlatans, faith healers and prophets of every kind. Each one of these German shamans had his own style. Every call to action, however eccentric, resonated with somebody, even in the middle classes, in industry and in the military. Saviours had never had it better. People had never longed so much for someone to come and heal the wound that was Germany.

What impressed me as symptomatic and significant about the miracle men was that, whether they were healers or alchemists, clairvoyants or bucket-shop swindlers, all of them claimed to have a patriotic mission, the restoration of Germany to greater strength than ever before.

The Rasputin-like Ludwig Haeusser from Württemberg, an itinerant preacher with a beard and a monk's cowl, found disciples all over the Reich. He styled himself Germany's saviour and the 'Dictator of the United States of Europe', and ran for the Reichstag, hoping to become president. In Berlin, Joseph Weissenberg, mesmerist and religious reformer, rallied more than a hundred thousand followers to join his 'Union of Serious Researchers from this World to the Next'. In Bavaria, the alchemist Franz Tausend formed a nationwide network of political esoterics, all delirious at his promise of producing gold by chemical means. Tausend was looked to as a source of hope, especially in the circles of war hero and prominent nationalist leader Erich Ludendorff—here was a way of paying off all reparations at one blow and casting off foreign rule. In Thuringia, Saxony and Anhalt, Friedrich Lamberty, known as 'the inflation saint', tried to breathe new life into Germany. Lamberty was a kind of Pied Piper, singing and dancing and preaching his way across the country, followed by a growing flock; in the early 1930s he would forge alliances with right-wing groups. And in Munich, Adolf Hitler caused a stir by working his way up from local beer-hall revolutionary to widely respected extreme-right leader. Despite the strident posturing of such nationalist prophets, the Great Depression drove more and more people into their arms.

It was financial expert Heinrich Brüning, though, who became chancellor in March 1930. Brüning was no charismatic saviour; his gaunt face, narrow-lipped mouth and cold eyes behind rimless glasses were those of a man of reason. His task was to bring an end to the economic chaos, and his method was to starve the country until its debts were discharged. One emergency decree followed another, until even salaries and pensions were whittled away. Brüning stuck to this course with iron resolve, longer than any other Weimar chancellor, and ended his stint in office believing himself only a few feet from his goal.

He had, however, failed to convince the Germans of the necessity of this tremendous feat of discipline. He had none of the qualities that impress people—neither rhetorical prowess nor personal charm, let alone the talent to seduce. Rather than inspire hope, he was stern, severe, exacerbating people's bitterness and demoralising Weimar's supporters. Brüning was not the longed-for saviour.

• • •

The Hamms, from the small university town of Giessen, led a politically uneventful life. In the whirl of his parents' conviviality, ten-year-old Reiner barely noticed the political goings-on in Germany. That changed in the early 1930s, when the local and general election campaigns grabbed his attention. Party symbols leapt off the hoardings at Reiner: the Communists' hammer and sickle, the Social Democrats' slanting arrows and, increasingly, the Nazi swastika. Against a backdrop of stucco-faced houses, the electioneers shouted till they were hoarse.

Brüning's emergency decrees pushed politics into family life. Reiner's parents talked at the dinner table of the 'hunger chancellor' and his excessive demands, and Reiner's father, a hardworking municipal employee, often raised his voice. Before long, the family were having to economise. There were no new clothes to replace the old, worn ones. The larder was empty. At home, Reiner heard the injured pride in his parents' voices when they talked politics; on the school playground, the name Brüning had become a byword for austerity, bitterness and fear of the future. This fear became palpable when hard-faced strangers tried to push their way in at the Hamms' front door. Reiner remembers being seized by terror.

> Would-be intruders frightened me by putting their feet in at the front door so that I couldn't close it. I was told to put the chain across on the inside before opening up to anyone.

The Great Depression surpassed anything suffered in Germany since 1918. In small and middle-sized towns like Giessen, all hell broke loose. Reiner's father came home in the evening with stories of unemployed people hammering at the doors and windows of the town hall, where he had his office. Reiner imagined them with twisted mouths and wide eyes. In the summer of 1932, after months of scrimping, the young boy was looking forward to a holiday on the North Sea. But there are no sandcastles in his memoirs—nothing that suggests a typical twelve-year-old's summer holiday. There is only the description of a motorboat journey around the port of Bremerhaven.

> It was depressing. Usually there were ships coming and going, and cranes on the quays loading and unloading cargo, but everything seemed dead. The freighters were lined up in a long row, and nothing moved.

Germany was at a standstill. But the election campaign of summer 1932 brought movement to Giessen. In June, Adolf Hitler paid the town a visit. Reiner Hamm's parents were in the audience that evening when he addressed a crowd of fifteen thousand. The next day, Reiner could tell how impressed they'd been by his speech.

Until 1929, the Nazi Party had little clout in Giessen. That had changed when the Great Depression hit, and in the 1930 elections the Nazis had won almost twenty per cent of the vote. Now, just two years later, on the eve of another election, Reiner saw brown SA uniforms everywhere. The 'movement' appealed not only to the desperate of Giessen, but also to the town's conservatives. It was these conservatives who'd recently organised Hessian Grenadier Day, when, for the first time since the defeat, the traditional regimental flags were carried through the streets. Reiner's father had taken him to see the parade, and they stood in the crowd, watching the heavy old flags pass by in solemn silence. 'My father was moved to tears,' Reiner later recalled.

Those wistful tears betrayed a longing for a leader who could cross the gulf between the camps and steer the drifting country on a new course. The more mainstream this vision became, the more Adolf Hitler stood out from the mass of cheap prophets and political one-day wonders. Throwing off the mantle of professional revolutionary, he came out into the open, leaving the reek of the beer hall behind him.

. . .

Gerhard Starcke was a penniless student and sick of his lack of prospects. He threw himself into the political fray and began to write about a free fatherland and national unity for his fraternity newspaper. Democracy and dry reason were not enough; he was seeking direction, inspiration—an animating spark. He wanted to feel alive. 'We Germans prefer professions of faith to cool consideration and patient watching and waiting,' he said.

Starcke's own moment of faith came in 1930, at the Sportpalast arena in Berlin. As he pushed his way through the mass of bodies at the entrance doors, he felt a thrill of excitement. It took him a long time to find a seat. Surrounded by thousands of people brought together by a common hope, he had the feeling he was a minute part of a greater whole, a single atom in a buzzing body made up of thousands of heads and arms and legs. It felt good. He made no attempt to resist. 'It was mass hysteria of such thrilling intensity that when Hitler finally appeared we sighed with relief and listened to his words as if to a revelation,' he said. Hitler's rhetorical skill was such, Starcke added, that he could talk to ordinary people in a way they understood without seeming superficial to the educated. That was one reason for his popularity; another, Starcke said, 'was that he said out loud what all Germans felt about Versailles', and about the failure of the Weimar Republic.

As the applause broke over Starcke's head, he knew he'd found what he was looking for. For the first time in his life he had direction. That same year he joined the National Socialists, membership no. 226,814. A profession of faith, as opposed to cool consideration. He became a party official in Berlin-Gesundbrunnen, designing flyers and writing for the party newspapers. Before long, something happened that had never happened to him before. He was in demand; he was praised and promoted.

• • •

In the election races of the early 1930s, Hitler was the focal point of a powerful campaign driven by the party machine. To set himself apart from the austere Brüning, he dashed from one event to the next, by car or plane. Soon every German child knew his name and face. Renate Finkh hadn't yet started school when the word 'Nazi' became common currency at the family dinner table. Her parents attended all the Nazis' political meetings in Ulm, and Renate noticed that they came home different people. 'When they talked about it, Mum's eyes, usually so dark and sad, lit up. If the Nazis won the elections, she said, then things would be better for everyone, including us.' The communists—the peaked-cap men and their hungry wives—would vanish, because they'd all have work again. There was relief in her mother's voice, and her father, a goldsmith, who had recently been grumpy about the dwindling number of customers in his shop, began to talk of 'the good Lord'—something he'd never done before. 'He said the good Lord had sent us a man called Adolf Hitler,' Renate recalled. 'He'd sent him to save Germany.'

'Germany, that's all of us,' her father said.

One evening, a packed Lindenhof was in turmoil. But this time, instead of peaked caps, Renate saw brown uniforms in flickering torchlight. She was a little scared, but left her curtains open. 'Songs are sung, over and over. They are tunes that rouse me. There is joy and excitement among these people. I can sense it, even without understanding what's going on.' A flag hung from her window. Renate saw her parents waving to her from below.

> There is something different in their joy as they come hand in hand up the wide stairs, their faces bright. All of a sudden, I know what it is: they are happy with a common happiness. I am six years old. Behind my closed eyelids, the fire is dancing.

In mid-1932, the Brüning government collapsed. Hitler emerged victorious in the July elections. More than thirteen million Germans followed the cult of his personality to the ballot boxes. He was the only person they trusted to lead Germany out of crisis. Letters of homage arrived in Hitler's private office, addressing their 'redeemer' in a naive, confiding tone. One follower, a man named Hoffmann, wrote a long poem to the Führer in rhyming verse, entitled 'The Saviour':

> I have become a child again,
> Trusting, helpless and silent.
> Germany bleeds from a thousand wounds.
> At the eleventh hour, I have
> At last found a saviour.

Although the majority of Germans were still undecided, they did nothing to halt Hitler's advance. Democracy had not put down roots—that was the view of René Juvet, a thirty-year-old Swiss notary employed in a factory in Augsburg. Hardly any of his colleagues were ardent Nazis. 'But no one was prepared to champion any other conviction, and all too many had no convictions whatsoever.' Then Juvet's boss, Waldmeyer, an educated man, asked his employee whether he'd got himself membership papers. There was no point, he said, in denying the coming reality. From that day on, Juvet felt a gradual change in Waldmeyer's behaviour. The confidently superior, sarcastic Prussian grew cagey, strategic.

No one on the factory staff mourned the defeat of Chancellor Brüning in 1932. But they all felt that something had come to an end with his downfall.

> Brüning may not have had many sympathisers, but we had
> a vague feeling that the ground was starting to slip now that
> he'd been removed from office. And nobody doubted that
> Hitler would be the beneficiary of that landslide.

Soon the first brown shirt appeared in the factory, worn by a weedy bookkeeper called Neder. Some of Juvet's office colleagues now had gleaming badges pinned to their lapels, the size of a thumbnail. Director Waldmeyer grew even cagier.

Torches in Winter, Violets in March

Hitler came to power on 30 January 1933, the so-called Day of National Rising. 'I have nothing sensational to report about this day,' René Juvet noted, ten years later, 'because I spent it not in Berlin, but in southern Germany.' While the Second World War was still being fought, Juvet recorded his memories of Hitler's early days in power. He concealed all names behind pseudonyms, but said his text was otherwise a 'factual account'. He was interested in the behaviour of the Germans—in their words and attitudes. His aim was to show the effects of the various phases of Nazi rule on his colleagues at the factory, to give some insight into the minds of these people he had been living among for twenty years. Although Juvet had been born in Frankfurt am Main and raised in Munich, he thought of himself as Swiss, not German, and wrote as an outsider, looking on.

The day passed without event at the factory in Augsburg. No new brown shirts, and only seasoned Nazi colleagues like Neder and Hofmann had enamel badges gleaming on their chests. 'On the whole there was little enthusiasm among us; a lot of people were apprehensive, waiting to see what the future would bring. The workers were very dejected indeed.'

In much of Germany, the election of Hitler as chancellor did not at first make much difference to the prevailing wait-and-see attitude. People were sceptical; they had seen too many governments come and go, and the spectre of economic crisis loomed too large. But in Berlin, the change of government was more than a mere radio report or newspaper headline; it was a kind of son et lumière show. The new chancellor's supporters made their way to the centre of town for the National Socialist movement's first victory parade.

. . .

Ilse Cordes attended the torchlight parade in the Tiergarten with her son. For her, the day was to mark a change of fortune for Germany. Hermann-Friedrich was eleven and had already seen so much—the war veterans' vengeful anger, the grief and the hatred, the hunger and the despair. From an early age, he had looked on as failure pushed his father to drink and his mother into depression. Two islands of hope had remained to Ilse Cordes, and to these she clung: her great fatherland and her little boy. The two were closely linked in her mind. She made sure that Hermann attended a nationalist secondary school and was pleased when he joined the Freischar Junger Nation, a nationalist youth group. She let him help out with the Nazis' election campaign, in spite of the fights that broke out there. She put all her hopes in him.

Right-wing paramilitaries marched past in seemingly endless columns, their heels ringing on the cobbles, their torches shining bright in the frosty January night. Ilse and Hermann-Friedrich pushed their way through the eagerly watching crowd at the side of the road. A lot of people were shouting and singing along to the march songs. Ilse Cordes felt joy and relief rise inside her. Everyone was laughing and smiling and cheering, she said—as if a huge weight had been lifted from their shoulders; they were no longer burdened by despair or the uncertainty of unemployment.

From the Tiergarten, mother and son continued on to the Brandenburg Gate, where the torches cast dancing shadows in the archways. They felt the hope of a new beginning for Germany— and of an end to the rift dividing their homeland. It looked as if the Germans really had become one people at last, Ilse Cordes said.

. . .

It was the new chancellor's express desire to overcome the fragmentation of the country. After years of internecine war, people were longing to live side by side in peace, and that is just what the Nazis promised with their idea of 'national community'—though their gangs of thugs had been a driving force behind Germany's street and pub warfare. It meant more than unity, though. It was also about equality, and the abolition of the old class structures. During the election campaign, it had caught the imagination of people all over the country.

'No rallying cry ever fascinated me as much as that of national community,' Melita Maschmann said. She first heard it from the Maschmanns' seamstress, who had called round to alter a dress. On previous occasions Melita had glimpsed the seamstress's embossed metal party badge under her coat collar, but now she was wearing it openly.

Her dark eyes twinkled as she spoke of Hitler's victory. My mother wasn't pleased. She thought it presumptuous of uneducated people to concern themselves with politics.

> But it was precisely because this woman belonged to the
> common people that she appealed to me.

Melita's parents expected the same deference from their children as from these 'common' people—their maid, for example, or their chauffeur. Their conservative upper-middle-class authoritarianism drove a wedge between them and their daughter. When the seamstress sat at her sewing machine extolling national community, it stirred Melita's youthful sense of justice, prompting feelings of which her parents would never approve.

That evening, Melita's parents took her to the torchlight parade. The sombre solemnity of the red and black flags, the glow of torches on people's faces, and the sentimental and rousing tunes threw her into a tumult of emotions. As the columns passed, she felt at first only the eeriness of the night. Then she saw boys and girls no older than her, solemnly marching in the parade, and she felt shame flush her cheeks. There she was, standing next to her parents like a little girl, while her contemporaries shouldered flags. Melita sensed that she was missing something.

> What was I—allowed only to stand at the edge of the road
> and watch, a chill at my back from my parents' icy reserve?
> Barely more than a chance witness, a child who was still
> given little girls' books for Christmas. And yet I was dying
> to throw myself into the current, to drown in it, drift with it.

She wanted to be part of it all like the others, serious-faced and involved in serious things. The next moment, she saw someone break ranks and begin, without warning, to club an onlooker. The man must have said something he shouldn't have. Melita saw him fall to the cobbles, bleeding; her parents didn't pull her out of the way quickly enough to protect her from the sight. The image fixed itself in her mind, but beneath her horror was a tiny thrill of danger.

'It was a matter of life and death—not clothes or food or school-work, but life and death.' Although frightened by what she'd seen, it made her determined not to stand on the sidelines anymore. She'd just turned fifteen, and she'd had enough of being too young. 'I wanted to break out of my narrow child's life and get involved in something big and important. It was a desire I shared with countless of my contemporaries.'

She liked the idea of a national community, in which everyone would live together like brothers and sisters—but if she wanted to get involved, it would mean going against her parents.

. . .

Stéphane Roussel, the foreign correspondent from *Le Matin*, had also fought her way through the crowd of spectators. She hadn't believed that Hitler would ever be chancellor, but now his troops were marching in proud ranks, ten abreast, their boots pounding in time to the battle songs. She could barely make out the uniformed men beyond the crowd who had gathered to watch them—only the light from their torches, and the flags they carried floating along in the air as if by magic. For a moment she had the impression that the Germans' self-loathing had subsided.

> People shout and laugh and sing and chant the party slogans.
> A lot of couples have brought their children. The men put
> them on their shoulders or hold them at arms' length, as if to
> bring them as close to Hitler as possible.

Roussel had trouble weaving her way out of the crowd. In the back rows, a little way off from the action, she saw behaviour of a kind that wasn't recorded in any of the photographs taken that evening. Not everyone was rallying behind the new government. Roussel saw people avert their eyes as the brown-shirted troops passed. People in a hurry to get back inside their flats. People having trouble concealing their anger, helplessness, distress or fear. A young girl with tears pouring down her face.

On the way home, Stéphane Roussel noticed a thin covering of new snow on the roads. Now that the crowd was no longer there to keep her warm, she felt the cold creep over her.

. . .

The spectacle was repeated all over Germany, thrilling fans and alarming sceptics. In many towns, local party units organised their own triumphant marches. In some places there were counter rallies and clashes between police and the Brownshirts. The politically undecided made do with watching and waiting, indifferent or tensely impatient.

Raimund Pretzel had no firm political views, though if asked he tended to lean to the right. For him, 30 January 1933 was neither cause for celebration nor a national disaster, but simply another change of government. Like many educated middle-class people, he abhorred the National Socialists and refused to take them seriously. He didn't go to the torchlight procession that evening, but discussed the news with his father in the drawing room. They saw little reason for concern, agreeing that Hitler was a mere puppet on an oversized stage. He couldn't possibly last long. 'There are few things as comic as the calm, superior indifference with which I and those like me watched the beginnings of the Nazi revolution in Germany, as if from a box at the theatre,' Pretzel would later write.

At the same time, he thought he smelt a warning whiff, a premonition of what was to come—'but I did not have an intellectual framework that would allow me to interpret it'. The next day he went as usual to the Court of Appeal in Berlin, where he worked as an articled clerk, poring over the clauses of the Civil Code, page by page. It reassured him that the judiciary continued to grind away—that his life kept chugging along on the same old tracks. Even the sensationalism of the press left Pretzel strangely unmoved.

> All this was still something one only read about in the papers. You did not see or hear anything that was any different from what had gone before. There were brown SA uniforms on the streets, demonstrations, shouts of 'Heil', but otherwise it was business as usual.

It was true that the government vilified Jews as *Untermenschen*, but when Pretzel glanced up in the quiet of the courtrooms, there was the scrupulous Appeals Court judge—a member of Berlin's Jewish community—still passing sentences that were carried out on behalf of the state. The newspapers could write about breach of constitution, and the Brownshirts could carry on like maniacs, but everyday life went on regardless. Pretzel decided not to take any notice.

He was not alone. After Hitler's appointment as chancellor, something strange began to happen. Although Germany's new leaders had made no secret of how they intended to deal with opponents or what radical methods they would favour, most people played down the risks. The desire for security and stability was so great that the Germans preferred to turn a blind eye to certain aspects of this new reality, as long as they weren't personally affected. They didn't probe too deeply. They didn't stop to ask what the changes meant, what was going to happen next. Life went on.

. . .

No sooner had Hitler taken his place at the head of the cabinet than he announced the dissolution of the Reichstag and called for new regional elections. Only forty-eight hours in office and already he was campaigning again. This constant drive was typical of him; he was always on the move.

British journalist Sefton Delmer had seen Hitler campaign on earlier occasions. He found it difficult to resist the energy of this extraordinary politician, who, when interviewed, would pitch into his answers with great fervour, letting each one swell to a speech, as thought after thought came bubbling out of him. Before long, Hitler would be shouting at his interviewer as if he were addressing a crowd.

Delmer accompanied him on a campaign tour by plane, observing his transformation from shy private individual into public dynamo. On the aeroplane, Hitler was sunk in morose apathy, like a listless travelling salesman on his way to a tedious appointment. But almost as soon as the plane touched down, his energy came flooding back, and by the time he was on the stairs to the tarmac, he was holding himself in his 'Hero-Führer posture', upright, serious, shoulders back.

> His eyes widened to show their whites and a 'light' came into them. A light intended to denote kindly understanding of his people's needs, fearless confidence, the light in the eyes of a Messiah predestined to lead Germany to its place in the sun.

The crowd responded as if electrified. There were roars of welcome as Hitler made his way down the steps, past dignitaries—shaking hands as he went—and into the car that was waiting to rush him to a nearby assembly room. Sefton Delmer tore off after him, through rows of outstretched arms to the stage with the huge swastika banner. The spectators didn't have a chance to draw breath before he launched into his speech. Afterwards, Hitler stood for a moment, soaking up the cheers, head held high. Then he was gone. Delmer had to dash after him again and speed to the airfield.

Hitler himself seemed to me to enjoy this racing around in cars and aircraft. It gave him a sense of dramatic urgency and fitted in perfectly with his great act as the twelfth-hour saviour of the German fatherland.

Nothing was more fundamental to Hitler's nature than the principle of movement. In his political treatise *Mein Kampf*, he uses the word well over a hundred times, describing the National Socialist organisation itself as a 'movement' rather than a party—a movement dynamic enough to set the masses in motion, and drive them to ever greater speed.

In the first hundred days of Hitler's government, the German population was confronted with a dizzying series of dramatic events largely orchestrated by Nazi propaganda experts. After the launch of an aggressive election campaign, the Brownshirts and the SS formed an auxiliary police force in Prussia to combat the Nazis' political opponents. When the Reichstag was set on fire a few days later, state terror against communists and other opponents of the regime escalated. An emergency decree annulled almost all basic democratic rights. By mid-March, more than a hundred thousand people had been arrested. Despite its lack of a majority, the government set about dissolving all regional parliaments. The same day that newspapers announced the opening of a concentration camp in Dachau intended to house five thousand political prisoners, Hitler celebrated the inauguration of the new Reichstag in Potsdam, just outside Berlin, where, in the eighteenth century, Frederick the Great had his summer residence and, in the nineteenth century, Bismarck inaugurated the Second German Reich. Two days after that, Hitler's Enabling Act was passed by a majority vote in the Reichstag, effectively dissolving the national parliament. In April and May there followed the first public boycott of Jewish businesses, a ban on employing Jewish and dissident clerks, and book burnings in Berlin and a number of university towns. On 1 May the Reich celebrated 'National Labour Day' in the name of national community, with parades, beer tents, singing and competitive sports. The next morning, the Nazi authorities broke up the unions.

This storm of events swept over a breathless population in the space of less than three months.

• • •

Reiner Hamm was thirteen when Hitler came to power. In his hometown of Giessen, the Brownshirts and the SS staged their own torchlight parade on the evening of 30 January, and when the Reichstag burnt in Berlin, they fanned out to hunt down communists. Local party activists did what they could to ensure that the major events in the capital resonated even in a provincial town like Giessen. 'In 1933 we were all completely absorbed by the rapid changes at home. What was going on around us in Europe took second place,' Reiner said. At the grammar school he attended, the pupils worshipped politicians like film stars. Reiner had pictures of his heroes hanging on the walls of his room— Frederick the Great, Bismarck and Hitler. The new chancellor provided a constant flow of news; there was always something to talk about at break or over dinner. He also fuelled the boys' collecting mania with a glut of likenesses.

> We were surrounded by Hitlers in every shape and size, from toy figurines, each with the trademark black moustache and a movable right arm, to the two-storey-high painting of the Führer that I saw in the Haus der Kunst in Munich.

In art class at school, Reiner drew a picture of a worker—to represent the German people—hámmering a huge *Ja* out of a stone block. *Yes* to Hitler. Hamm had found the idol of his youth. Like millions of others, he dreamed of meeting the man himself.

. . .

At the conclusion of the election on 5 March 1933, the National Socialists were, with forty-four per cent of the vote, still in a nominal minority. Only three weeks later, it looked as if Hitler had the majority of Germans behind him. In the space of a breath, wary astonishment had given way to excited approval and even euphoria. It was the time of the 'March fallen' or 'March violets'— the much-derided opportunists who rushed to join the party only after the March elections.

In the middle of the month, René Juvet had an appointment with his manager. Waldmeyer wasted no time on factory matters, but immediately launched into a political lecture. Democracy, he said, was a thing of the past; it was time for a change of attitude. Juvet had never been asked to deny his democratic convictions; now his boss was demanding it straight out. Lying low wasn't enough; to satisfy Waldmeyer, Juvet would have to make a commitment. The threat was unequivocal. 'The faster you act, the better it will be for your career,' Waldmeyer told his employee.

> Jettison any unnecessary ballast. There'll be no more standing on the sidelines here. In future, anyone wanting to get anything done will do so on National Socialist terms. I for my part am convinced that Hitler is the man of destiny and I will stand by my conviction.

Juvet didn't know what to say. The talk shook him more than anything he'd heard or seen since the change of government. He knew Waldmeyer as an educated, erudite Prussian with an eclectic circle of friends, a boss who was respected by his staff for his intelligence and sarcastic sense of humour. And suddenly here he was, urging Juvet to toe the party line. He even told him to avoid his Jewish friends, having decided to do as much himself. Juvet couldn't bring himself to reply. He silently resolved to keep his views to himself and watch his step.

In the days that followed, Waldmeyer came to work sporting a shiny new party badge. He helped set up a Nazi cell at the factory, run by the former bookkeeper Neder, an early party member and now the head of purchasing. Half the office staff and a quarter of the workers readily signed up. Except for some foreign correspondence, business letters were now signed off with 'Heil Hitler'. A few days in March had been enough to transform an ordinary factory into a model Nazi business run by party loyalists.

. . .

The dizzying excitement that had gripped Melita Maschmann at the torchlight parade in Berlin had left her thoughts in a whirl. Now she began to look for facts to shore up her new 'faith'. She greedily lapped up any news that offered 'proof' of the leaders' spirit of enterprise. She believed their promises to free millions from misery and unite the German people. She believed them when they said they'd do away with the Treaty of Versailles. She was on the threshold between childhood and youth and felt ready for great ideas.

But her upper-middle-class parents stood in her way. Though they rejected Weimar, they looked no more favourably on the National Socialists and their revolutionary carry-on. When Melita wanted to join the Hitler Youth, they wouldn't let her, pointing her instead to a monarchist girls' league. And so Melita made a lonely decision that was to separate her from her parents' world.

As my parents wouldn't allow me to become a member of the Hitler Youth, I joined secretly. That was the beginning of my private 'time of struggle'. At last I was catching up with my comrades who had joined before 1933; I, too, was paying for my allegiance to the National Socialists with a personal sacrifice.

In early 1933, the Hitler Youth organisation had more than a hundred thousand members. Since Hitler's inauguration, an advertising campaign had been underway to lure young people into its ranks with camps, sporting activities, parades, drama groups and frequent celebrations. Fed up with the tedium of dull Sunday outings with her family, Melita Maschmann initially looked forward to these social activities, but her time as a member of the Hitler Youth proved a disappointment. The social evenings held in a dingy basement were excruciatingly primitive and the coarse language of the other girls grated on Melita's patrician ears. They were salesgirls, seamstresses, maids—all from the working-class backgrounds she had romanticised. Melita's late entry into the Hitler Youth saw her branded as a March violet, making her an object of derision to the 'old guard', who expected her to admire and respect them.

> Because I was a March violet and a schoolgirl, they treated me with scorn and made it quite clear to me that I didn't belong. Some of them were distressingly uncouth and, I realised to my dismay, corresponded in every detail with the picture my mother often drew of hoi polloi.

The only way Melita could reconcile her fantasy of a classless national family with bitter reality was to pin all her hopes on the future. 'That's why I stayed in the Hitler Youth. I wanted to help realise the idea of a national community in which people would live together like one big family.' After all, the future was only just beginning.

. . .

In the early spring of 1933, millions of Germans cast aside their reservations and joined the Nazi Party in droves. The party offices were overwhelmed with applications. Between January and April, membership numbers exploded, reaching 2.5 million. The old guard had nothing but contempt for the March violets, whom they regarded as unprincipled bandwagon jumpers.

But the people who flocked to join the 'movement' did so from a variety of motives. There may have been a certain amount of cool calculation, but, at the same time, it was spring; people were feeling upbeat and hopeful and keen for something new. The desire for unity was officially fulfilled on the 'Day of Potsdam', when the former president, Hindenburg, shook hands with the young chancellor. In every city in the Reich, symbolic acts marked the spread of Nazism: lime trees were planted, known as 'Hitler lindens', the Führer was welcomed as an honorary citizen to towns across Germany, and the Hitler cult passed into the realms of kitsch and sentimentality. This enthusiasm penetrated the tiniest hamlets and infected even the most reluctant. Those who kept their distance began to be noticed.

Soon fear had become an ingredient of the collective frenzy. No one had failed to notice the wave of terror against the 'enemies of the national community', and although it met with widespread approval, it created an atmosphere of unease that would prove persistent. This unease was partly provoked by the unacknowledged fear of marginalisation. The margins were dangerous. Everyone could see that.

Stéphane Roussel had a large circle of German acquaintances, and wherever she went in those weeks in March 1933, she encountered recent converts. 'Many who had hesitated end up doing the same as everyone else,' she noted. Some people got hold of brown shirts and party badges so quickly that it made Roussel wonder. Her good-natured concierge, Herr Hellmann, suddenly began to wear a uniform under his coat. A friend in advertising showed her his party badge and talked of a campaign he was working on for 'the German patriot's soap'. Some of the March violets seemed to feel the need to justify the step they had taken, and cast about for alibis.

On one occasion, Roussel heard a wealthy woman—a Prussian nobleman's widow—talk openly about this fear of marginalisation. This woman had never made a secret of her abhorrence of Hitler—his oily way of speaking, his base origins—but she was beginning to realise that most of her friends had joined the party. Her invitations to social events were dwindling, and the excuses she received when she tried to hold a tea party herself were chilly. The widow was advised to join a Nazi women's organisation, at least in an honorary capacity, and she began to feel afraid. A few weeks later, on a visit to Roussel, she said she'd heard it rumoured that Hitler was the illegitimate son of a Hohenzollern, and thus of noble blood after all. That story did the trick, Roussel noted: 'The next time I see her, she's wearing swastika earrings and has a magnificent diamond-studded swastika pinned to the lapel of her tailor-made suit.'

The euphoria which spread to every corner of the Reich that spring showed how great the Germans' capacity for excitement was. They were prepared to follow Adolf Hitler anywhere. Yet at the same time, right from the start, they were driven by fear. The only way they could live with this contradiction was to ignore it, to invent their own version of reality.

Part of Something Greater

An October evening on Ulm's Lindenhof, dusk swallowing the shadows. Renate Finkh stood on the square where, not so long ago, she'd seen the communist protest marches and the processions of Brownshirts from her nursery window. Now it was her turn. Aged ten and a half, she was to be accepted into the Hitler Youth and join the Young Girls' League. So far, she hadn't been able to muster much enthusiasm. The games bored her and she was no good at asserting herself. She felt the old pain gnawing at her again, the pain of not being needed. Not by her parents, not by her older brothers and sisters—and not by the girls at school, who always avoided her. She was used to feeling lonely. But feeling unnecessary was worse.

The young girls and boys of Ulm stood in a rectangle, waiting to be sworn in by the youth leader and receive their knotted neckerchiefs. Renate waited indifferently, her shoulders drooping. Large crowds had always frightened her, and this was no exception; she felt out of place.

Then suddenly it happened: 'The solemnity of the occasion, made more solemn still by the singing and music, sweeps me off my feet, raises me high and gives me an undreamed-of sense of importance.' Staring right through the speaker who is earnestly addressing them from within a circle of torches, Renate thinks she can make out the figure of the Führer, calling her, needing her. Her, Renate Finkh. She feels her little girl's forlornness and weakness fall away from her and, as she speaks the oath she's gone to such pains to learn, her voice is clear and confident. The stilted lines that speak of faith and pride and strength suddenly make sense. 'It is the first ceremony of my life, and it pierces me to the heart.'

She feels all at once very close to her parents, who admire the Führer, though they argue so much she sometimes wishes she were invisible. Now there is something uniting them all. She is no longer shut out of their world. She feels strong enough to endure anything.

> I am no longer a pebble thrown into a pond, encircled by rippling rings that vanish into uncertainty. I am tied fast by my knotted neckerchief, part of a whole. Only one ring encircles my life. Its name is Germany.

Belonging. Being a part of things. The feelings described by Renate Finkh were central to the experience of millions of young Germans. Solemn initiation ceremonies like the one on Lindenhof made them feel like people in their own right, able to share in grown-up life. They felt less dependent on adults, less in thrall to their parents and teachers, who never gave them that kind of recognition. Renate suddenly saw herself in a different light—more grown-up, more important. But she had entered another form of dependency: she was now in thrall to her country and her Führer.

· · ·

By attacking the grey dignitaries of Weimar, the Nazis styled them-selves a party of youth. After Hitler's inauguration, the number of people joining the Hitler Youth soared. Soon it was on its way to becoming the only state youth organisation. Slogans like 'Youth Leading Youth' and 'Dawn of the New Generation' inspired members with high expectations for the future and helped many to endure joyless lives. After joining in April 1933, Hermann-Friedrich Cordes spent all his free time with his troop, organising hikes, finding places for the boys to camp, deciding who slept in which tent. He devoted weeks to such preparations, and his enthusiasm didn't go unnoticed. Aged twelve, he became leader of a group of ten boys his age. 'We lived like the robber barons in the March of Brandenburg!' he wrote in an enthusiastic letter to a friend. The Hitler Youth became a kind of home to him.

His actual home, meanwhile, had degenerated into chaos and misery. His parents stumbled through the ruins of their marriage, unable to break away from each other. Hermann's father descended into drinking and gambling, couldn't hold down a job and barely managed to scrape together the money for clothes and rent, while his mother seemed incapable of taking her fate into her own hands. For a time, Hermann-Friedrich's only clothes were his Hitler Youth uniform and a cousin's hand-me-down shirt. The bailiff was at the door again. The Cordes drifted from flat to flat like urban nomads, each dwelling more wretched than the one before. The economic boom of the early Hitler years passed the family by.

'Just look at the boy! Skin and bone from all that running around, and quite frighteningly pale.' Ilse Cordes knew that her son's quiet temperament stopped him from protesting against the constant sacrifices and frequent humiliations he suffered, but seeing no way out for either of them, she clung desperately to him—and to his love for her, which helped her to bear her own burden. 'These are difficult times for him, but now, more than ever, he is a fond and solicitous companion to his mother. May these memoirs serve as a monument to his deep filial love.'

The only bond holding the family together was their obsessive love for the fatherland. Ilse Cordes clung to her son's success in the national movement, hoping it might make up for his life of privation.

For younger people, who knew no life but that of the Third Reich, the Nazi initiation rituals were accepted as a matter of course. Johann Radein, from Siefersheim, was born in 1932. 'Like all those of my generation who grew up in the National Socialist age, I felt as if life always had been this way and always would.'

The Nazis' highly emotive language, their symbols of strength and power, their flags, parades and songs were all part of everyday life, and seemed somehow eternal. When the ten-year-old Johann and his friends gathered in the hills outside Siefersheim to be inducted into the Hitler Youth, membership had been mandatory for some time. But though the organisation had grown into an immense machine with several million members, the induction ceremony had lost none of its dramatic pomp. Johann Radein was impressed by the highly decorated men standing on the hill before him, flanked by standards, waiting to receive the boys' oaths of loyalty.

> The oath of allegiance, sworn in the middle of nature, feels to me like an irrevocable bond—a sublime, memorable and unforgotten experience of a symbolic, almost religious act. Even as I return home, the feeling is overwhelming.

Johann felt like a discoverer, pushing open the door to a new world together with his sworn comrades. After the ceremony, the troop leader had pressed a collection of songs into their hands. They soon knew them all by heart. 'It's quite an experience to march in closed ranks down the road and through our village, singing as we go.' The lyrics were sombre, momentous. They spoke of the future, of danger, time and eternity. Aged eleven or twelve, Johann Radein sang the song of death, yearning to sacrifice his life in battle for his country. That was another advantage of being part of a greater whole: you could give back something of what you had received.

. . .

A sense of being needed, of belonging, and deriving self-esteem from it—this was the lure of the 'new era'. If certain unreasonable demands were also part and parcel of the system, they paled into insignificance beside such advantages. Anyone deemed worthy by the regime to participate in 'project Germany' was offered some kind of formal place within it. There were organisations for women and students, teachers and doctors, war victims, clerks and workers. The spirit of national community could be enjoyed by all ages.

In May 1933, on her fifteenth birthday, Lore Walb, a young girl from Alzey, began to keep a diary. The blank notebook was a birthday present; she was also given a quoit, a towel, a brown 'Hitler jacket' and a swastika brooch of hammered metal. Lore came from a warm, loving family, but they had their prejudices, too—against communists, and Roman Catholics, Jews, gypsies and the working class. Her father had helped found the local branch of the party; her mother was in the women's league, her brother in the Hitler Youth. She herself was a member of the League of German Girls. When Hitler came to power, the family was overjoyed. Lore was gripped by the spirit of the new era, fascinated by the Führer's character and ideas.

Decades later, Lore Walb put herself through an unusual experiment. She wrote a book attempting to come to terms with her former self, the small-town German girl who had kept the diary. The thoughts and feelings she had recorded in it knocked her sideways. Like so many others her age, she'd been a bandwagon jumper, a 'follower'.

> My youth in the Third Reich passed unspectacularly. My diaries document what was going on in the minds and hearts of millions of Germans. They are representative of the exultant and silent majority.

Political events had such a strong effect on young Lore that they took up more space than her private life in her diary. For her, the political and the personal were inseparable. She wrote about solstice celebrations and summer holidays, Versailles memorial days and Easter eggs, Hitler's evening radio broadcasts and her dates with boys. The diary entries were interleaved with copies of school essays on the role of art in the national community or the wonders of 'Winter Relief'.

Winter Relief was a charity run by the Nazis to benefit the poor and unemployed. It called on young people to do their bit for the national community by collecting donations or selling badges. The winter ritual was driven by a massive publicity and doorknocking campaign. Like hundreds of thousands of other young people, Lore Walb walked the streets with her collecting tin, doing the rounds of homes, shops and restaurants. 'I have a clear memory of the joy I felt at taking an active part in the street collections. It was satisfying to be needed; it was inspiring to be able to use my talent for speaking.' Lore liked the idea of sacrifice for the community. In an essay on Winter Relief, written in March 1936, she made an appeal to the children of the Reich: 'One for all and all for one! That must be our motto. No one must exclude himself! For without individuals, there's no community.'

That year her father died. She had always accepted his nationalist convictions without question; now the values of national community provided her with a substitute for her lost father. 'Just as, in my dream, I had been a weak little girl holding up the heavy picture of my father, I now put all my strength into holding high Hitler's picture.' In the summer of 1938, Lore Walb signed up to do national labour service. She found herself having to cope with strangers and strict superiors, but more importantly, she felt useful and valued. 'We were very popular. The girls treated us a bit like leaders, always asking our advice, I don't know, we were somehow special.' In the labour service camp she felt the magic of belonging. Being surrounded by a group of contemporaries made her feel more confident.

• • •

The young lawyers in the Court of Appeal in Berlin received recognition and appreciation without having to make any effort at all. In autumn 1933, Raimund Pretzel's training was nearing its end. It hadn't escaped his notice that the Jewish judge had left and been replaced by a younger man, tall, blond, ruddy-cheeked. The older lawyers were uncomfortable with the young man's brash manner, but it was no concern of Pretzel's. He and his fellow clerks 'rose daily in importance', he said.

> The Association of National Socialist Lawyers wrote us all (me included) the most flattering letters: we were the generation who would build the new German justice. 'Join us. Help us in the historic task assigned to us by the Führer's will!'

The clerks were gathering confidence. They sensed that there were advantages to belonging. Raimund Pretzel lost some of his friends to the movement and others to exile. Then, in October 1933, he found himself with a few dozen other articled clerks in the little town of Jüterborg in Brandenburg, attending an eight-week course on politics. While he was there, he wore black boots and a uniform. He marched behind a flag, singing marching songs. This wasn't something he was used to; he didn't know any marching songs. In the past, he'd always taken refuge in doorways when flags were paraded down the streets. 'Now we were the ones embodying an implicit threat of violence against all bystanders. They greeted the flag or disappeared. For fear of us. For fear of me.'

In the articled clerks' camp, Pretzel learnt to do drill and give the Nazi salute. He went along with all this because he had to, if he wanted his degree—and because he found a strange sense of security in Jüterborg that he'd never felt before. When he stood naked in the shower room with the others every morning, when they tussled with each other, covered up for one another or grumbled about the instructors together, it instilled in him a feeling of camaraderie.

> We trusted one another without reserve in all the actions of the day, and had boyish battles and fights. We were all the same. We floated in a comforting stream of mutual reliance and gruff familiarity...Who would deny that that brings happiness? Who would deny that men yearn for this, a yearning that is rarely satisfied in ordinary, peaceful civilian life?

Camaraderie was the cement that held the national community together, whether in the Hitler Youth, the labour service, the army or the articled clerks' camp.

Pretzel woke from this reverie feeling hungover and disgusted with himself. Usually a critical thinker, he felt that he'd fallen into a trap. 'You are under a spell. You live a drugged life in a dream world. You are terribly happy, but terribly demeaned; so self-satisfied, but so boundlessly loathsome, so proud and yet so despicable and inhuman.' By letting others dictate how he spent his days, how he dressed and what words he used, he had shed not only his worries and burdens, but also responsibility for his actions. It was only when Pretzel returned to Berlin that he realised the fatal appeal of renouncing responsibility in this way. In the weeks that followed, he began to think about leaving.

An Inner Rift

The ambivalence that had marked the beginning of Melita Maschmann's career in the Hitler Youth often came back to haunt her. She
threw herself with enthusiasm into her new job of running the press
office and collaborating on the youth magazines, but was shocked
by the mediocrity of the other junior workers; she found herself
surrounded by a bunch of naive souls—keen, but slavishly obedient
to party slogans. On a training course, she caused a stir by rejecting
the popular conspiracy theory that the German poet and philoso-
pher Schiller had been poisoned by his friend Goethe, who happened
to be a Freemason. The old guard poured scorn on Melita: it was
common knowledge within the party that the Freemasons were
enemies of the people, on a par with Jews and Marxists. Maschmann
found herself on the wrong side of the unspoken law that if you
didn't belong—because you were different, or had different views—
you were ostracised. She chose to bury her objections rather than be
excluded, telling herself it was the right thing to do:

One has no right to turn one's back on the party because of such disappointments. Little by little the spirit of truth will prevail over untruth. One must fight the battle wherever one happens to be. As time went by, I often found myself reflecting along these lines.

Such contradictions became part of Melita's life. She had joined the Hitler Youth soon after making friends at school with a Jewish girl called Marianne Schweitzer. Although Melita believed that Jews were a threat to Germany, and went around saying so, this did not at first affect the girls' friendship. Melita made no connection between the anonymous spectre of 'the Jew' and real-life Jewish people like Marianne or the nice man who lived next door, Herr Lewy. Millions of children in Germany had grown up accepting this paradox, Melita later explained.

Our parents may have grumbled about the Jews, but it didn't stop them from feeling genuine liking for the Lewys or socialising with my father's Jewish colleagues. For as long as we could remember, we had watched the grown-ups act out this contradiction as if it were entirely natural.

In the same way, Melita told her Jewish friend all about the Hitler Youth. It was only when Marianne's brother became involved with communists that the tension began to weigh on her. Gradually, Melita eased herself out of the friendship by devoting more and more time to the Hitler Youth. When her parents sent her away to board because she wasn't doing well enough at school, she decided to make a clean break. She was a youth leader; she didn't want to be friends with a Jewish girl anymore. When she said goodbye to Marianne Schweitzer at Halensee station in Berlin, she felt dull, traitorous. Outwardly all was in order now, but her conscience suffered. 'At the time I thought: So being guilty is a part of life, then.'

. . .

The National Socialists left the Germans in no doubt about who belonged in their country and who didn't. Anyone considered a 'comrade of the people'—and that was the vast majority of the population—could stride out with them into the great new age. Anyone who didn't belong would be ostracised and, in the long term, eliminated. Ordinary Germans observed such distinctions daily. They might register it with approval or disapproval, relief or indifference, without having to change the course of their lives. But they couldn't avoid it entirely. Many began to feel an uneasy apprehension.

. . .

Renate Finkh's father had been an early supporter of Hitler and was keen to remain on the 'right side'. He said openly that the Jews should emigrate. But then he found himself having to ask a popular player to leave the Ulm tennis club, of which he was chairman. It had come out that the man's mother was Jewish. Renate's parents discussed the dilemma over lunch. It was one thing to be against the Jews. 'But it went against common decency to take action against someone they knew and who'd done them no harm.' Renate was confused. How often had she been in Gold's chocolate shop on the way to school to buy a few pennyworth of sweets? Now her mother happened to mention that Herr Gold was Jewish. Renate felt caught out, as if she'd been lying. She'd spent money in a forbidden shop. She never set foot in Gold's again.

She came up with a plan to make amends for her transgression. Out playing in the yard, she crept into a shed belonging to their Jewish neighbour Fräulein Liebel and left behind a turd. When this woman broached the matter with her, Renate denied it rudely. For a long time, the young girl was terrified that Fräulein

Liebel would talk to her parents. But she didn't. Renate never told anyone this story.

> I pushed it to the back of my mind, hid it away behind the 'Jews Unwanted' signs and the newspaper reports which blamed all the ills in the world on the Jews. But the stench pervaded.

Johann Radein took part in Nazi events with an enthusiastic if somewhat uneasy alacrity. The overblown language, by turns cloying and cruel, left him uncertain whether to feel happy or despondent. He had no defences against the rousing imagery, and the words and tunes went round and round in his head. Even during his first days as a member of the Hitler Youth, he swung from one mood to another. As his troop marched through Siefersheim, singing, their spirited young voices echoed off the rows of houses, and the farmers had to pull their carts over to let them pass. Johann's heart was in his mouth every time.

> We sang the same aggressive songs over and over. Nobody stopped us. Sometimes the songs gave me a heavy, queasy feeling in my stomach that often took hours to subside, like a fit of depression.

When the last song was sung, Johann made for home, no longer part of the column. Now the farmers looked down at him from their carts, dark and silent. Führer, flag and loyalty were far away. The magic had flown. Once the parade was done and the feeling of camaraderie had evaporated, Johann said, he often 'fell into a deep emotional hole and felt very lonely'. The weight that settled on Johann's shoulders as he headed home was as much a part of his memory as the high-spirited hours that had gone before.

• • •

For most Germans, life after 1933 went on largely unchanged. As Raimund Pretzel observed, the facade of ordinary life was left intact. People went about their business. They went to the pictures or the theatre, sat in cafes, danced in dance halls, walked in parks or relaxed by the seaside. The tension and anxiety were hidden away beneath the surface. 'Strangely enough,' he said, 'it was just this automatic continuation of ordinary life that hindered any lively, forceful reaction against the horror.'

Although Pretzel himself felt the horror, he too went about his business. He passed his state examination, did some occasional work as a lawyer, went to cinemas and cafes. He tried to remain friendly in his dealings with others and not to let himself be swept along by the hatred directed against those perceived as outsiders.

> The only way is to turn a blind eye, block your ears, seal yourself off. You become so spineless as to be inured to what is going on around you and eventually you descend into a kind of madness and lose all grasp of reality.

For five years, Raimund Pretzel dragged himself around in a state of inner conflict. Then, in August 1938, he left Germany.

The Happy Years

The six and a half years of peace from 1933 to 1939 shine out in the memories of many who lived through them as an era of happiness. The bleakness of the preceding years gave way to relief, optimism, even exuberance; Germans were swept off their feet by the can-do attitude of Hitler and his youthful team. Their society's transformation was so rapid it left no time for reflection. The Nazis were initiating social reforms that had previously seemed doomed never to get off the ground. Workers' holidays, days off, family allowances, tenants' rights protection—ordinary people were profiting from the new welfare policies on a broad scale. Owning a house—and perhaps even a car—was no longer a utopian dream; travelling was no longer a privilege. The leisure industry was booming. Upward social and professional mobility were possible as never before. Despite the repression of dissenting voices and limits on intellectual freedom, many felt that their country was more open now, as a result of its growing prosperity.

In late 1933, faith in economic recovery asserted itself. The decline had in fact begun to slow under the Weimar government, and the economy was only just beginning to pick up, but a lot of demonstrative first-sod-cutting gave the impression that Hitler alone was responsible for the upturn. In Demmin, his appointment as chancellor had sparked euphoria. Until then the town had been in debt and the streets full of unemployed people. After the handover of power, Demmin experienced its own provincial version of events in Berlin: its own torchlight parade, its own communist hunt, its own Jewish pogrom, its own rallies and May Day celebrations. At the Reichstag elections in March, the proportion of Nazi voters in Demmin was higher than in the Reich as a whole. Party members formed a living swastika on the square in front of the town hall. The new city fathers set about enforcing conformity and dismantling what remained of their democracy. They renamed Anklamer Strasse 'Adolf Hitler Strasse', planted a Hitler oak and drew up a 'kitsch law' to prevent the production of embarrassing fripperies such as Hitler cups or swastika sweets. Meanwhile, two colossal swastikas flanked the pediment over the entrance to the town hall.

Marie Dabs, the furrier's wife, hadn't forgotten Brüning's brutal austerity drive. The queue of the unemployed had reached all the way from the Baustrasse labour exchange to her family's shop on Luisenstrasse. Marie Dabs had struggled daily to make ends meet, borrowing a bit here and a bit there, chasing up IOUs. She had come to live in fear of bills and rent day. All around her, businesses were going bankrupt. Without her, her husband Walter would have thrown in the towel; he wasn't cut out for a life of struggle.

When the town hall began to fill with brown uniforms, Marie Dabs was sceptical. She liked to think of Demmin as the elegant garrison town of imperial times, where noble-born officers from the Uhlan regiment could be seen strolling in and out of Luise Gate. The Nazis' vulgar flamboyance wasn't something she took to.

> There was something coarse about those hands raised in salute. But even one year on, a lot had changed for the better. The large numbers of unemployed had disappeared, young people were working for the labour service. At Tutow, only half an hour from Demmin on the local railway, they built the largest military airfield in Germany.

Tutow was a classic case of Nazi rearmament. The flying school was used by combat squadrons, training squadrons and a flak training regiment. Housing sprang up around the airfield—sports grounds, a swimming pool. Local building firms moved further out of the red with every contract signed. The garrison swelled to more than three thousand men, who all came into Demmin to do their shopping. Marie and Walter Dabs seized the moment and got hold of a licence to sell military decorations and medals. 'I filled the two showcases at the shop door with everything the airmen would need, and they weren't long in coming,' Marie Dabs said. The fur shop suddenly had its own arms business.

There was such a rush of airmen that the shop was soon too small, and they had to rent space next door. Marie rose to the top of Demmin society. Walter was declared the town's 'king of the marksmen' in 1936, and they attended the big winter ball as a 'royal couple', Marie in a champagne-coloured evening dress with a dark-red rose. 'Everyone wanted to dance with the queen, who was much complimented that evening,' Marie would later recall. At dinner she was put opposite a prominent district councillor, a member of a noble family, and had soon made a customer of him. Queen of Demmin. Marie Dabs had climbed higher than she'd ever dreamed. The German economic miracle was entering its fifth year.

Business was also picking up in the goldsmith's shop run by Renate Finkh's father. In Ulm, the after-effects of the Depression had subsided.

> Dad was full of optimism and confidence at that time. I knew he was one of the ones who'd believed in the Führer before the takeover. He made a point of that. Now he was proud and happy to have been proved right.

People everywhere could be heard telling each other that everything was better, *thanks to the Führer*. Renate's father was even able to grant his wife her wish for a little house with a garden. She drew up the plans and he found a plot of land. After years of conflict, they had a common goal at last. Renate felt that things were looking up.

> I often sat astride the bare roof ridge, relishing the warm wave of joy that swept through me. One day, there would be a real home here. When the house was finished, I wrote a long illustrated poem about the building of it and gave it to Dad for Christmas. I could tell he was proud of me.

Renate's father had been aloof and irritable. Now he could do anything again. His wife found that the garden gave her a zest for life and new-found courage. Renate gained a sense of security from the house unlike anything she'd known before.

• • •

But the German people's happiness had another, more public aspect to it in the 1930s. This was Hitler's string of foreign-policy successes, which produced a continual buzz of triumph and satisfaction among the Germans. As Hitler pulled off coup after coup, at almost yearly intervals, he rekindled the nation's desire to restore Germany's lost greatness.

Like the spectators at a sporting event, the German people were themselves part of the show, part of the action. In one of her first diary entries in June 1933, Lore Walb describes a memorial day held in her hometown of Alzey to mark the anniversary of the Treaty of Versailles. It was like a national day of mourning. The flags hung at half-mast, the radio played solemn music. At school, lessons came to a standstill, and the children were given a speech about the abhorred treaty. The government's foreign policy had pushed its way into the classrooms of Alzey Secondary School. Lore Walb was fourteen.

In January 1935, a referendum was held in the Saarland to decide if the region should be reintegrated into Germany after fifteen years of administration by the French. By then the feeling of enthusiasm had been growing for some time. Standing in the crowd at the Saar rally in October 1933, Lore glimpsed the Führer twice. He was standing in his car, serious and upright, shoulders back, arm raised. She felt giddy.

> The sight of him brought tears to my eyes. I don't know why, but I think I sensed how wonderful it feels to trust a leader of our people. I almost believe it was the most beautiful, moving and powerful moment of my fourteen years of life.

. . .

In her diary, Lore Walb chronicles the revision of the Treaty of Versailles. Every one of the country's risky manoeuvres is also hers; when Germany leaves the League of Nations in October 1933, she leaves too. She fills several pages on the subject of the Saar Referendum on 17 January 1935, noting, reporter-like, any anecdotes that strike her as relevant. At 6.30 am she sees the 'blood flag' of the Saarland being carried through Alzey towards Berlin.

'We are living in great times. Things are happening thick and fast,' she writes when German troops march into the Rhineland in March 1936. The rapid pace of events is dizzying, but it inspires her with confidence. Until the annexation of Austria in 1938, she reports enthusiastically and at length on each event. In the space of a few years, Hitler has overcome the ignominy of Versailles, expanded Germany's borders and made it a military nation again—all without bloodshed. The sense of relief is as great as the triumph. Lore Walb reveres her Führer as a man of peace. 'If he could only bring peace to the world. His greatest desire, his goal.'

• • •

For more than six years, it seemed to be ever upwards for Germany. Meanwhile people rushed from one celebration to the next. There was an endless succession of national holidays, when people gathered to assure one another of their loyalty. The cycle was ushered in on 30 January with the Day of National Rising. There followed the tenth anniversary of the party's foundation in February and Heroes' Memorial Day in March, the Führer's birthday in April, the Day of National Labour in May, the summer solstice in June, Reich Party Day and Harvest Festival in September, Memorial Day for the Movement's Fallen in November and finally the winter solstice in December. All were excuses for drums and marching bands, paramilitary parades, flag-waving children, mass choirs, blazing torches and Albert Speer's *Lichtdome*—spectacular 'cathedrals' constructed from beams of light. Reports of recent successes punctuated this calendar of festive rituals like stories of miracles, providing regular boosts to German self-celebration.

In February 1934, René Juvet, the Swiss notary living in Augsburg, was asked to make a speech about Hitler at a party at the factory. He had no hope of extricating himself. At eleven in the morning, Juvet's colleagues were waiting. He choked out a few sentences about the fight against unemployment, the government's achievements, and how it should be everyone's duty and pleasure to support it in its efforts. He felt that he'd got out of the predicament as best he could. Even a democratically minded outsider like him couldn't deny Hitler's success in getting the German people back to work. 'Anyone who had witnessed the cruel misery of unemployment was inclined to give its vanquisher a chance, even if he didn't see eye to eye with him ideologically.'

Foreigners who visited the Third Reich during those years of peace were impressed by the mood of optimism. René Juvet's friend from university, Ernst Scheitlin, who came to stay from Basel in the autumn of 1937, was bowled over by the changes he saw in Germany. He hadn't expected what he found: magnificent buildings built to last for millennia, modern expressways for long-distance travel, and everywhere cheerful people who had put the Depression behind them. When Juvet pointed out that the Germans had paid for the boom with personal and public freedom, Scheitlin waved his objections aside. 'You've grown small-minded, old chap. Maybe you're too close to things to see them. All I can say is, I'd be jolly glad if Switzerland had a Hitler.'

During Germany's 'happy' years, the Munich Agreement of 30 September 1938 was considered the keystone of Hitler's peace-keeping politics. Under the terms of this agreement, Hitler absorbed the Sudetenland—at the time, a part of Czechoslovakia—into the German Reich. Again, there was no bloodshed. René Juvet's boss, Waldmeyer, was full of optimism, convinced that peace would never end. Neder and Hofmann, the factory's keenest party members, raved about world dominance, eager at the prospect of colonies in the east.

Not long afterwards, in Munich on a business trip, Juvet attended the Oktoberfest. He'd been many times before, but never had he seen such high spirits. In every beer tent he visited, the festive mood ran higher. Long rows of beaming people stood arm in arm, swaying to the music. Beer flowed in torrents, roast chickens seemed to fly through the air. In the oompahpah music and the clinking beer steins, the merry faces and the sweaty bodies, Juvet thought he saw the secret of the Germans' happiness under Hitler.

He had conquered a great Reich for his people without resorting to the sword, triumphed over the obstacles of the detested peace treaty, and, it seemed, transformed yesterday's enemies into friends of the Third Reich. Unemployment, that grey guest of the last years of the Weimar Republic, was banished. Wealth reigned supreme, the people of Munich could eat their fill... and if they compared all that with the little bit of democratic plunder they had sacrificed, they could, on the whole, be satisfied.

Of those six happy years, 1938 was considered the happiest.

In Love with the Führer

'Germany... was thriving and happy. On its face was the bloom of a woman in love. And the Germans were in love—in love with Hitler.' After leaving the German Reich in 1933 to run the Paris offices of the *Daily Express*, British newspaper correspondent Sefton Delmer returned in 1936. He found people transformed. Three years had been enough to put them under the Führer's spell. 'They were adoring his firm ruthless rule. They were in raptures at being told what to think, whom to hate, when to cheer.'

Delmer knew all about the appeal of Hitler's drive, having felt its effects himself, almost physically, during the election campaigns. He could see why people were grateful to Hitler for pulling them out of humiliation and putting them back into work, restoring their confidence and hope. He saw the glow of satisfaction on the workers' faces as they cycled to the factories in their blue denim jackets, their enamelled coffee cans slung over their shoulders. Gone were the days when they hung around on the streets. The class struggle and internecine hatred seemed to have vanished. '[T]hey all, children and grown-ups alike, were enjoying the little jobs, the titles and the offices Hitler had given them, the bit of authority over others.'

The Germans' unbounded admiration for Hitler didn't surprise Delmer; after all, they regarded him as personally responsible for every new political success. It was Hitler alone—not the *Gauleiter* or the generals—who was the vanquisher of chaos, economic miracle maker, rearmament engine, people's conciliator and avenger of stolen pride. The Führer had become a myth.

His lowly origins made him a man of the people. His service in the Great War meant that he had experience of life in the trenches and understood the trauma of what was seen as unearned defeat. His rise to power came at a time of a profound identity crisis for the Germans, and he lived through that crisis with them. He shared their experiences and sufferings. He knew, and knew how to galvanise, their feelings, yearnings and prejudices—how to transform depression into exhilaration. As a man of the people, he spoke their language. He was the faith healer they had been waiting for.

All this catapulted him out of the herd and into the firmament. In the glow of his success, Hitler became a Messiah. Religious symbolism and language—*awakening, resurrection, amen*—characterised his public appearances. The words he addressed to the 140,000 faithful at the Nuremberg Rally in 1936 were close to mystical: 'It is the miracle of our age that you have found me... among so many millions! And that I have found you is Germany's great good fortune!'

Each of his appearances was as carefully choreographed as the liturgy. Each encounter between the Führer and his people was a piece of highly orchestrated drama, familiar and moving to the initiated, though sometimes disconcerting, repellent or ridiculous to outsiders. During the 1933 election campaign, Stéphane Roussel got herself a seat in the Sportpalast to hear Hitler's speech. Rather than sit in the press stand, she decided to mingle with the crowd. As the Führer's car approached, a rumbling could be heard in the distance, like a gathering storm. 'Suddenly, the storm broke. All the doors burst open and the waiting crowd poured in.' Everyone stood up, disciplined and excited at once. Hitler appeared at the back of the hall, surrounded by his aides, and began to advance, stately as a priest. His outstretched arm made it look as if he were dividing the crowd—not that anyone showed any sign of getting in his way.

> Since Hitler has arrived, the atmosphere has changed. We are no longer in the Sportpalast where Berlin's big bicycle races are held. We are in some 'elsewhere'. And slowly, a mysterious bond is formed between the audience and this man who stands alone, motionless, as if unaware of the waves of applause that roll towards him and break at the foot of the stage, without reaching him.

Silence in the arena, as his voice swelled. He spoke of victory over the past, of the present and the future, work and happiness—and every member of the audience seemed to feel as if he were addressing them personally. Roussel noticed the way he transformed their vague but urgent feelings into something more tangible. People's longings and resentments were laid out before them, on public view. Their most secret thoughts were no longer anything to be ashamed of; they belonged to everyone in the hall. '[T]hey're yours, he seems to say, and yours and yours.' Roussel glanced at the woman next to her and saw sweat pouring down her face. Oblivious to her surroundings, she was rocking her body in time to the Führer's words. The common man's dream had come true: everyone felt understood.

When it was over, the audience looked drained. Dark rings under their eyes showed how intently they had listened. Roussel hurried to escape. Not for a second had she felt tempted to succumb. When she mentioned this to a German colleague, he gave her a faint, condescending smile: 'It wasn't you he was talking to.' The myth of Hitler, and of Germany, was intended for others. Stéphane Roussel, a Frenchwoman of Jewish origin, was not one of them.

. . .

By the spring of 1934, the Führer cult had taken root across the country. The people's infatuation was genuine and remarkably durable. Their leader was untouchable, a fixed star. The failures of everyday politics were blamed on others—on the party or on Hitler's vassals, the 'little Hitlers'. Minor inconveniences and major atrocities were dismissed with the same simple phrase: 'If the Führer only knew!' He was exempt from all criticism.

Johann Radein's earliest memories of his childhood were bound up with memories of Hitler. He remembered standing in the dining area of his family's flat, gazing up at the picture of the Führer that hung next to the dresser and feeling trust and affection. When he was four, his mother took him with her to the local women's league leader, who thanked her in the name of the Führer for her achievements as a mother of four. That Christmas, a troop of Brownshirts called at the house with a washing basket full of presents—with the Führer's compliments. On Hitler's fiftieth birthday, Johann's mother reciprocated by hanging a homemade flag from the roof.

Johann felt deep love for the Führer. Despite his Catholic upbringing, his faith in the Führer held an important place in his life. When Hitler's speeches were broadcast on the radio, it seemed to him like a time of communion and prayer, as if Hitler spoke to him directly.

> The Führer's emotive language appeals directly to the feelings and emotions that my faith in him arouses in me. His highly impassioned voice seems in harmony with my thoughts. Sometimes the tone is quiet and solemn, at others loud and rousing; shouts strained to the point of hoarseness are followed by passages in an almost tearful undertone, low and lamenting, yet full of energy.

In the cold, dark winter months, when Hitler's speeches were full of talk of providence, Johann drew comfort from the familiar Christian term. In his childish faith, he thought he was hearing the word of God from the Führer's mouth.

The media did their bit to sustain this larger-than-life image; Hitler's charisma was the product of continual orchestration. The Nuremberg Rally film, the weekly newsreel, the living-room oil portrait—all these kept him far removed from the banalities of everyday life, portraying him as a leader without human flaws, who didn't smoke, didn't drink, ate no meat, and had neither a woman nor a family. Here was a man who would sacrifice himself for his people. This sentiment was echoed in the heaps of love letters and letters of admiration that arrived in the Reich Chancellery and party headquarters every day, part hero-worship, part cosy familiarity.

Hitler understood his role as the movement's central force. He knew, too, that he needed the majority of the population behind him, and so he carefully honed his image—manner, style, bearing, language—avoiding any hint of weakness or sordid intrigue. He played his role so perfectly that he himself was taken in. He began to see himself as the man he wanted to be seen as, believing in his own infallibility and divine election. Reality grew steadily more remote.

. . .

Gerhard Starcke had supported Hitler since a rally in the Sportpalast in 1930. He'd stood on a box of grit at the side of the road and watched the January 1933 torchlight parade pass through the Brandenburg Gate, hugged complete strangers and kissed women he didn't even know. Soon afterwards he became editor of the factory cell newspaper. He saw it as his task to contribute to the work of peace promoted by Adolf Hitler. One day, along with a group of other journalists, he met the chancellor himself in the garden of the Reich Chancellery. There he was in front of him, suddenly. 'His blue eyes went straight through you. It felt as if the man could look into the bottom of your heart and see every flaw.' The magnetic effect of Hitler's eyes became a myth in its own right. His gaze was described variously as intense, twinkling, piercing, penetrating, deep, hypnotic and terrifying. If Starcke had ever had doubts about Hitler's vision for Germany, they were forgotten at this moment.

. . .

Ordinary Germans seldom had the opportunity to glimpse the real Hitler. Martin Sieg was a boy like millions of others. His childhood in the East Prussian town of Rastenburg was unspectacular. When, years later, he sat down to write his autobiography, he felt as if he'd spent the first decade of his life on another planet. 'Those years were something like a rich overture, the calm before the storm. But the storm broke soon enough, and a very different kind of reality set in.'

Sieg's parents never discussed the political situation, so in 1937 he was put into a Hitler Youth uniform without being asked—but without protesting, either. He was proud of his uniform, because it gave him access to a higher social sphere. He liked marching with his friends, and he loved the spirit of freedom breathed by the scouting games and excursions. The Hitler Youth also gave him the chance to realise his dream of gliding.

Towards the end of 1940, his hometown gained special standing when one of the Führer's headquarters, the 'Wolf's Lair', was built deep in the woods near Rastenburg. The high security, the atmosphere of secrecy and most of all the proximity of the Führer put the boys in a permanent state of quivering excitement. Life near the Führer's bunker felt like a perilous adventure. Word got around whenever Mussolini, Göring, Rommel or other revered war heroes came to visit.

The day Martin Sieg met the Führer in Rastenburg, he was expecting no less than a demigod. Hitler's supernatural aura had made him a figure of legend. Sieg knew his voice from listening to his radio broadcasts in the living room with his grandmother, letting the words gush over him like a waterfall. That day, news had leaked that Hitler was going to inspect a new kind of tank at a nearby military training area. All excited, the Hitler Youth boys positioned them-selves at the roadside. Martin saw a gleaming black Mercedes in the convoy, advancing at a crawl. The crowd went wild and poured onto the road, pushing Martin onto the mudguard of the Mercedes.

I saw Hitler right in front of me, separated only by the glass of the window. The cameras clicked without let-up and I sat there like a rabbit before a snake, staring at the 'Übermensch' in a state of some shock. Suddenly the almost mask-like earnestness melted from Hitler's face, he smiled slightly, cranked down the window and gave me his hand.

Then Martin saw nothing but black uniforms—SS men who beat a path through the crowd with fists and boots and shoved him aside. He heard voices shouting themselves hoarse, but he couldn't cheer

anymore. His joy was gone. A feeling of emptiness and disappointment came over him, and he didn't turn to look for the Mercedes,
or for his friends. He wanted to be alone.

> I felt somehow stiff inside; the flood of feelings had frozen
> in mid-flow. In a way I was disappointed in myself because
> no new emotions were released in me. I tried to make sense
> of what was going on around me, but failed. I left the scene
> almost numb.

Recalling this episode later, Martin Sieg felt uneasy. The invisible
bond had snapped. He had got too close to Hitler.

The Smell of Fear

In the happiest of the happy years, the dark side of the regime was revealed, unequivocally, to everyone. On the evening of 9 November 1938, Melita Maschmann took part in a rally outside the town hall in Frankfurt an der Oder. She was bored, but stuck it out. By this time, she had built up something of a career as a Hitler Youth official; she no longer had to prove herself politically. A man in uniform hinted that something bigger was planned for later that evening, but she ignored him; she had an early appointment at the youth leadership offices in Berlin the next day.

In the morning, as she made her way from Alexanderplatz along a narrow lane with shops and bars, Melita saw in astonishment that all the windows were smashed. She picked a path through piles of broken glass and splintered furniture, but didn't see a soul. When she asked a policeman what had happened, he replied curtly that public feeling had run high the night before. Against the Jews. Melita recoiled.

For a second, I felt clearly that something awful had happened. Something frighteningly brutal. But almost in the same instant I abandoned my misgivings and switched to accepting what had happened as a fait accompli.

The unease she felt at the vandalism mustn't get the better of her. The longer the moment of horror stretched, the more dangerous it was. Dangerous to her inner self. So before the policeman could take a closer interest in her, she went on her way, her mind already hard at work, explaining away what she had seen. The Jews surely had only themselves to blame for their misfortune. Melita turned the corner, back into *her* world, where there was no broken glass, no blackened facades.

> I pushed the memory from my mind as fast as I could. As time went by, I got better and better at switching off quickly like this. It was the only sure way of keeping moral doubts at bay. I suppose that, somewhere below waking consciousness, I knew that any serious doubts would have swept away the foundations of my life.

On the afternoon of 10 November, Renate Finkh set off on her own initiative to the site where Ulm's synagogue had been torched. When she'd heard from her friends in class that morning what had gone on in 'Jews' Alley', and that the 'Jews' church' was still on fire, she couldn't keep her mind on the lesson. 'All this could happen, here in our town, while I was fast asleep?' A dull fear rose in her, she said, but she couldn't put her finger on the cause.

She was hit by a revolting burnt smell. A few Brownshirts were guarding the site; a handful of civilians stood around, staring in silence at the walls. Renate was afraid and turned to head back. On her way home, she saw the shattered windows and looted shops. That evening her father guessed where she'd been. Renate felt as if she'd done something forbidden and kept a sheepish silence. Never again, her father shouted at her, was she to go and look when something like that happened. The Jews had only themselves to blame. 'But you and I, we're nothing to do with all that, do you hear!' he said. He was very worked up, but didn't say why. The dull sense of unease was still with Renate in the morning.

After that, her father was a changed man. He grew more and more bad-tempered and refused to say a word to Renate about the Jews. She was left to mull things over alone. For days the cold, pungent burnt smell lingered in her nose and mouth—a smell that frightened her.

. . .

Lore Walb's 1938 diary ends with an entry on 6 November, a few weeks after she returned to Alzey from doing labour service. The last pages of the year are blank. Decades later, she filled in the missing events. There had been riots in Alzey, as there had all over Germany. The windows of the synagogue in Augustinerstrasse were smashed; Hitler Youth boys broke into the flats of Jewish families and hacked furniture to pieces. Gawpers pushed their way through the town's Jewish prayer room in long lines to see the devastation up close. Lore Walb's only response was a defensive fear. 'I clearly recall the feeling of panic that rose in me—fear, defensiveness: I'm not going in there, I don't want to see it, I've nothing to do with any of it!'

The silent blank pages in her diary expressed her feelings better than words could have done.

. . .

Confronted with the pogroms of 9 November 1938, many German people felt a similar shock at the outbreak of violence in their midst. René Juvet, who was on a business trip in Nuremberg, went round to the flat of some Jewish friends of his on the morning of 10 November. The flat had been ransacked, the woman beaten up. Her husband died in hospital. Back in Augsburg, Juvet discovered that most of his colleagues in the factory condemned the riots. Waldmeyer seemed unusually pensive. Hofmann, one of the old guard, made no secret of his disgust. The workers were horrified. One of them, a Brownshirt, confessed to Juvet how glad he was to have been out of town that night. 'I ask him whether he'd have joined in if he'd been around. "Of course," he said. "Orders are orders." When I heard that, a lot became clear to me.'

. . .

Fear, disguised as vague apprehension, was spreading fast. Although it had retreated after the demise of the Weimar Republic, it had never disappeared altogether. Each new shift in foreign policy was attended by the fear of war. People's cheers had, as much as anything, been cheers of relief that everything had passed without bloodshed. In the years following 1933, the mood in Germany didn't follow a steeply rising curve, but a frenzied zigzag that kept the regime on its toes as it tried to sustain public support. In the tumult of events stirred by Hitler, people were depressed one week and buoyed up the next. When he spoke of peace, it was a concession to the changing moods of the population.

The Sudeten crisis in the autumn of 1938 had strained nerves to the limit. The SS report on the public mood spoke of 'war psychosis' and described the population as depressed and pessimistic. For the first time, doubts were registered about Hitler's politics. Relief at the signing of the Munich Agreement was all the greater: it looked as if Hitler had managed to avert war before it was too late. On 20 April 1939, spectacular celebrations were held in honour of the Führer's fiftieth birthday. A few months later, the Germans got the war they had feared.

Marie Dabs had been a child during the First World War and a young woman in the Weimar years. Her generation was haunted by the memories of war and the aftermath of defeat. They knew what it meant to be at war and feared nothing more than to see the horrors return. Marie Dabs had spent the summer of 1939 recovering from a bout of tuberculosis. She hadn't long been home in Demmin when her husband was called up to the navy on 24 August. All summer and all the previous year they had pushed the rumours of war from their minds. Now it was upon them. Walter packed his case, Marie said, and caught the next train.

> Dear God! Were we to see another war in our lifetime? It didn't bear thinking of. But it came. On 2 September 1939 Poland was invaded and that horrible war began. I was paralysed with horror and couldn't sleep for nights on end.

Marie Dabs had a lot on her mind. There was the fur shop that she'd been left to manage alone—the full storerooms, the outstanding IOUs, the ongoing obligations. There were her children. There was the hated blackout that forced her to line her lovingly dressed windows in black paper. She was stunned that it had come to this. She'd believed every word spoken by the 'man of peace'. The Führer couldn't let all this happen, she said. 'He couldn't let it come to war after doing so much to help us build everything up these last years! How naive I was!'

September 1939 began on a gloriously fine day. In Augsburg, news had spread that the Führer would speak on the radio at about ten in the morning. René Juvet slipped out of the factory to avoid having to hear the speech at the mandatory 'community listening' session. He knew his colleagues abhorred war, and he didn't want to have to look them in the eye when the news came. He felt more than ever like an outsider. And so, when Hitler spoke of peace efforts, sacrifices and forebodings of death, Juvet was hiding out in the corner of a local cafe. As the familiar voice filled the room, he sat and stirred his coffee. The speech was received with thundering applause, but Juvet didn't see anyone clap. 'Nobody joined in the applause in my little cafe in Augsburg. Indeed, nobody stood up for the national anthem either.'

Back at the factory, Waldmeyer seemed to feel duty-bound to make a show of optimism. Juvet could see no other signs of enthusiasm. His colleagues spoke in hushed tones. They were waiting to be called up to the Werhmacht. Some of them had hung up their uniforms twenty-one years ago, hoping never to have to put them on again.

. . .

News of war reached Melita Maschmann far from home in a park in Potsdam, where she was on a training course for leaders of the League of German Girls. It came as a shock. Politics since 1933 had hardly been uneventful, but now she felt that the die was cast. Her parents had been evoking the malign shadow of war since her childhood. In those September days on the lake in Potsdam, she felt the same as everyone.

> I remember the silence that suddenly gripped our cheerful group. We scrutinised each other's faces: what were they thinking? The same fright was apparent everywhere.

Her horror subsided, giving way to grave composure. The war mustn't deter her from the faith she had set her compass by. She resolved to follow the unwritten law of her country: if you don't want to suffer wrong, you must do wrong yourself. She was convinced of the moral superiority of Germany's position. She believed the propaganda that Germany wasn't to blame for the war—to blame were the country's opponents, who wouldn't let them live in peace. She managed to push fear from her mind by submitting her fate to a higher authority. It didn't matter what happened to her, as long as the overarching whole remained intact. 'Anyone who has something to live for can put up with almost any way of life,' she said.

A few weeks after the outbreak of war, Melita Maschmann followed the Wehrmacht into conquered Poland.

Victors

'Last great test of fate.' At dawn on 1 September, Gerhard Starcke accompanied German forces over the border into Polish territory. As one of the Wehrmacht's fifteen thousand 'propaganda troops', Starcke sent home accounts of the action from the very first day of the war. He heard Hitler's speech on the radio. He'd been seven when the First World War broke out, and its aftermath had shaped his life. His reaction, too, was one of dread. 'It was only now, hearing Adolf Hitler, that we knew war had begun!—So now, we thought to ourselves, we shall share the same fate as our fathers.'

There was no rebellion in this thought—only the humble faith of a man bowing to necessity. Over the years Starcke had got used to entrusting his life to a higher power—providence, or the sacred nature of things—everything the Führer stood for. Now that higher power was testing him and Starcke wasn't going to question it.

The Germans followed their Führer into the detested war without protest, because they believed in his genius and in the justice of the cause. They may have feared him, but they had no qualms. As a part of the propaganda machine, Gerhard Starcke adjusted his political views in the reports he wrote. He saw the rapid advance of the troops greeted by cheers from the German population of Posen and West Prussia. 'It didn't occur to us for a moment that the confrontation with Poland wasn't natural or necessary.'

. . .

The swift victory over Poland took Melita Maschmann east in the wake of the German army. The area around Posen inhabited by a German minority had been annexed and renamed 'Reichsgau Wartheland'. Maschmann was asked to help set up the Hitler Youth there. The prospect of colonising the new eastern province caused her no misgivings.

> I said to myself, if the Poles were fighting with all possible means not to lose the disputed eastern provinces that the German people claimed as 'Lebensraum', then they remained our enemies, and I saw it as my duty to suppress any private feelings that conflicted with political necessity.

When she arrived in Warthegau, she found plenty of reason to withhold her private feelings. The barefoot, hungry children she saw in the dark streets and stinking backyards of Posen pursued her even into her dreams. An old beggar man keeled over face-first onto the snow in front of her and didn't get up again, but lay there, stiff as a board. She remonstrated with a German guard who wanted to beat an eight-year-old girl for stealing cabbage. Maschmann's young driver horsewhipped a deaf old farmer. She realised she would have to close her eyes to all this if she wanted to get on with her work. 'I developed the fateful ability to suppress the spontaneous sympathy I felt for the troubled people of that foreign nation.'

Thanks to this ability, Maschmann found that she enjoyed her work. She was twenty-one. Her job in the occupied zone made her a conqueror and a pioneer. There was no bureaucracy, no old guard, and plenty of scope for courage and initiative, encouraging Melita's belief in herself. The young ethnic Germans in Wartheland had never met anyone from Germany before; for them, her stories from the Reich sounded like fairytales. She developed the arrogance of a missionary.

> Our life in those days seemed like a big adventure. We were all the happier because it wasn't an adventure we had sought out ourselves to satisfy some private quest for action. We felt called to a fine and difficult duty.

It was only when Melita returned east after being home on leave that her feelings were more ambivalent. She was frightened at the thought of having to slip back into that cold, hard shell she had learnt to hide within. But the fascination of her work was stronger. The war opened up worlds.

• • •

The invasion of Poland gave many a thrill of power and adventure. Destruction held a new and strange appeal. For boys, fighting offered the chance of personal fulfilment, outside the grey tedium of everyday life and the hardship they had grown up in. At the start of the Polish campaign, Hermann-Friedrich Cordes volunteered with Infantry Regiment 111, the historic unit in which his father had served in the First World War. Cordes was eighteen and hoped to be able to slough off his childhood in the war. Behind him lay years of grim deprivation. The drama of his parents' marriage had left him quiet and introverted. Life had taught him to avoid getting involved with anyone, so that no one could land him in trouble.

His mother sensed his relief when he marched off to fight. A love of Germany had been the one passion she and her son had in common, and to see that love as a calling was perhaps the most important lesson that Ilse Cordes had passed on to Hermann-Friedrich.

After the 1940 campaign against France, which Hermann-Friedrich Cordes spent on the front line with his regiment, he could at last feel victorious. It was in part a personal victory over his former life, and the feeling was as powerful as a drug. His letters home are full of pride and satisfaction and happiness. In spring 1941 he told his parents he'd been put in charge of a small infantry squad. 'My dears, remember this date! Rejoice with me! Jump for joy! I've made it!' At last he could show his mettle. He had known only bleak privation, but war brought him recognition, respect.

> It is a proud feeling, to be allowed to think for others and educate them and take responsibility for them—i.e., for everything they do. But through all this I have remained my silent old self, reserved and detached.

In his New Year's letter to his mother in 1941, Cordes tells her that it is his dearest wish to feel again the elation of battle—to charge once more against the enemy and sweep the field clear.

. . .

The lightning victories of 1939 to 1941 brought new heights of euphoria. Once again, Hitler's onwards-ever-onwards principle proved effective. The reports of success from battleground after battleground—Poland, Denmark, Norway, France, Africa and the Balkans—threw the German people into a frenzy of joy, happiness, satisfaction and triumph, a blend of emotions which left them susceptible to that particular sense of superiority that the Nazi ideologues had been inculcating in them for years.

'Isn't it terrific?' Lore Walb wrote during the French campaign of May 1940. 'No sooner has one event sunk in than the next one's upon you.' She had grown used to victory by then. Decades later, she would recall the day war broke out. It was a late summer's morning and she was sitting in the kitchen with her mother, stoning cherries. From the radio, Hitler's voice boomed on about retaliating against Poland, bomb for bomb. 'The words and cadences, forever retrievable, are closely tied to the feelings spreading inside me: trepidation—"so it is going to happen, after all"—and apprehensive sorrow. I am twenty years old. I weep…'

Yet there is no sign of sorrow in the diary written by Lore's twenty-year-old self. Page after page is filled with explanation and justification: the reasons for the invasion are set out in detail, written in the style of a war correspondent, as if Lore had adapted her voice to fit the occasion. She traces the course of events in clipped sentences, listing prisoners' names and charting frontline movements, so that her diary reads like a military dispatch. The act of writing allowed her to savour the feeling of being a victor all over again. 'World history has never known such a campaign—the opponent eliminated in a bare four weeks. It is just wonderful to be German.' The newspapers ran death notices for men killed in action, but these seemed somehow unreal. The phrase 'For Führer, people and fatherland' evoked a sacrificial ritual. Occasionally, though, a personal connection to one of the millions of prisoners, the many thousands of fallen soldiers, would penetrate this unreality. The deaths of Lore's dancing-class partner, Klaus, and her slender blond schoolmate, Gerhard, receive only a brief mention, but such moments of chill reality stand out starkly against a general mood of intoxication, almost delirium, at Germany's victories.

When victory over France came in June 1940, half of Europe was under German control, but more importantly, the humiliation of defeat was wiped out. United as never before, the Germans hailed Adolf Hitler as their idol. A breathless Lore Walb did her best to keep pace with events, flitting from one news item to the next.

> It's strange to think that these are moments of historic signif-icance and that we ourselves are getting to see something of them. I don't believe we've fully grasped what great times we are living in.

She dreamt of peace, believing after each victory that the happy ending was in sight. But the war showed no signs of stopping; instead it began to gnaw its way into day-to-day life. When Lore went to Munich to study, she saw young men with amputated arms and legs and battle-scarred faces, sometimes only a few seats away from her in the lecture theatre. Victors could also be losers.

The war went on, but after a while no further headway was made. People weren't used to that. Lore Walb may have been polit-ically naive, but she was good at gauging the general mood. When she sat down to write in her diary on 3 October 1940, she had no progress to report—no victory, no turning point. Even so, she sensed that something had happened. 'For the first time since war broke out, my perpetual optimism is shaken. We're not getting anywhere with England. It looks as if there's something wrong.'

A Sense of Foreboding

One Sunday morning, Renate's mother shook her awake. She never usually came into her room to wake her. Half-asleep, Renate heard her say they were at war with Russia. She looked up through the skylight at a blue oblong of clear summer sky. 'Mum's standing in front of me. She looks even graver than usual and a little helpless. I suddenly realise that it's war for real.'

As they sat at the wireless, dread gripped them. The tinny voice coming from the radio spoke of the million-strong 'red hordes' and of the chain of German soldiers reaching from Finland to the Black Sea—the iron chain against Bolshevik Russia they'd heard so much about. Renate's father was optimistic, reassured by the victories against Poland and France. Her mother remained grave. Renate Finkh had the impression that what had gone before had been no more than a prelude to real war.

. . .

In all the diaries and memoirs of the time, the beginning of the Russian campaign on 22 June 1941 is like a thick, black dividing line. At dawn, the Wehrmacht invaded the Soviet Union on a broad front. Later, everyone would remember the moment of shock—where they were, how they heard, what they felt. It marked a deep caesura. Everything that had come before paled into insignificance. No one would be left untouched. It wasn't so much the surprise that made for such a violent shock; after all, rumours had been circulating for some time. It was the fear of the suddenly gaping abyss. This war would be different. It would determine Germany's fate.

'That moment on the morning of 22 June 1941 was the only time until 1945 when I seriously wondered whether Hitler had acted wisely and responsibly,' Melita Maschmann said. In Lindau, on the shores of Lake Constance, where she was on leave with her parents, she heard snatches of a loudspeaker broadcast from a cafe garden. A few holidaymakers were gathered round a radio set. She recognised Hitler's voice, announcing the invasion of the Soviet Union. It all flashed through her mind at once: the demoralising two-front war twenty years before, the terrifying vastness of the Soviet Union, the ghastly Bolsheviks, Napoleon's retreat in that icy winter. No one in the cafe garden said a word.

> The people around me had gloomy faces. We avoided one another's eyes and stared out across the lake. The opposite shore was hidden by grey cloud. There was something cheerless in the air on that dull summer's morning. Before the broadcast was over, it had started to rain.

Melita walked dispiritedly along the shores of the lake, the water lapping listlessly against the quay wall. She was exhausted after spending the night on the train and felt very small. She knew what this new campaign meant. The war would go on for many more years. It would claim an incalculable number of victims.

. . .

Only in January, Hermann-Friedrich Cordes had quoted to his mother the Führer's prophecy that 1941 would bring ultimate victory to the Germans. On 21 June he wrote to his parents from the Soviet border region where his infantry regiment had been posted.

> My dears, by the time you get this letter, you too will have heard what we already know. This morning we learnt for certain that the attack on the USSR will begin tomorrow. Strange feeling, knowing twenty-four hours in advance.

Over the next four weeks, Ilse Cordes received regular letters from her son telling her about Russia's boundless expanses, the exertion of the march, the encounter with the enemy and what he planned to do after the victory. On 8 July he sent her a fond birthday letter. 'I'd like to embrace you with all my heart and thank you for what you've done for your little rascal of a son, and for the big rascal. Keep well and happy and don't let the sun of your heart go down on your Reich!'

It was his second-to-last letter. On 18 July he died at Karoly, in an insignificant battle that got no mention in any report. The account Ilse Cordes wrote of her son's brief life includes two photographs. In one, a boy in uniform is laughing, his face turned shyly from the camera. The other shows a cluster of roughly hewn birch crosses in front of a group of trees. Somewhere in a Russian copse, Ilse Cordes lost her only child.

'Despite the hard blows that fate deals him and his parents, he is always smiling as he walks his short path through this world to his premature end.' On the twenty-two closely written pages of her little book, Ilse Cordes struggles repeatedly to wrest some sense out of Hermann-Friedrich's death. She writes of his faith in Germany, of his willing devotion to the great cause, the crowning of his life, the ultimate sacrifice, of God, eternity and her son's last deed. She explains everything with reference to his end. 'He didn't give his life in a rush of fleeting enthusiasm or in the heat of youthful passion. He gave it in all clarity, in the calm consciousness of higher things.'

But despite the high-flown protests and the patriotic words of comfort, Ilse Cordes' despair shines through. The greatest loss of her life forced on her the implacable question of meaning. She couldn't bear the thought that the sacrifice she and her son had made might be in vain. What remains is a broken mother's stifled scream.

Hermann-Friedrich Cordes' death in a nameless copse was lost in the ocean of death and suffering brought by the war of extermination in the east. An average of two thousand soldiers died every day on the German side; among the Red Army soldiers, the figure was five times higher, and the killing of civilians added to the death toll. Every day, several pages in the German newspapers were filled with the notices of men killed in action. The deeper the soldiers penetrated into enemy territory, the more lost their lives and the wider the repercussions at home. Until the summer of 1941, the war had barely touched daily life in Germany. The war in the east changed everything. The horror that gripped people in that first instant of shock was there to stay.

When Marie Dabs heard about the attack on Russia on 22 June as she breakfasted on a hotel terrace, she cut short her holiday in Eisenach and caught the sleeper back to Demmin. She was deeply shaken. The foundations on which she had laboriously built her life were crumbling, the walls cracking and caving in, one by one. Her husband, a soldier since the beginning of the war, had more or less vanished from her life. When the advance continued into the winter, she had to empty her fur shop. The coats and muffs she was so proud of were driven off to the front. One of her seamstresses had to be dismissed; her apprentice was called up. She, meanwhile, had to stand in the gym at the boys' school with her sewing machine, repairing furs for the war effort. 'We received quantities of furs, piles and piles, but did they ever reach our freezing soldiers who were in such bad need of them? I rather think not.'

The streets of her beloved hometown were changing. Shops closed down and didn't reopen. Windows were black and sightless behind blackout blinds. Young and middle-aged men vanished. Their parents looked distraught. Marie Dabs saw women with mask-like faces, their make-up harsh against their pale skin. Her nephew Siegfried was missing in Russia; so was Wilhelm, her daughter's heart-throb. Her youngest apprentice, Kurt, had to leave the Hitler Youth because of his Jewish roots. Then the labour exchange sent a letter, calling him away to do 'labour service'. Marie Dabs, who was on good terms with the local group leader of the party, asked for Kurt to be allowed to stay on in her strategically important business, as he was her last remaining male employee. 'By then, even we small-town people had worked out where the "labour service" would end up.'

Her children, Nanni and Otto, spent the summer doing harvest work, before being called to do 'service in the east'. Marie Dabs' salesgirl and the last of her seamstresses were also called east. 'They all had to go off and shovel ditches to halt the Russians' advance,' she complained. 'Nothing could stop the Russian steam-roller.' The shop and flat in Luisenstrasse stood empty. For the first time in her life, Marie Dabs felt abandoned. 'It was horrible for me,' she said. 'I was suddenly all alone.' Marie Dabs fell sick and had to close her shop. She spent her birthday in an empty flat, lonely and despondent.

. . .

When the blitzkrieg against the Soviets came to a standstill in late 1941, disillusionment with the Nazi regime began to set in. But it wasn't a sudden loss of faith that gave people the strength and courage to resist; it was gradual, excruciatingly slow and passive.

In Augsburg, where Swiss notary René Juvet did his work in the factory and recorded his impressions of Germany, the mood had changed dramatically, but so had working life. The reality of fighting a war on two fronts came as an immense shock to the people of Augsburg. 'The war had carved deep furrows in the face of the German nation. Even our little factory didn't go untouched.'

More and more men were called to the front, and the empty factory was filled with forced labourers from abroad. The threat of receiving call-up papers loomed over the heads of the managers, who made no secret of envying Juvet the Swiss passport they'd so often teased him about. Waldmeyer was fierce and arrogant one moment, nervous and cagey the next. His optimism had dried up. Juvet noticed that he'd stopped wearing his party badge except at official events. Hofmann, the old-guard Nazi, was a broken man; something had changed in him since his son had fallen in the march on Moscow. None of them could mention the war to him.

The wounded who returned from battle told stories different from those in the press—tales of monstrous losses, savage carnage and opponents who fought with more conviction than the Germans. In April 1942, Weinmann, the senior accountant, returned from the Eastern front on leave. Juvet found him robbed of all hope.

Germany, he said, could only bleed to death hopelessly in this lunatic enterprise. The Russians' power was completely unbroken and he didn't see the point of this war.

In the face of joyless reality, the Nazis' propaganda made frequent and determined efforts to rekindle the Germans' hatred for the enemy and a belief in purpose and victory. War reporter Gerhard Starcke, who had been allocated to the army in the east, was convinced that there was no option other than National Socialist rule or a Bolshevik reign of terror. He never gave anyone cause to doubt his faith in the party line, but it didn't escape his notice that the German military used methods identical to those he reported on daily in the land of the Soviet beast. He would write of 'Bolshevik looting' as his countrymen looted and murdered right in front of him. He would condemn 'Bolshevik exploitation', knowing that the Germans were preparing to enslave populations in the east on an unprecedented scale. The Russian campaign brought home to him more than ever the lying, deceitful nature of German propaganda. Little of what he read and wrote tallied with what he saw.

Back at home, the news of the inexorable forward march of the Germans and their liberation of enslaved eastern peoples formed part of a set ritual. The 'travelling cinema' brought weekly newsreels to villages like Siefersheim, where Johann Radein lived. He and his friends from the junior branch of the Hitler Youth sat next to each other in the semi-darkness of an improvised projection room, thrilling at the triumphal fanfare with which each reel began. The speakers' voices were charged with tension. They bombarded the audience with figures that surpassed the limits of imagination—numbers of prisoners, numbers of dead, quantities of looted material. As Johann Radein watched the endless winding columns of Soviet POWs pour over the horizon on their way to German captivity, they seemed to him like alien beings.

His child's mind could make no sense of the excesses. 'I was often overwhelmed by a stifling fear, too immense to express or describe. I went around feeling a faint, numb inner tension at the monstrousness of what was happening.' But he wanted to be a soldier all the same—to risk his life for his country. Almost all the boys from Siefersheim dreamt of dying heroes' deaths at the front. It was only next door at the Espenschieds' that the swastika flag never waved. When Ernst Espenschied was called up soon after his elder brother Philipp, the Radeins heard the boys' father cursing loudly. Johann's mother sometimes sent him round to ask if he could do anything for the neighbours. Frau Espenschied always received him with undisguised grief, showing him mementos of her sons, as if she'd already lost them. The twelve-year-old boy stood there, mute and helpless, hoping she wouldn't notice the tears in his eyes.

> Fear, pain and grief catch up with Frau Espenschied at every turn, as she talks of her sons and waits daily for post from them. On one occasion she's so distraught that I turn away from her and set to work because I can't bear to see her grief.

Death and violence put down roots in family life. Grief and fear on the one hand, hatred and ruthlessness on the other, had German society in their grip—and as the war went on, and family after family was affected by it in some way, their hold only strengthened.

On the way to the funeral of her sister-in-law, who had died in childbirth, Renate Finkh felt the strangeness and unfamiliarity of the dark clothes she and her parents were wearing. But they were not, she realised, the only ones; the streets were filled with people dressed in black. She was suddenly aware of the grief all around her. So far, the boys in her family had remained unscathed. Her brother-in-law Werner had recently been wounded again, narrowly escaping the disaster of Stalingrad. Rainer, who was home on convalescent leave, refused to speak of the front. 'He turned up on the doorstep one day and I didn't recognise him,' Renate said. 'The slender, rather soft boy had hardened into an aloof stranger.' She noticed others around her who seemed similarly afflicted by grief. 'Grey, stony women's faces. Weeping mothers. Eyes full of uncertainty. But towards me they remained cool.'

Renate Finkh continued her work for the Hitler Youth, which was doing its best to rouse Germany's weary youths into action with sports and cultural activities. She went along with it all, though she was starting to feel drained, and was so pale and tired that she fell asleep at her school desk. 'The days ticked on like clockwork and I was driven along, with no way of stopping.'

In summer 1943, the obligatory 'service in the east' jolted Renate out of her apathy. She, too, was sent to Wartheland to help Germans who had been settled on the farms of displaced Poles. In Posen she was met by a pretty, bubbly representative of the League of German Girls, eager to whip up support for her mission. This girl talked of the Poles: there was no need to be shy or polite in the presence of these creatures; they mustn't be allowed to forget that the Germans were members of the master race. Listening to her, Renate remembered a conversation she'd heard at home, soon after the 1939 invasion of Poland, about settling the new territory. You could just throw the rich Poles out of their flats, someone had said. *Get out, pigs.* Easy as that. 'I remember shivering at the feeling of power that crept through me when I heard that. I was thirteen. It gave me the chills.' Four years had passed since then, and Renate was no longer a child, though not yet a woman, when she arrived in the remote village on the eastern border. By then most of the Polish inhabitants had been driven out.

Renate was sent to the only German family who had been living there all along. She was horrified at the dirt and mess, and at the superstitions of these people—Germans, like her, and representatives of their shared culture—but she gritted her teeth as she'd been taught and wiped and swept her way through the filth, looked after the sick peasant woman and taught her the basics of hygiene. On one occasion, a local Nazi leader called in to check on her work. Greedy-eyed, he began to grope Renate, holding her arms tight, while the peasant woman watched from her bed, laughing. With some effort, Renate wriggled free of his grasp. She swallowed her shock and her shame, and wrote not a word on the matter in her enthusiastic reports on her time in the east; she was ashamed of her fellow Germans.

Towards the end of Renate's stay in Wartheland, the peasant woman sent her out to the cow pasture to give the Polish herd boy a beating. If she didn't, he'd let the cows run away, the woman said. You had to beat Polacks or they disobeyed. Renate went hot and cold. 'A German girl can do anything,' said a voice in her head. 'A German girl must be able to do everything!' Slowly she walked onto the pasture, clutching the stick the woman had given her. Her legs were like jelly; fear pounded in her throat. The boy— her height, skinny and ragged—was far out in the fields. He only grinned and shrugged when she drew near and addressed him. She summoned all her courage and hit him on the leg with the stick—brushed him with it, really, rather than hitting him, but she'd done it. She saw his wild eyes flash with anger and hatred. He raised his hand. She stood there as if rooted to the spot. Then he dropped it again and walked off. 'His hate-filled eyes haunted me day and night,' Renate said. 'I only had to look at myself to learn that completely ordinary people can become tacit supporters and thugs. Why not murderers, too?' This was another episode that she left out of her report on her adventures in Wartheland. She didn't want anyone to know.

. . .

The service camp that Melita Maschmann was in charge of during her time in the east was in the middle of nowhere, forty kilometres from the railway. Apart from a handful of German officials, there were only Poles living in the village. A few days after Melita's arrival, she heard a siren and, coming out of the camp into the village, saw columns of smoke over the thatched roofs. 'That day, I met the evil in myself, without realising.'

People came pouring out of their houses, running into each other, all shouting at once. Some of them pulled their animals out of the sheds or dragged furniture onto the road. Melita pressed herself up against the wall of a house. A woman with tangled hair and torn clothes clung to her, but Melita pulled herself free and pushed the woman away as hard as she could. She ordered the villagers about, chivvying them as they put out the flames. With nothing to lose in the fire herself, she felt remote, superior.

> What was evil was the chilliness with which I moved about among those unfortunate people. I saw their fear and plight as if in a film: none of it touched me. I remember having particularly acute powers of observation. I wanted to know exactly how people act in such a desperate situation.

The villagers who lost their houses and livestock to the fire were her enemies. A few weeks later Melita Maschmann stood alongside a truncheon-wielding SS officer, helping him to expel Polish farmers from their farms as part of a resettlement drive. She felt their disgust, but they feared her too. She felt like a soldier at the front, fighting an enemy nation.

The Shadow of Others

Not only did the soldiers returning from the front paint a picture of war that in no way resembled a final drive for victory. Not only did they speak of unprecedentedly bloody battles, of hunger, cold and tedium. They also spoke of crimes committed against civilians in the name of the German people—crimes against men and women and children. Whenever Waldmeyer and the other party members were out of earshot, René Juvet and his colleagues heard about the things the soldiers had seen in the hinterland.

> For reasons that were unclear, whole villages were wiped out. There was talk of unimaginable numbers of victims. Many of the soldiers present at the executions were left with lasting psychological damage.

A former colleague of Juvet told him about a colonel who had dispatched each of his men in turn to shoot civilians dead. He'd wanted to toughen the men up.

• • •

No German needed rely on third-party reports to know about the mass deportation of the Jewish people. In the 1930s, the regime had run several successive propaganda campaigns, preparing people for their removal, and when hostilities broke out in the east, the 'race war' against Jews and Bolsheviks was elevated to a life-and-death struggle. In September 1941, it became compulsory for Jewish people to wear yellow stars, so they could be distinguished at a glance. The Jews' disappearance, too, was visible; they were removed in full public view.

Standing on a street corner where they'd arranged to meet, Renate Finkh and her friend Greta went quiet when they saw a long line of people pass. Cowering figures, their eyes fixed on the ground, the stars of David on their coats and jackets a bright, shining yellow. Men in uniform were herding them to the station. A friend of Greta's mother happened to pass by at the same time and stopped to whisper something in Greta's ear. When the two girls were alone again, Renate didn't have to pester her friend for long. 'Those people'—she jerked her head at the group of Jews, now only visible from behind—'they're going to Poland. They'll all be killed there.' Renate shuddered, but later said she didn't know what she was afraid of. Soon after this monstrous secret was revealed to Renate, the street corner was full of everyday bustle again, as if the line of people had never existed. The memory of an old Jewish schoolmate pushed its way into Renate's mind. But the image was blotted out by a shadow.

> From then on, I knew. For the first time, I thought to myself:
> A lot of what happens shouldn't be allowed to happen. But
> we young people were being called on to pit good against
> evil. I kept the evil I wanted to fight hidden in shadow.

Renate pushed a great deal of what she saw and heard into this shadow. It was like the silence that confronted her at every turn. The silence of her mother, who stifled her sympathy and told her they couldn't afford to show compassion until after the war. The silence over afternoon coffee with Frau Cornelius, whose goddaughter had been committed to a psychiatric clinic. The girl had been sent home from her service in occupied Poland after six months, a physical and psychological wreck. 'What did the Poles do to her?' Renate asked in horror. The two women look at her and said nothing. Eventually Renate managed to worm out of them that it had nothing to do with the Poles.

She thought of her own service in the east, of the peasant woman and the Polish boy in the cow pasture. Immediately the shadow descended. She knew not to ask any more questions if she didn't want to compromise her faith and loyalty. Soon afterwards, her brother-in-law Werner came home on leave from the Eastern front. He paced up and down in his room, holding his ears and shouting, to drown out the screams in his head. Renate was told only fragments of what he had seen. Her sister said curtly: 'We have to win this war or it will be awful.'

. . .

Violence was so ubiquitous as to have become normal. Johann Radein, still a member of the Hitler Youth, felt sucked in by it; the violent acts condoned and even glorified by the grown-ups seemed to him inevitable, intrinsic to human nature. But this didn't make them any less frightening. The cold tyranny of the law of the strongest left Johann feeling numb and scared and helpless.

On his way home from the neighbouring village of Wonsheim one evening, he and a schoolfriend saw a group of local SA men at a crossroads, haranguing some foreign labourers—Poles and

Russians who'd been doing heavy farm work in the area for years; Johann knew most of them by sight. Suddenly, as if at a signal, the Brownshirts began to punch and club and kick them until, one after the other, they fell to the ground. Then they kicked them some more, ramming their boots into the men's bellies and heads, with dull cracking sounds. Johann and his friend watched from a distance, struck dumb with horror. They crept away over the fields until all they could hear was men's voices and laughter.

It was a long time before Johann's pulse steadied. He and his friend trotted along next to each other in helpless silence, until suddenly one of them said into the quiet of the night: 'If the Führer only knew.'

'He can't know everything,' the other replied.

'Maybe he knows more than we think.'

They couldn't believe what they'd witnessed. The next day they heard that the Brownshirts had wanted to send a warning to forced labourers. The boys saw the injured and bandaged men around for some time to come. 'That traumatic incident left its mark on my friend and me,' Johann said.

Part of the reason that belief in final victory flickered up one last time towards the end of the war was people's presentiment of their own guilt. That presentiment made Germany's impending defeat a taboo subject. Instead, people told each other of their hope. Talk of providence and God's support took on more urgent overtones. 'But what will come after defeat?' Johann Radein wondered. It seemed beyond the imaginative and intellectual powers even of the adults around him.

. . .

It wasn't only the leading figures of the regime who burnt their bridges at the start of the war of extermination. *Victory or downfall—*

the slogan captured the national mood. René Juvet noticed that, having heard about the crimes in the east, his colleagues were afraid of retribution. Hardly anyone denied these things in private. 'We have to stay the course,' they said. 'There's no knowing what form the Russians' revenge will take if they win the war.' This argument persisted, Juvet noted, because there was a certain logic to it.

Juvet's factory colleagues were a good example of the paradox of German staying power: the worse the war was going—the crueller the executions and the more brutal the mass slaughter—the more frightened the German people became, and the more urgent their desire not to lose the war at any price. René Juvet often heard people say: 'If Germany loses, every German will be killed.'

Fuelled by subliminal feelings of guilt, shame and complicity, reinforced by a long-fomented hatred of the enemy, the Germans' fear of defeat fed a final, grand, collective delusion—that defeat could still be averted.

Frozen Soul

At some point in the course of 1943, René Juvet decided to return to Switzerland to escape disaster. Everyone in the factory in Augsburg envied him his emergency exit route. Waldmeyer had often made spiteful remarks about his lowly home country and its political conscience, but his congratulations were sincere. Juvet had lived twenty years among the Germans, half of them under Hitler. He concludes his memoirs by relating a late-night encounter on a branch-line train journey to Augsburg.

The train stopped at a station and an SS man entered Juvet's empty compartment. It was so dark that Juvet couldn't make out the man's face except as a shadowy blur, but he could see that he was drunk and keen to talk. The man, who was on leave, had to drink to endure his job and get to sleep at night. He was stationed at Mauthausen, a concentration camp near Linz, in northern Austria. The inmates—Jews and Eastern Europeans—were whipped to make them work harder. Anyone the guards wanted rid of they drove into the high-voltage wire fences around the camp. Some inmates went of their own accord. 'I have to go back to the camp tomorrow,' the SS man told Juvet, 'but maybe I'll end up running into those wires myself one of these days. I can't take it anymore. How's all this going to end?'

The guard was Catholic. He spoke of God, who surely wouldn't let such deeds go unpunished; of the gloves worn by those high-and-mighty gentlemen so they wouldn't dirty their own fingers; of the murderer they'd made of him. The drink had plunged him into self-pity; he felt used and betrayed, a victim of the Führer. The only way out he could think of was to commit suicide—to anticipate the end, now that victory was no longer attainable. Juvet said nothing. 'No aspect of the German psyche was more clearly brought out by the war than the tendency towards contradictions and extremes.'

. . .

The hype of victory had died down, drowned out by the news from Stalingrad, Africa, Italy and the western coast of France. The Germans' belief in their military omnipotence vanished, along with their trust in their leaders, who had, they felt, misled them with their propaganda. With no new triumphs to announce, the Führer made fewer speeches, staying out of the public eye. The sun that had warmed the German people became a distant star, and their love for their leader cooled to respect.

Then, on 20 July 1944, a bomb was detonated at Hitler's field headquarters in East Prussia. Though Hitler escaped virtu-ally unscathed, many of those present were injured and several were killed. The attempted assassination and the coup d'état that was to follow had been planned by the German resistance, and among the conspirators were many powerful military and polit-ical figures. The Gestapo would eventually arrest thousands of people in connection with the conspiracy, and execute around two hundred of them.

News of this failed attempt on Hitler's life reignited the German people's love for him, and the regime made the most of it, fanning the flames of their fury. The security service's secret reports recorded an outpouring of shock and anger: all over the country, furious people gathered in spontaneous demonstrations of loyalty to their leader. Grave men and weeping women and children offered up prayers of thanks for Hitler's survival.

Listening to the news of the attempted assassination on their radio, the Radeins had felt a sense of doom. Twelve-year-old Johann was shocked, as were his parents—as was everyone in the village. No one showed any sign of relief. His friend's mother said out loud what they were all thinking: 'What's to become of us all?' The mute tension persisted when they heard that the Führer was still alive. Johann Radein felt as if the world were holding its breath.

> This speechlessness revealed an even greater depth and complexity to our connection with the Führer—a wholly personal spiritual and emotional bond—and a profound empathy for him as the target of the attack. I felt it myself.

In the dining area, next to the dresser—and opposite the crucifix— hung the Führer's portrait. Johann had often stood and looked at it, enjoying the strength of resolve and confidence it had given him. Now the aura of invulnerability seemed even stronger. The attempted assassination brought the Germans closer to their Führer again. Like Hitler himself, they saw his survival as confirmation that God was on their side. Johann clung to the idea that God would see Germany safely through.

The possibility of defeat was never mentioned, even in the final months. In the last winter days of 1945, Johann stood in his Hitler Youth uniform in a crowded, freezing hall. An injured war veteran had come to talk, an indomitable spirit in a broken body. He spoke of fighting and staying the course, his voice rising and falling imploringly. Johann Radein felt awe rise in him again, though he shuddered too.

. It was the last such event he was to attend. A few days later, as enemy forces advanced, his mother set him the task of getting Hitler out of the house.

> Reluctantly I take the Führer's portrait off the wall and wrap it in newspaper and a piece of roofing felt to protect it from damp. I bury the parcel in the garden. The picture leaves a pale oblong on the whitewashed kitchen wall.

Later, when Johann secretly tried to disinter the portrait, it had vanished from its grave.

. . .

When Renate Finkh heard on the morning of 21 July 1944 that the Führer was safe, she too believed it was divine intervention. She thought with chagrin of the doubts she'd had about the war, the sacrifice of human lives, the youth work she'd come to feel burdened by, and the temptation not to give a damn about any of it. 'I was ashamed of my despondency and weariness. I knew I was now needed more than ever.'

Renate built a high wall inside herself to keep her thoughts at bay—to keep out the line of people with their stars of David, the Polish herd boy, the stinking turd in Fräulein Liebel's shed; the ghosts she felt so defenceless against. She took refuge in the protective shadow of this wall. 'In the chill of this shadow, my soul was frozen.'

It was in this state that she went through the events of the next months—her sudden release from school so she could go to

Bavaria to do labour service, the bombing of her hometown, the rooting around in the pile of rubble where her father's goldsmith's shop had been, the Christmas party at the labour service camp—and the arrival of Allied troops on German soil. Renate saw all this with acute clarity, and yet she felt somehow detached from herself. 'I could see that the end had come and that it would be a terrible, unthinkable end. But I wanted to stand by all I had said.'

• • •

Renate was dismissed from labour service and returned home to Ulm, thinking she'd report back to the Hitler Youth office there. Her father, who had never lost faith in the Führer and found hope even in the darkest situations, was in shock. Führer and Reich no longer existed for him. But Renate carried on regardless. She knew nothing else. 'We'd got into a way of thinking that simply didn't allow for collapse,' she said. After all those years extolling duty and loyalty, she refused to believe that she might have been spouting empty words. In the almost deserted Hitler Youth office, she met the regional leader, who sent her home again. There was nothing left to do. 'Everything I'd built my life on, my entire youth—it was all falling apart,' Renate said.

When she returned to her childhood home, her father wasn't welcoming. Something told Renate that he wasn't sure whether to let her in. He, too, had lived for an illusion. His anger and shame at this made him brutal. He couldn't share his despair with Renate. When the French arrived at the city limits, the two of them took flight on their bicycles. Renate's father pedalled away like mad, without turning to look back at his daughter. The distance between them grew and grew.

• • •

The mythology surrounding Hitler had been revived after the assassination attempt in 1944, but it had lost the glow of hope and happiness associated with new beginnings. The Germans' demigod became a grim god of hatred and revenge, a guard against Bolsheviks and 'Anglo-Americans', Jews and traitors. Many young people remembered the euphoria they had felt in the early years of the war; Hitler had lifted them above drab, everyday life and instilled values in them that had given their lives meaning. Now they looked to him to uphold those values; abandoning them was unthinkable. Any thought of what might come afterwards was terrifying. Adolf Hitler hadn't allowed himself to contemplate armistice since the war had begun. After him there could be nothing. No Reich, no movement, no national community. He thought it only logical that he should take his people with him to his death.

Gerhard Starcke had seen the horrors of the eastern campaign and given a sketchy outline of them in his memoirs, but he'd kept them at arm's length, not stopping to think too deeply about them, not questioning his own part in things. Starcke didn't blame the Führer or the system; he blamed the traitors and sceptics. He had the regime to thank for his terraced house, and his position as company commander—and yet, despite all this, a small part of him remained vigilant, ready to sound the alarm.

In spring 1945, some days into the Battle of Berlin, Starcke found himself in a barracks lecture theatre with other propaganda officers, listening to propaganda minister Joseph Goebbels prepare them for the final battle. Starcke had come across Goebbels several times over the course of the years, and always been bowled over by his rhetorical skill. 'Even at this stage of the war, he remained an unrivalled rhetorician. A frightening fascination filled the room.' Goebbels spoke once again of the necessity, the compulsion to emerge victorious, and of the fate of the German people, who could only win or go under. For that reason, he concluded, every one of them must stay at his post.

Starcke was all too familiar with the circular nature of this logic, but when the speech was over and he was about to leave, he was approached by Goebbels himself. Goebbels had recognised Starcke, and they fell to talking. If Starcke hadn't heard the speech with his own ears, he wouldn't have believed this was the same person. One on one, Goebbels was quite prepared to admit the possibility that the war was lost; he and his family would take the necessary steps and wouldn't live to see the collapse of the Reich. Starcke was thunderstruck. Here was the Führer's right-hand man and closest confidant, telling him that his own death, and that of his family, was as good as settled.

> Those who had led the fight for Germany's place in the sun had, in the end, only the darkness of death in their eyes, and dragged those who trusted them into the darkness with them.

Starcke knew now that there would be no final victory and resolved to think only of himself. To survive, he would have to forget everything else—Führer, fatherland, loyalty, betrayal, disappointment. Fate, in the form of Joseph Goebbels, had given him a glimpse of the truth which, like so much of reality, he had chosen to ignore. Gerhard Starcke managed to smuggle his family out of the city before the Soviets started their major offensive. On 3 May 1945, he surrendered to the Americans in Ratzeburg.

. . .

'I was quite certain I wouldn't survive the Third Reich. If it was doomed to go under, I would go with it.' For twelve years, Melita Maschmann had been devoted to the Hitler Youth. Since being drafted to the Reich's youth leadership in Berlin in 1943, she had been swallowed up by the bureaucratic apparatus. Her office had been repeatedly bombed out and relocated, and she had gone from one temporary office to the next, working with a kind of frantic compulsion on one project after another, only to see them thwarted by the war, meddled with by management, or dropped altogether. But, determined not to admit that anything was wrong, she and the others in her office continued to throw themselves into their work. Melita saw her offices as a termite mound pervaded by an unacknowledged sense of imminent collapse.

> A swarming frenzy of activity filled every cell of the termite mound. We came up with plans and more plans, to keep ourselves from stopping and thinking, even for a moment— for then we'd have had to admit that all this industriousness was starting to look like the throes of a danse macabre.

Melita Maschmann kept up the frenzy—anything not to hear that voice inside her telling her there was no future. In September 1944, her parents were killed in the cellar of their house during an air raid. Melita, who was staying with them at the time, was the only one to escape alive. Hope died in her that morning, to be replaced by a grim fatalism. When she'd left home twelve years before to make Germany—and the world—a better, happier place, she'd been little more than a child. Now she was twenty-six, and as she stood contemplating the ruins of her parents' house, she could no longer justify the sacrifice. After that, she was silent on the subject of Hitler and Germany. She didn't rebel or ask questions, but from that day on, her support was no more than tacit.

During the Red Army's offensive on Berlin, Melita accompanied Hitler Youth music groups into the trenches to entertain the soldiers. Later, she couldn't recall a single conversation about impending defeat. She stared, as if hypnotised, into the abyss that was swallowing her up. She took to leaving the protection of the trench, ignoring the snipers and artillery fire—waiting for the bullet that would kill her.

> I was filled with the hazy notion that 'my world' would be knocked out of its orbit like a star in a cosmic catastrophe and that I—a tiny speck of dust—would be swept away with it into the darkness. At times I must have felt a vague fear that I would miss my destined 'downfall' and end up surviving.

On 19 April 1945 she attended a ceremony in the domed hall of the Reich Sports Field in Berlin. The boom of Soviet artillery was already approaching from the east as the initiation of ten-year-old girls and boys into the Hitler Youth was celebrated one last time. The next day, Melita Maschmann left Berlin for southern Germany in a truck full of casualties. She moved as if through a thick fog. 'I had no plans for the future.'

. . .

The Germans' incomprehensibly long resistance was not only a result of the regime's coercive terror and propaganda. They were also driven by a fear of the void and by the loss of a sense of purpose in life. They wanted to postpone the inevitable.

The future they had been promised was evaporating before their eyes. The Führer had left them, and the Reich was collapsing, leaving behind it a gaping void. After twelve years imbibing Nazi ideology, those who had believed in it, identifying as part of the national community and subscribing to its moral and social norms, faced not just a collective loss of meaning but the threat of personal disintegration. The emptiness they felt was palpable. Many genuinely believed that the victorious Allied forces would wipe out the German nation, and the best they could hope for was a life of oppression. Unwilling to face this reality, they chose suicide as a final act of resistance, of renunciation.

• • •

Lore Walb, the student diarist from Alzey, had shed her mask of optimism. Fear was now the dominant note in her journal. It had already been present in her hysterical outpouring of 29 November 1942: 'What fate is in store for us??? Must we bow down again? Can heaven allow us to be destroyed???' It had started to seem that the destruction the Germans had wrought on others would now be turned against them—against Lore herself. For her, the name Stalingrad evoked a monstrous, hulking figure with a brutish face and shorn head, bent on revenge. She hoped that German soldiers taken prisoner by the Russians would have the strength to commit suicide.

The question of the meaning of life was a recurring theme in the young woman's diary. She sensed that her longing for a normal life, for a family and children, was at odds with world events, which seemed to be growing closer and closer.

> But we *mustn't* lose the war—what horrors would face us then! It's no good thinking beyond the present day—it's not even possible. Who'd have thought that the future would one day be so veiled in grey. What's in store for us—if, that is, we're ever to see the end of the war?

In March 1945, Lore's fear of destruction made it impossible for her to imagine life after the collapse of the regime. Her fear of the Americans was scarcely less acute than her fear of the Russians. It was terrible to have to admit that all those victims had died in vain. For Lore Walb, 8 May 1945 was a black day. Germany's unconditional surrender brought her no relief—only grief and distress. Her usually neat handwriting is shaky, uncontrolled, a clear sign of her turmoil. 'My mind alone can comprehend this end—my heart will never manage. Victory celebrations—what a relief for the others. Peace—only for the others, not for us—never again.' She almost weeps the words.

. . .

Martin Sieg, the boy from Rastenburg in East Prussia, had once seen the words 'Better dead than slaves' written on a beam in a Hitler Youth training home, but his own desire to survive was strong. On 2 May 1945, he swam across the Elbe into American captivity. It was the first day for years that he had no duties to carry out, no orders to follow, no need to fear for his life. He wasn't prepared for the questions that besieged him, though, when he had time to stop and think.

> What possible reason could there be to carry on living? Wasn't it best just to put an end to it all? A lot of people were wondering that. Sometimes, after a long stretch of despair, I too found myself overcome by such dark thoughts.

No one tried to help him find a way out of the emptiness and confusion. He was left to deal with the question of meaning alone, turning it over and over in his mind, filling reams of paper with his thoughts. Martin Sieg had yet to hear the fate of his mother, who had hanged herself in January 1945, when the Red Army invaded Rastenburg. She had taken her life in the attic, together with two other women. Martin wouldn't find out until months later, in a letter from his grandfather:

> Your mum said goodbye, crying and kissing us and thanking us for all the good things. She had your father's picture with

her, and little Ilse's and yours too, kissed them all and tucked them away, the tears running down her face. She was afraid to lose all three of you, or that she might have lost you already.

Marie Dabs, the furrier's wife from Demmin, had never had any doubts about the meaning of her life. Her robust nature had got her through economic crises, illnesses and wartime hardships. She had adapted herself to life in the Third Reich without losing heart or mind; the Nazis' death cult was alien to her. But when, in the last days of April 1945, she was caught up in the wave of suicide that crashed over Demmin, the mood of doom almost got the better of her. If she'd had poison to hand, she would have killed herself and her children.

Part IV

THE PULL OF SILENCE

Curtaining off Reality

'Our philosophy is a matter of the heart. Feeling is more to us than reason.' This simple Hitler Youth principle helps to explain the power of the Nazi movement. When the Germans' world came to an end in 1945, they had spent twelve years being driven from one extreme emotion to the next: the hope of upturn, the joy of belonging, the pride of being special, the euphoria of success, the arrogance of power, the rage of destruction. They had been in a state of permanent intoxication with never a moment to sober up; there was no respite in those densely packed years, no time to reflect, and when everything ended in collapse, the overblown emotions collapsed too. What remained were the beginnings of other, less exhilarating feelings that had sprouted in the shadow of success: guilt at having taken part, shame at having looked away, hatred and self-hatred, fear of revenge and violence, despair at the emptiness that now faced them.

The suicide epidemic that had rolled in waves across the dwindling Reich—from east to west, Königsberg to Berlin, Demmin to

Siefersheim—was a radical response to this emotional collapse. Untold numbers of Germans turned on themselves the violence that had become part of their everyday life. The epidemic, which claimed tens of thousands of victims, was an extreme expression of the meaninglessness and pain people felt in the face of defeat, humiliation, loss, shame and personal suffering.

But millions of Germans survived the downfall and had to carry on with their lives. Although long-announced, the end had come abruptly for them. The awakening was stark and sober. Contemporaries who look back on that time speak, as if in a daze, of a broken spell, a vanished illusion, banished ghosts. The past years suddenly seemed unreal.

After swimming the Elbe, Martin Sieg ended up in a POW camp in Gorleben. He and the other prisoners sat around, staring blankly into space, wrapped up in their own thoughts. They mulled over the hopelessness of their situation, but couldn't speak about it; they had withdrawn inside themselves. 'The past, which had left only a void, seemed to me an illusion.' Martin tried to think his way back to an earlier time, back to the lovely world of his childhood. He held imaginary conversations in the lost paradise of his grand-parents' garden and went on imaginary walks with his parents in the forests of East Prussia. In this way he kept alive the will to carry on.

As Christmas 1945 approached, the first Christmas since the fall of the Reich, Martin Sieg felt uneasy. Memories overwhelmed him; he was afraid that the feelings at this supposedly festive time would prove too much for him. Not long before, news had reached him that his father had been sentenced to twenty-five years' forced labour in a Russian POW camp. Then there had been the letter from his grandfather, telling him of his mother's suicide in Rastenburg. 'That letter forced me to look back with a heavy gaze,' Sieg said. 'As soon as I'd read it, I knew I would never come to terms with the past.'

What had the last twelve years meant? He found no answer. 'Life had slammed shut and locked the door to yesterday.' He was eighteen. He decided to look ahead, to set himself some kind of task and slog his way forward, to accept these new times, to live on.

Later, when his father returned from the prison camp, Martin Sieg realised how hard it was to reconcile the old with the new. His father found himself in an alien world, unable to feel at home. The sunglasses he'd once worn into town stayed on permanently. He couldn't cope with the colours of this strange new place.

• • •

In July 1945, the Americans arrested Melita Maschmann in Bad Reichenhall. Until then she'd been on the run, from the Allies but also from herself. It was in a prison in Heidelberg that the full horror of her situation hit her: everything she had lived and fought for was in pieces. But she was still alive. She lay on the floor of her cell, weighing up her options. She could take her life. She could abandon herself to despair and madness. Or, she thought, she could summon all her strength and shut herself off to the onslaught of misery.

> That way I would survive the collapse of the world in which I'd been happy. To be sure, it would only be possible if I kept a tight control on my thoughts and emotions. There were boundaries they must never cross again. Beyond those boundaries lay self-destruction.

During her three years in Ludwigsburg Women's Camp 77, Melita never once crossed those boundaries. The routine of prison life in the company of other high-ranking functionaries and concentration camp guards allowed her to put off confronting what she'd been through. Her time in the camp with these other true believers in the Nazi cause only made her more self-righteous. Not once in those long days divided between idleness and interrogation, she said, did these women pause to question the foundations of their faith. They saw themselves as loyal patriots and stood by their convictions. When their guards showed them photographs of heaped corpses and dying prisoners in concentration camps, they pronounced them fakes. The only weakness they permitted themselves was self-pity. Melita Maschmann wasn't ready for reality. Only occasionally did a nagging inner voice press her to justify her beliefs. 'There was only one way to protect myself—to stop thinking altogether.'

. . .

In 1945, Allied soldiers occupied a Germany ravaged by years of air raids and battles drawn out past the point of absurdity. Most city centres had been bombed to rubble. But the behaviour of the Germans, as they picked their way through the ruins of their former greatness and glory, was surprising. Julius Posener hadn't been in Germany for twelve years. He came from an upper-class family with Jewish roots and had spent his youth in a smart residential area of Berlin before fleeing the country in 1933 and enlisting in the British army. In April 1945, he returned to his native country as a military engineer; later he would become a political intelligence officer and help to establish Germany's new political culture. Before crossing the border, he was handed a booklet about the Germans' character, warning him of all the hazards of a deluded nation prepared to die. But Posener found his fellow countrymen in an altogether different state; years afterwards he would write laconically about returning home to pyramids of rubble and how strangely contradictory he found the German people's response to it all. 'The destruction was to be expected, but the way people looked and behaved came as a shock. It didn't add up.'

The way the German people looked and behaved didn't add up

They didn't look defeated; they looked more like people opening the windows after a long, hard winter. Perplexed, some of Posener's British comrades asked him where the cannibals were. They'd been expecting brutal monsters, but all they could see were friendly old people and sweet young girls. Before coming to Germany, they had been in Italy with their unit and seen pale, ragged figures on the verge of starvation. 'What was that,' Posener asked, 'compared with the rows of nice girls dressed in white, going for an evening walk outside the ruins of their town, as flirtatious and unassailable as if the town were still intact and their fatherland weren't at the bottom of an abyss?'

Posener explained the Germans' outward wellbeing by pointing to the Nazis' wartime pillaging and plundering, which had enriched German towns and kept the people's morale high. But how was he to explain to his British comrades the Germans' callous reactions to the destruction of their own country and the monstrous crimes committed in their name? When the concentration camps were discovered, the Allies hung pictures of the atrocities outside town halls and showed films. Julius Posener recalled that all the Germans he spoke to guilelessly told him they'd known nothing about it. But they'd all had a friend or cousin at the front or in the hinterland who'd passed on this or that to them.

> A lot of Germans knew something. They'd hear something, from some cousin or other, and suddenly a curtain would be drawn back before them—but because they didn't really believe it, the curtain would fall shut again. Who, after all, would probe into a truth as awful as that?

During his time in Germany, Posener saw people try to wriggle out of their guilt, to justify what they had or hadn't done. The trials of the perpetrators and the accounts of the atrocities were used to blame the crimes on 'the Nazis'; it seemed a large majority of the population had not been involved in any way. Once again, a curtain was pulled across reality.

. . .

Hannah Arendt returned to her former homeland three years after Posener. She had grown up in Königsberg and emigrated in 1933. After sixteen years away from the country, she returned in August 1949, aged forty-two, to do some work for a Jewish organisation. She, too, was struck by the Germans' denial of reality. 'Nowhere is this nightmare of destruction and horror less felt and less talked about than in Germany itself,' she said. 'A lack of response is evident everywhere.'

In the three years since Posener had made his observations, things had moved on. While Posener had made tentative efforts to understand, there is something harsh and brusque about Arendt's forty-page report. The ghostly scenes she describes, as she hunts for clues amid the ruins of a country that was once hers, are brimming with disillusion.

> Germans mail each other picture postcards still showing the cathedrals and marketplaces, the public buildings and bridges that no longer exist. And the indifference with which they walk through the rubble has its exact counterpart in the absence of mourning for the dead, or in the apathy with which they react, or rather fail to react, to the fate of the refugees in their midst.

Everywhere she looked, she saw Germans running away from reality. When she spoke to them, they totted up their suffering and compared it with that of others. When she criticised them for this, they icily deflected her remarks. When she asked about the reasons for the catastrophe, they dodged the question with vague talk of the wickedness of mankind. Arendt caught them shuffling out of responsibility with a variety of tricks: self-pity, distraction, apathy. Their refusal to confront what had happened came at the cost of genuine feeling.

An Inability to Feel

Arendt was brought to the newly established Federal Republic of Germany by her work as director of Jewish Cultural Reconstruction, an organisation set up in 1947 to trace and distribute 'heirless' Jewish property within the US occupation zone. She spent more than six months there and her report shows that she put a great deal of energy into grappling with the psychological devastation of the people she encountered. She was astonished by the emotional vacuum left by Germany's defeat.

She often started conversations by telling people she was a German Jew and explaining what had brought her to Germany. Not once did this prompt questions about her fate or her family's fate. Nor did it evoke sympathy or pity. Instead people trotted out well-rehearsed stories about the Germans' suffering.

This general lack of emotion, at any rate this apparent heartlessness, sometimes covered over with cheap sentimentality, is only the most conspicuous outward symptom of a deep-rooted, stubborn, and at times vicious refusal to face and come to terms with what really happened.

Arendt observed the same reaction of chilly indifference towards the millions of refugees and uprooted people who were drifting across the country from the east. The younger generation struck her as emotionally paralysed, incapable of expressing themselves appropriately or putting their feelings into words. Instead they bridged the depths with platitudes and clichés. Arendt found it difficult to say whether this signified 'a half-conscious refusal to yield to grief or a genuine inability to feel'.

. . .

The Germans' refusal or inability to yield to grief had, in a way, begun on 1 May 1945. At about half past ten that evening, Hitler's death had been announced over the radio. The wording of the announcement transformed his unglamorous suicide into the death of a hero, fighting to the last against Bolshevism. Even so, the announcement of the century met with indifference; few of Hitler's many millions of supporters mustered more than a shrug. If he'd fallen victim to the assassination attempt of 20 July, he would have been revered as a martyr. But by the time he actually came to die, the masses had turned away. Surreptitiously, they took down their Führer portraits and buried them in their gardens. As if by arrangement, all the other icons, symbols and devotional objects vanished too, suddenly reduced to mere trinkets and trash. Hitler's myth had died in the weeks of the final battle, before the man himself. Nobody grieved.

By the time Lore Walb heard the news of the Führer's death on 2 May, French troops had occupied her homeland. The few lines she devotes to Hitler are divided between pity and reproach. He gets satisfactory marks for domestic policy, but a clear 'poor' for foreign affairs. 'He's at peace now, which is surely the best for him. But what about us? We're adrift and abandoned and it will take us more than a lifetime to rebuild what the war has destroyed.'

This entry and the last in the diary are a week apart. During that week, Germany's military defeat was accomplished and the surrender signed. And within the same space of time, Lore Walb made a complete break with the leader she had believed in. He had featured in the first entry she ever made in the blank book she received for her fifteenth birthday, on 23 May 1933. Later that year, at the Saar rally, she had been moved to tears by the sight of him and blessed with the most beautiful and poignant moment of her life. She had heard his voice on the radio and wished he'd go on speaking for hours. She had paid tribute to his achievements in carefully composed school essays. She had admired his will and his peacetime strength. He was her comfort and support when the war frightened her. His genius as a statesman gave her faith in his genius as a commander.

Lore Walb had loved Hitler like her own father and asked God to protect him. For twelve years he had been the focus of her diary. On 8 May 1945, as the spring sun shone and the birds sang, Lore wrote her last entry:

> Hitler is dead now. But for the rest of our lives, we and those who come after us must bear the burden he has inflicted on us. This, then, is what has come of his rule. God seems not to love us anymore.

Lore felt as if the perpetrator had slipped from the dock, leaving the judge to pass sentence on his minor accomplices.

...

Gerhard Starcke devoted no more than a single dry sentence to the death of Hitler—the man who had been his inspiration, his protector, his leader. At the 1930 rally Starcke attended as a penniless student, Hitler had appeared before him like the Old Testament God. Hitler had given him a purpose in life and set his nerves quivering. Starcke had followed him first along the way of peace and then along the warpath. He had the Führer to thank for all that he'd achieved in life.

But as soon as he realised that Hitler wanted Germany to fall with him, Starcke's only thoughts were of survival. When he surrendered to the Americans on 3 May, he drew a line under his life as a Nazi, like someone quitting a job. It cost him no inner anguish. During his two years in the former concentration camp of Neuengamme, where he was imprisoned by the British for being a Nazi propagandist, Starcke wrote his life story. In the conclusion he refers to Adolf Hitler as a black magician who put a spell on his life.

> Until we awoke from the spell cast on us by a madman on the cusp between putative genius and lunacy—a madman whose propaganda concealed that lunacy from his people— we, too, were struck with blindness.

As a Nazi propagandist, Starcke had spent twelve years helping to sustain the madman's magic.

...

Ten days after Hitler's suicide, Melita Maschmann heard the news of his death on the radio. She never forgot the moment. She was in a remote Alpine valley when she heard and, looking out of the window at the evening light on the mountains, she half expected the craggy rocks to rear up and fall crashing into the valley. Hitler, the man of the people, had epitomised her ideal of national community and given her life meaning. She had devoted her life to the organisation that bore his name. Recalling the shock of 20 July 1944, when her knees had given way and she'd had to fight back tears, she waited to see how she would react this time. 'Hitler was dead! But nothing happened. The Alpine sunset faded. An almost black purple settled over the peaks. Then, calmly and coldly, it began to rain.'

A feeling of emptiness gripped her. She recalled how he'd looked in the previous week's newsreel: an aging man with a stooped walk, casting distraught glances about him. She felt no tears rising. She had been dreading this moment, but when it came, it left her cold.

In almost all German memoirs that describe this period, his death is a gaping void. Those writers who do mention it sound as if they are fulfilling a duty. They refer to him in passing, devoting a few brief words to him as if he were some overbearing relative— one-time family patriarch and tyrannical centre of the clan, now long gone and little lamented. Some wiped away a fleeting tear. But they were done with high-flown emotion. No laments, no eulogies. No one asked about the funeral.

. . .

'What had happened to their love? For the Germans loved Hitler.' In 1938, after five years in Berlin, Stéphane Roussel had been forced to shut her correspondent's office, and made up her mind then to have nothing more to do with the Germans. She'd had enough. They all—every one of them, from her concierge to the ladies in her *kaffeeklatsch*—idolised Hitler. Their love for him aroused fear and disgust in her—and not just because of her Jewish roots. Despite the show and hyperbole, their devotion was real; what

Roussel had witnessed among the spectators at the Sportpalast was neither acted nor forced. But she had been afraid of him. He had driven her out of Germany.

But soon after the establishment of the Federal Republic, she returned to run *France Soir*'s office in the new capital, Bonn. No one showed less interest in her earlier experiences in Germany than the Germans themselves. Conversations on the subject soon dried up. 'When I tell people that I lived under Hitler until the eve of the war, it rarely elicits a reaction,' she said. Stéphane Roussel searched in vain for the old devotion. Gone were the women who had put up little altars in front of Hitler's portrait, adorned with flowers and candles. Gone were the men who had trusted and admired him. Gone were the boys who had worshipped him, smitten with him because he pronounced them men. 'It was best to forget, to draw a line under the past, avoid explanations, rewrite one's part in things,' Roussel said. 'Disappointed love can produce talented authors.'

People's love for Hitler had vanished overnight. The cult of the Führer was gone, along with the displays of public devotion and euphoria, the confessions of faith in market squares and forest clearings. Sensationalism and sloganeering had become suspect, as had collective frenzy. The dream that everything was possible had died a death, leaving people with nothing. Holy Germany, a fatherland mythicised out of all proportion, had forfeited its power to create meaning. The sacrifice demanded of its worshippers had been for nothing.

Collective passion gave way to the sober desire for a quiet, circumscribed life, without risks, without intense surges of feeling or near-uncontrollable emotion. To some outsiders, the atmosphere in postwar Germany seemed severe and sterile, and its people stony, joyless and cold.

Victims

Those happy years of peace between 1933 and 1939, when success had followed success, were now shrouded in a distant, unreal mist. Stéphane Roussel, who had documented those years for her French readers, returned to Berlin to find them lost in a thick cloud of forgetting, no more than an inconsequential prelude to what came after.

> For most Germans, the drama began in 1944 or '45, when the country was destroyed, the cities bombed, military bases established. They'll talk freely about the great 'trek'—the exodus of people from the east, fleeing the advance of the Red Army. In fact, they'll talk about anything that makes victims of them.

Roussel had come up against a phenomenon that increasingly troubled neutral observers and deeply embittered the regime's victims and former opponents. Not long after the end of the war, most Germans considered themselves victims of the Nazis.

. . .

During her journey through postwar Germany, Hannah Arendt had the opportunity to study this phenomenon. In her conversations with Germans, she often found they had a blind spot when it came to the causes and origins of the totalitarian experiment, and their own participation and involvement in it. Her questions on these subjects were met with angry bewilderment.

> This is usually followed by...a deluge of stories about how Germans have suffered (true enough, of course, but beside the point); and if the object of this little experiment happens to be educated and intelligent, he will proceed to draw up a balance between German suffering and the suffering of others, the implication being that one side cancels the other...

The final months of the war had been apocalyptic: carpet bombing and low-flying aircraft, enemy armies advancing on all sides, futile defensive battles, the horrors of the Soviet army in the east and, on top of everything else, the ruthless terror of Germany's own regime. The feeling of existential threat—not knowing whether the next day, or even the next hour, would be survived—was burnt deep into people's minds. No one who had lived through the intense events of those last weeks would ever forget them, while what had come before—the rejoicing, the happiness, the successes—soon faded from memory. It was the tragic moment of collapse that shaped the way the Germans perceived themselves. They had been afraid of the war; they hadn't wanted it. The worse their experiences, the more ill-used they felt, and from there it was only a short step to believing that they themselves had been targeted by the regime. The way the Germans saw it, the orgy of violence at the end of the war had left them the ultimate nation of victims.

'But what about us? We are adrift and abandoned.' Decades later, Lore Walb couldn't believe that her twenty-five-year-old self had complained about being let down by the Führer, like a small, dependent child. Even before the war was over, she had started to think as millions of Germans soon would. Her generation saw themselves as deceived, cheated of their youth, betrayed in their ideals and values, exploited and used—after putting all their energy into the movement's ideas. 'What a course things have taken. Now the people have to suffer for it. If Dad had lived to see this!'

Lore Walb's father, who had died in 1936, was spared having to witness the bankruptcy of the idea he had supported as a party member. Unlike millions of other party officials who had held jobs of various descriptions, he never had to justify his part in things. Even before the guns had fallen silent, the Germans had begun to distance themselves from the regime. People flocked to defect— from Hitler Youth boys to those in the highest echelons of power. At the Nuremberg war crimes trials, generals, *Gauleiter*, ministers and commanders-in-chief pleaded forgetfulness and ignorance or claimed to have been oppressed and manipulated. Even the Nazi elite insisted they'd merely been following orders. Every finger was pointed at the man who had misled his people with lies and betrayals, coercion and terror—who was to blame for their lost homeland, the destruction of their family homes, their fallen brothers and sons, the rape of their mothers, sisters and daughters.

The idea that they were victims freed the Germans from the need to examine their own consciences. This willingness to renounce the Nazi cause made the job of the occupying forces easier in some ways; the Allies were relieved not to face resistance from diehard loyalists or underground guerrilla units. But hardly anyone would admit to having been involved in the Nazis' crimes, and the Allies' ineffective attempts to distinguish the guilty from the innocent only reinforced the Germans' collective refusal to face up to the past. The practice of denazification ended up creating even more 'victims'.

The bureaucratic notion of using questionnaires to distinguish Nazis from non-Nazis failed. Membership of a Nazi organisation such as the civil servants' league, the teachers' league or the motor vehicle corps was no indication of the extent of a person's involvement in the Nazi system, and neither was their rank. Whether innocent or guilty, Germans did not consider such information sufficient evidence to support a lay judge's verdict for or against them. Many regarded denazification as an absurd theatre of injustice—and as a threat to their families and futures, leading as it often did to imprisonment, or exclusion from their previous professions.

When Melita Maschmann appeared before the court of arbitration during her internment in the women's camp at Ludwigsburg, she vehemently disputed the judges' right to assess her case. She saw the German judges as henchmen of the occupying powers, accusing her not of any crime, but of fighting for a political ideal. She scorned the idea that it was possible to determine guilt or innocence by bureaucratic means. 'I despised those courts of arbitration so much that I wouldn't have hesitated to fight them with every lie and trick in the book, if I'd thought it necessary,' she said.

Charged with being a 'major offender', Maschmann did everything in her power to be ranked a follower instead. She had no qualms about bringing her rhetorical skills to bear to get the judges on her side, and the success of this strategy left her acutely aware of Germany's political helplessness. The court found Melita Maschmann guilty of poisoning the minds of the young people of Germany with her work for the Hitler Youth, but she got off with a light sentence.

. . .

Gerhard Starcke's decision to submit to denazification was practical rather than moral: he was keen to work as a journalist in postwar Germany and thought serving time in prison a wiser move for his future career than going underground like some of his comrades. He acted entirely strategically. Having turned away from the church in the early 1930s, he began to get involved again while in the camp at Neuengamme. 'I saw my return to the Protestant Church as another way to speed my release.'

Because Starcke had been a party member and worked in propaganda, his denazification was long and drawn-out. He was just going through the motions; it would never have occurred to him to question seriously what he had done. All the same, he must have been surprised when the court of arbitration found that he had been a follower who had lent no substantial support to the Nazis. 'The English can't have probed very deeply,' he would later comment. Now he began a second life, in provincial West Germany, unshadowed by the past. He continued to work as a journalist. Nobody asked him about his early writings. His autobiography of more than four hundred pages ends on a note of near incredulity: 'However bleak and sad things may have looked when I was released from Neuengamme in 1947, they soon took a rapid and quite spectacular turn for the better.'

The Third Reich may have splintered into millions of pieces as it went down, but it was not without a legacy. A new community of suffering was born out of the shared experiences of hunger and cold; a community of victims emerged from the sense of betrayal, injustice and helplessness; a community of interests sprang up as reconstruction began. Wherever she went in Germany, Hannah Arendt saw people working away, even on Saturdays and Sundays.

It was as if they were under a kind of compulsion to keep themselves busy, toiling away from morning to night. There was something unnerving about the speed at which the Germans had got back into their hardworking routines.

> Watching the Germans busily stumble through the ruins of a thousand years of their own history, shrugging their shoulders at the destroyed landmarks or resentful when reminded of the deeds of horror that haunt the whole surrounding world, one comes to realize that busyness has become their chief defense against reality.

The great appeal of the 'zero hour' metaphor that was adopted for 1945 was its twofold promise: on the one hand, the severing of all ties with an overwhelming past, and on the other, a fresh start for a society that felt its downfall absolved it of responsibility for its actions. The idea of a 'zero hour' encouraged the revival of the old psychological metaphor of the inner rift. As in the Nazi years, the people of Germany acted as though a part of reality didn't exist. This time they were in denial about their own history.

Ghosts of the Forgotten

In the sober atmosphere of postwar Germany, the frantic emotions of the Third Reich felt like a stale and aberrant memory, discredited by the shock of reality. As Hannah Arendt travelled the country, she found no genuine expression of feeling, not even grief at the loss of friends and family. It was as if all emotion had been replaced by assiduous detachment, or trite sentimentality. Arendt had been studying the young Federal Republic for eight months when she left in March 1950. It had been a painful reunion. She wanted to cry out, to tell the Germans: 'But this is not real—real are the ruins, real are the past horrors, real are the dead whom you have forgotten.' But they were living ghosts, she said, 'ghosts whom speech and argument, the glance of human eyes and the mourning of human hearts no longer touch.'

Renate Finkh was nineteen when the war ended. Hitler's suicide had left her almost unmoved, but she was still loyal to the Nazi cause; she was determined to stay the same old Renate. The world around her and the people in it had changed, though—so much so that she 'hardly recognised anyone'.

She could no longer stand the company of her family and left to find herself a job on a farm. After keeping his hatred of Hitler a secret for twelve years, the farmer could finally express his pent-up anger, raging about German megalomania and the torture and extermination of thousands, even millions, in the concentration camps. Renate refused to believe him, just as she had refused to believe the photographs of heaped corpses in the newspapers and on billboards. All lies, she said to herself. The good she had done was being lied away. All summer long, she had to listen to the farmer's fierce triumph as he poured scorn upon her former idols. 'I had to keep silent. My family were frightened. They begged and begged me not to upset anyone.'

But if Renate Finkh kept silent, she also swore to write everything down, so that her children would know of the fire that had burned within her, of the faith that had been more for them than for herself. There were, of course, truths that even faith could not deny. Her brother-in-law Werner had been killed late in the war, leaving her sister alone with their three children. Her brother's wife was dead, her brother in a prison camp, and their son practically an orphan. Her father's goldsmith's shop had burnt down. Disappointment and exhaustion had carved deep furrows in all their faces. No one wanted to hear about the fire of faith anymore.

Renate moved back to her hometown with her father, leaving her mother in the countryside with her sister and the children. Her father had grown lonely, taciturn and grumpier than ever. In the house he had built all those years before, in happier times, he and Renate lived their separate lives, no longer able to talk to each other. Renate couldn't understand why he suddenly renounced his former beliefs. Even when her brother came home from the POW camp, there wasn't a lot to say. Andreas packed his things and went on his way to see his mother and son. The father's joy at seeing his son again was marred by silence.

Eventually, Renate Finkh could no longer evade reports of the Nazis' crimes. In her father's silence, in her own silence, she tried to find peace. She came to accept that her search for a sense of safety and belonging had trapped her in a big lie. All this time she had been pursuing a chimera, trying to escape reality, but she had gained nothing, and instead lost even herself.

> Guilt and shame sealed my mouth shut. They grew with time and awareness. I knew I had aligned myself with evil. The evil hadn't been mitigated by my loyalty; it had made my loyalty evil too.

It took her fifty years to break her silence. By then Renate Finkh knew that although her feelings had left her isolated and lonely, she had never been alone. 'Many had felt the same way. Many were dead. I had been spared and left to live. But how do you live after a youth like that?'

. . .

Melita Maschmann spent more than ten years looking for an answer to this question. That was how long it took her to detach herself from the Nazi movement. When she was released in 1948, she tried to settle down in Darmstadt. She travelled, attended university on and off, wrote the occasional newspaper article. The postwar world seemed to her hostile, West Germany's incipient democracy pathetic and the way she was treated unjust. But once outside the prison walls, the self-righteousness she had cultivated in captivity, in the company of like-minded women, crumbled. She began to have her doubts about the huge numbers of pointless sacrifices the German people had made. An army of forgotten dead and ghosts haunted her dreams. Right up to the last days of the war, she had kept fear at bay. Now it was eating her up.

> Sometimes I'd be out on the street and wouldn't dare walk any further, convinced that if I took one step more, the houses to the right and left of me would fall backwards into space. It's true that I only rarely had such specific fears, but for years I felt a vague and indeterminate dread that only very gradually eased off.

A paralysing depression kept her in bed for days. She made no attempt to stay in touch with her old Hitler Youth friends, but cut all ties. 'Emotionally and psychologically, I had reached rock bottom,' she said. For as long as she could, Melita Maschmann pushed away the questions about National Socialism that were trying to worm their painful way into her mind: What had it been? What it had done to her? These questions eventually led to a reckoning with herself.

In 1963, Maschmann published a book, *Fazit* (released in English under the title *Account Rendered*), about her time in the Hitler Youth. She was among the first to break the silence, to tell the inside story of her time with the Nazis. The book takes the form of a fictional letter to her real-life schoolfriend Marianne Schweitzer, the Jewish girl with whom she had severed all ties for the sake of her career in the party. Maschmann regarded the story of this betrayal as the tragedy of her youth. The result is a disturbing self-portrait of a young woman who wanted to love but allowed herself to be swept away by hate. Maschmann knew that many would see the publication of this book as an intolerable affront, but for her it was a matter of life and death. She felt she had paid with her suffering.

On 3 July, not long after the book's publication, Melita Maschmann sent a letter to Hannah Arendt in the United States, a kind of coda to her story. She had read Arendt's writings on Germany and wanted to help her understand the Germans who had continued to be passionate Nazis even after the collapse of the regime. 'The line between good and evil ran right through our midst, without our noticing,' she said.

Marianne Schweitzer and Melita Maschmann would soon meet for the first time in more than twenty-five years. Maschmann's confessions, the reason for their reunion, stood between them, a dark, impenetrable wall. After reading the book, Marianne knew too much to want to talk to Melita about it. Again, silence was the only answer. The two friends never saw each other again after that.

. . .

Silence also surrounded the German suicide epidemic of 1945, suppressed, like other distressing details of those times, by an unspoken pact governing what could and could not be said in the decades following the war. The black wave of self-destruction that had rolled over Germany receded from memory. The suicide taboo, abandoned in the last days of the war, was reinstated. Apart from the deaths of Adolf Hitler and his entourage, heavily laden with symbolism, none of the tens of thousands of suicides received close attention.

At no point, though, was the phenomenon entirely forgotten. In the vast collection of source material published in West Germany shortly after the war, *Documents on the Expulsion of Germans from Eastern Central Europe*, there were countless references to suicide in the former eastern territories. The first report by Demmin's new district councillor in November 1945 also mentioned suicide, putting the number of residents who killed themselves at seven hundred. Wilhelm Damann, the teacher, wrote a report for the town's local heritage museum in 1955, in which he described the wave of deaths that accompanied Soviet conquest. In the cemeteries of Demmin and the surrounding area, memorials were erected on mass graves to commemorate the victims of the suicide wave. In communist East Germany, it is true, any mention of the violence of Soviet soldiers was unwelcome, and studies that touched on the matter were kept under lock and key—but as long as no link was made to that particular topic, discussion of suicide itself was not taboo. In 1965, a local newspaper from Neustrelitz estimated that there had been around six hundred suicides in the town at the end of the war. And in the flood of Third Reich memoirs that followed capitulation—Leopold Reitz's diaries, for instance, which came out in 1959, or Marie Dabs' memoirs, published in 1984—further details came to light.

But no contemporary commentator attributed much significance to the phenomenon. Few devote more than a sentence or two to the subject—cursory marginal notes—choosing to focus instead on the drama of Germany's downfall. As they write of the people who hanged and shot and drowned and poisoned themselves, the authors of these accounts have a detached, factual tone. Suicide had been such a common response to the coming apocalypse that few contemporary observers stopped to ponder causes, reasons or inner motives. The suicides had no one to tell their individual stories.

And so they remained out of sight and out of mind. This didn't change even in the 1960s and 1970s, when a spate of films, television series, documentaries, radio features, articles and books sought to re-examine the history of the Third Reich. This reappraisal gained further momentum with the fall of the Berlin Wall and the opening up of East Germany and its archives. One by one, the painful taboos were overcome: the extermination of the Jews, the Wehrmacht's crimes, the lootings and deportations, the expulsions from the eastern territories, the mass rapes. The postwar code of silence gave way to an obsessive interest in the Nazis' crimes as the country came to terms with its history. Facing up to atrocities became part of German identity.

But this drive to acknowledge the past and commemorate victims of the war overlooked the suicide epidemic. There were, it is true, witnesses and local historians who spoke up in Mecklenburg and Western Pomerania after German reunification in 1990 and shed light on the events in Demmin, Neustrelitz, Neubrandenburg, Teterow and elsewhere. But their reports found no resonance beyond the local area. German society as a whole ignored the fact that one of the greatest mass suicides in history had taken place in a provincial town two hours north of Berlin. The dead of Demmin, Berlin, Leipzig and Siefersheim have no place in the German tableau of history, with its focus on culprits, victims and the occasional hero or heroine. They don't fit the accepted narratives, so their suicides have remained private tragedies. But every one of their deaths is proof of the depth of the abyss that had opened up before the Germans during the Nazis' rule. Take this last story, the story of Paul Kittel.

. . .

On 26 January 1959, a fifty-five-year-old clerk came before the court in Hanover. Paul Kittel was charged with committing multiple manslaughter fourteen years before in the small town of Malchin in Mecklenburg. He was standing trial in West Germany, where he had settled after ten years in a Soviet camp.

His former hometown of Malchin is about thirty kilometres south of Demmin and, like Demmin, lies on the gently flowing

Peene. Malchin and Demmin: two towns on the same river, with the same story. Malchin, too, was invaded by the Red Army on 30 April. Large parts of the town centre burnt down, and people flocked to the Peene to drown themselves. Later it was said that five hundred people had killed themselves within three days. On 1 May, Paul Kittel took the pistol of a neighbour who was already dead and shot first his wife and then his two sons, Ullrich and Joachim, aged thirteen and fourteen. According to statements given in court, all three had asked him to shoot them. He ended by turning the gun on himself, but nothing happened. There had been only three bullets in the pistol. Paul Kittel couldn't kill himself. He couldn't complete his murder-suicide.

The jury declared Paul Kittel of unsound mind at the time of the offence, though of course they had no way of knowing what had been going on in his mind, or in the minds of his wife and sons, in the preceding days and months and years. The *Hannoversche Zeitung* reported the case under the headline 'Alive Thanks to Missing Bullet'. The journalist saw the drama of a family's destruction as an almost unparalleled tragedy. Paul Kittel was acquitted of manslaughter. But the burden of memory he had to shoulder was, perhaps, worse than death.

Notes

RIVER WITHOUT BRIDGES

p. 3   '*We reached... Demmin*.' Irene Bröker, *So war's! Lebenserinnerungen 1922–1997*, Deutsches Tagebucharchiv Emmendingen, 131, p. 66.

p. 5   '*We got bogged... night's rest*.' Ibid.

p. 6   '*Wretched night... insoles*.' Gustav Adolf Skibbe, *Kriegstagebücher 1944–1945*, 13.3, Deutsches Tagebucharchiv Emmendingen, 1344, 1, n. pag.

p. 6   '*Everything at sixes... overcrowding in town*.' Ibid., 15.3.

p. 6   '*without much of note*.' Ibid., 24.3–27.3.

p. 7   '*She was forever... evenings*.' Marie Dabs, *Lebenserinnerungen*, Lübeck, 1984, p. 77.

p. 8   '*They joined... wife and daughter!*' Ibid., p. 78.

p. 8   '*It wasn't just... blessed, too*.' Ursula Strohschein, 'Rote Armee in Demmin', *Pommersche Zeitung*, 1. April 1995, 13/95, p. 16.

p. 9   '*Crammed full of strangers*'. Ibid.

p. 10   '*What will become... defend Demmin*.' Ibid.

p. 11   '*Things... fall apart*.' Wilhelm Damann, 'Die letzten Kriegstage

1945 in Demmin', Demminer Regionalmuseum, newspaper 5093, folio 2.

p. 11   '*beggared belief... a word.*' Marie Dabs, *Lebenserinnerungen*, p. 79.

p. 12   '*The Russians... River Oder!*' Ibid., p. 78.

p. 12   '*How naive I was.*' Ibid., p. 67.

p. 12   '*Why didn't I... ran its course.*' Ibid., p. 81.

p. 13   '*I had on my dark-grey... over my arm.*' Ibid., p. 80.

p. 13   '*for withdrawal purposes*'. Gustav Adolf Skibbe, *Kriegstagebücher*, 28.4.

p. 13   '*Murder. Manslaughter.*' Ibid., 30.4.

p. 13   '*hasty retreat*'. Ibid.

p. 13–14 '*Mum's birthday... allowed out.*' Ibid., 29.4.

p. 14   '*The telephone... around the town.*' Irene Bröker, *So war's!*, p. 67.

p. 15   '*But there we were... in a trap.*' Ibid., p. 68.

WAR WITHOUT LIMITS

p. 19   '*The time has come... a new war.*' Call from the 2nd Belorussian Front's Council of War, 16 April 1945.

p. 20   '*I do not... no longer tenable.*' Adolf Hitler, *Mein politisches Testament, Gegeben zu Berlin, den 29. April 1945, 4.00 Uhr*, folio 4.

p. 21   '*the potential suicide par excellence*'. Sebastian Haffner, *Germany: Jekyll & Hyde. 1939—Deutschland von innen betrachtet*, Berlin, 1998, p. 24.

p. 21   '*that the surrender... is impossible.*' Adolf Hitler, *Mein politisches Testament*, folio 6.

p. 22   '*I don't want... circumstance.*' Adolf Hitler to Otto Günsche, in: Walter Kempowski, *Swansong 1945: A Collective Diary of the Last Days of the Third Reich*, tr. Shaun Whiteside, London: Granta, 2014, p. 214. (Translation slightly modified.)

p. 22   '*Didn't sleep... make it?*' Gustav Adolf Skibbe, *Kriegstagebücher*, 30.4.

p. 23   '*Many, many people... rare sight now.*' Ursula Strohschein, 'Rote Armee in Demmin', p. 16.

p. 24   'Herr Stoldt... before they left.' Ibid., p. 44.

p. 24   'If only... future held?' Marie Dabs, *Lebenserinnerungen*, p. 81.

p. 25   'We managed... beloved Demmin.' Ibid.

THE EYES OF THE ENEMY

p. 28   'I myself... capitulation.' Adolf Hitler, *Mein politisches Testament*, folio 6.

p. 28–29 'It is our will... my people.' Ibid., folio 3.

p. 30   'We heard... in the distance.' Irene Bröker, *So war's!*, p. 67.

p. 30   'When we heard explosions... in my ears.' Ibid., p. 68.

p. 31   'He told us... into the sky.' Ibid., pp. 68–69.

p. 31   'When we got back... as far as Gnoien.' Gustav Adolf Skibbe, *Kriegstagebücher*, 30.4.

p. 32   'We young women... first Russian attack.' Maria Buske, 'Erinnerungen', in: Norbert Buske, *Das Kriegsende in Demmin 1945. Berichte—Erinnerungen—Dokumente*, Schwerin, 2007, p. 50.

p. 33   'He was too intelligent... in particular.' Wilhelm Damann, 'Die letzten Kriegstage 1945 in Demmin', folio 2.

p. 33   'Old Frau Rentner... a few Russians!' Ibid.

p. 34   'I see his act... played a part too.' Ibid., folio 3.

p. 34   'Gunshots cracked... out of the cellar.' Ursula Strohschein, 'Rote Armee in Demmin', p. 16.

p. 37   'His head... on her face.' Hitler's valet Heinz Linge, in: Walter Kempowski, *Swansong 1945*, p. 296. (Translation slightly modified.)

p. 38   'Look, that's... on fire.' Erich Mansfeld to staff sergeant Hermann Karnau, in: ibid., p. 297. (Translation slightly modified.)

p. 38   'Why they came... at the time.' Norbert Buske, 'Das Geschehen', in Norbert Buske, *Das Kriegsende in Demmin 1945*, p. 14.

p. 38   'A guard was posted... of his watch.' Maria Buske, 'Erinnerungen', in: ibid., p. 50.

p. 39   'My mother... all over Luisenstrasse.' Ursula Strohschein, 'Rote Armee in Demmin', p. 16.

p. 39   'but an uneasy... crept over us'. Ibid.

p. 40   'The Russians cut off children's tongues!' Karl Schlösser, conversation with the author, Demmin, 15 April 2014.

p. 41   'One of them ... with his rifle.' Ibid.

p. 41   'The lovely big farm ... Russians and Poles.' Marie Dabs, *Lebenserinnerungen*, p. 82.

p. 42   'Several Russians ... in a high arc.' Ibid., p. 83.

p. 42–43 'But in the end ... were saying.' Else R., 'Brief', in: Norbert Buske, *Das Kriegsende in Demmin 1945*, p. 31.

p. 43   'We immediately started ... for a good hour.' Ibid., pp. 31–32.

p. 44   'Ilse was ... it's not possible!'" Ibid., p. 32.

p. 45   'We cowered there ... bundle of fear.' Norbert Buske, 'Das Geschehen', in: ibid., p. 16.

TOWER OF DARKNESS

p. 47   'It was a cold ... burning town.' Marie Dabs, *Lebenserinnerungen*, p. 83.

p. 48   'Peering apprehensively ... Fire!' Ursula Strohschein, 'Rote Armee in Demmin', p. 16.

p. 49   'Day and night ... clouds of smoke.' Ibid.

p. 50   'Our beautiful tall ... to be seen.' Marie Dabs, *Lebenserinnerungen*, p. 86.

p. 50   'We must all get out of here.' Karl Schlösser, conversation with the author.

p. 51   'We're going ... your father!' Karl Schlösser, in: 'Tief vergraben, nicht dran rühren', *Spiegel Spezial*, 30.3.2005.

p. 51–52 'I am afraid ... awful truth.' Else R., 'Brief', in: Norbert Buske, *Das Kriegsende in Demmin 1945*, p. 31.

p. 52   'For you, Else.' Ibid., p. 32.

p. 52   'I was all confused ... hand in hand.' Ibid., p. 33.

p. 53   '"This is the last ... own blood."' Marie Dabs, *Lebenserinnerungen*, p. 84.

p. 53   'I asked them ... on their way.' Ibid.

p. 54   'When my father ... the Trebel.' Ibid., p. 85.

Notes

p. 57   *'My mother... like an avalanche.'* Lotte-Lore Martens, 'Erinnerungen zum Kriegsende in Demmin', in: Norbert Buske, *Das Kriegsende in Demmin 1945*, p. 26.

p. 57–58 *'With the smoke... in the water.'* Ibid., p. 28.

p. 58   *'Some women... I wonder?'* Ibid.

p. 62   *'Nobody knew... every night.'* Irene Bröker, *So war's!*, p. 70.

p. 62   *'Dr P. told us... washing ashore.'* Ibid.

p. 63   *'No one will ever... of darkness.'* Ibid., p. 71.

p. 63   *'At last... after that.'* Ibid.

p. 64   *'He pulled... at it bravely.'* Ibid., p. 73.

p. 64   *'When the woman... held me back.'* Ibid.

p. 64   *'All this sounds... will understand.'* Ibid.

THE GHOSTS OF DEMMIN

p. 66   *'The deserted dental practice... the horror.'* Ursula Strohschein, 'Rote Armee in Demmin', p. 16.

p. 66   *'A heavy blanket... dead bodies.'* Karl Schlösser, conversation with the author.

p. 67   *'The sight of the riverbank... worthless.'* Lotte-Lore Martens, 'Erinnerungen', in: Norbert Buske, *Das Kriegsende in Demmin 1945*, p. 29.

p. 69   *'Another thing... at a later date.'* Else R., 'Brief', in: ibid., p. 35.

p. 69   *'veterinary surgeon'.* Wareneingangsbuch der Demminer Friedhofsgärtnerei 1945.

p. 71   *'Death by suicide (hanging)'* etc. Sterbebücher des Standesamtes Demmin 1945, vol. 1 (1–300), vol. 2 (301–700), vol. 3 (701–1100).

A VOICE FROM THE BOMBED-OUT TEMPLE

p. 76   *'The parish hall was bursting.'* Jakob Kronika, *Der Untergang Berlins*, Flensburg, 1946, p. 40.

p. 76   *'Something of a sense... way they sing.'* Ibid., p. 51.

p. 76   *'We have no right... strange service.'* Ibid., p. 40.

p. 77 'There is risk... no way out.' Ibid., p. 41.

p. 77 'I can't carry on... madness and crime.' Ibid., p. 18.

p. 78 'But the tyranny... rule of evil.' Ibid., p. 19.

p. 78 'war's rebellion against peace'. Ibid., p. 9.

p. 79 'Wilhelm II... yesterday.' Ibid., p. 40.

p. 79 'Goebbels has changed... last resort.' Ibid., p. 39.

p. 79 'The brunt of responsibility... Dr Goebbels.' Ibid., p. 41.

A WAVE ROLLING OVER THE REICH

p. 80 'The thought of living on... hopelessness of victory.' Christian Goeschel, *Selbstmord im Dritten Reich*, Berlin, 2011, p. 213.

p. 81–82 'It was still hard... in public.' Hans Graf von Lehndorff, *Ostpreussisches Tagebuch. Aufzeichnungen eine Arztes aus den Jahren 1945–1947*, Munich, 2005, p. 9.

p. 82 'They must all... "and our country?"' Ibid.

p. 82 'The Führer... he'd sooner gas us.' Ibid., p. 18.

p. 82 'It doesn't really matter... now.' Ibid.

p. 83 'They are not... say, food.' Ibid., pp. 24–25.

p. 84 'We return to Juditten... Lord's Prayer.' Ibid., p. 25.

p. 84 'As we're coming... "with gas."' Ibid.

p. 85 'to fight the risk of contagion posed by suicide'. Ibid., p. 62.

p. 85 'A thorn is piercing... It is enough.' Ibid., p. 75.

p. 85 'There's nothing more... nothing impossible.' Ibid., p. 76.

p. 85 'All feeling... dead inside?' Ibid., p. 153.

p. 86 'Dead bodies... in the beds.' 'Erlebnisbericht aus L.S. aus Groß-Nappern', in: *Die Vertreibung der deutschen Bevölkerung aus den Gebieten östlich der Oder-Neiße*, Munich, 2004, vol. 1, no. 7, p. 25.

p. 86 'Shudder after shudder... all the family.' Ibid., no. 8, p. 31.

p. 86 'The most senior... last night.' Ibid., no. 14, p. 59.

p. 86 'In the course... in the tree.' Ibid., no. 53, p. 208.

p. 86–87 'When I said... that very day.' Ibid., no. 59, p. 229.

p. 87 'Mass graves... their own lives.' Ibid., no. 61, p. 237.

p. 87 'It's hardly surprising... that terrible night.' Ibid., no. 68, p. 266.

p. 87   *'In the forest… hanged themselves.'* Ibid., no. 72, p. 274.

p. 87   *'Several Germans… slitting their wrists.'* Ibid., no. 96, p. 360.

p. 87   *'Young Frau Lemke… his pistol.'* Ibid., no. 105, p. 399.

p. 87   *'In her despair… herself.'* Ibid., no. 116, p. 432.

p. 87   *'In the night… days later.'* Ibid., no. 122, p. 453.

p. 87   *'Countless suicides… indescribable.'* Ibid., no. 127, p. 468.

p. 87   *'My uncle… and ran away.'* Ibid., no. 129, pp. 475–76.

p. 87–88 *'The list of people… longer and longer.'* Ibid., vol. 2, no. 8, p. 29.

p. 88   *'On the evening… suicide.'* Ibid., no. 10, p. 35.

THE TEACHER AND HIS WIFE

p. 89   *'The war is over. The guns are silent.'* Hildegard Theinert, 'Der letzte Eintrag', in: Hans Richard Schnittny, *Erinnerungen*, Deutsches Tagebucharchiv Emmendingen 1106, p. 12.

p. 90   *'The rumours… "become of us?"'* Ibid.

p. 91   *'SS, field gendarmerie… upon us.'* Ibid.

p. 91   *'Johannes had… that evening.'* Ibid.

p. 91   *'Life would… did that.'* Ibid., pp. 12–13.

p. 91   *'We would… together.'* Ibid., p. 12.

p. 92   *'Glittering… rippling waters.'* Ibid., p. 13.

p. 92   *'I have said… happiness.'* Ibid.

p. 92   *'How lovely… the fortress.'* Ibid.

p. 92   *'The Russians… more and more.'* Ibid.

p. 92   *'Only a little… forever.'* Ibid.

p. 93   *'Who will… any meaning?'* Ibid.

HELL MACHINE

p. 94   *'I have shot… household.'* Suicide note from Generalmajor a.D. Karl Bernhard Wilhelm von Brozowski, in: Ursula Baumann, *Vom Recht auf den eigenen Tod. Die Geschichte des Suizids vom 18. bis zum 20. Jahrhundert*, Weimar, 2001, p. 377.

p. 96   *'I remember… all dead.'* Ludmila Woloshina, in: Eleonore Wolf, 'Das Kriegsende 1945 in Neubrandenburg,' in: *Zeitgeschichte* regional. *Mitteilungen aus Mecklenburg-Vorpommern*, 9:1, July 2005, p. 7.

p. 96 '*As I record… your hands?*' Renate Meinhof, 'Das Tagebuch der Maria Meinhof. April 1945 bis März 1946', in: *Pommern. Eine Spurensuche*, Reinbek bei Hamburg, 2006, p. 15.

p. 97 '*Sunday dawned… church.*' Ibid.

p. 97 '*Then the grandmothers… hanging.*' Ibid., pp. 54–55.

p. 98 '*Throw my children in after me.*' Ibid., p. 70.

p. 98 '*I could describe… fates.*' Ibid., p. 56.

p. 99 '*hell machine*'. Günter Jacobi, in: Nils Köhler, 'Das Drama von Alt Teterin 1945—ein Projektbericht', in: *Zeitgeschichte regional. Mitteilungen aus Mecklenburg-Vorpommern*, 14:1, July 2010, p. 93.

DEATH IN THE WEST

p. 101 '*Aged twelve… grown-ups.*' Johann Radein, *Wir sind wieder einmal davon gekommen*, Deutsches Tagebucharchiv Emmendingen 1300, p. 200.

p. 101–02 '*I don't dare… intimate scene.*' Ibid.

p. 102 '*My friend and I… told them so.*' Ibid., p. 201.

p. 102 '*It's over… to that.*' Ibid.

p. 103 '*I'll never forget… cemetery.*' Ibid.

p. 103 '*year of… and orphans*'. Leopold Reitz, *Jahre im Dunkel*, Neustadt an der Weinstraße, 1959, p. 46.

p. 103 '*Death is… matter of course.*' Ibid., p. 39.

p. 104 '*The motto… be dire.*' Ibid., p. 130.

p. 104 '*Not only… to blame.*' Ibid., p. 106.

p. 104 '*Hanged, shot… and drink.*' Ibid., p. 152.

p. 104 '*The list… talked out of it.*' Ibid., p. 199.

p. 105 '*I could see… clear eyes.*' Mathilde Wolff-Mönckeberg, *On the Other Side: Letters to My Children from Germany 1940–1946*, tr. Ruth Evans, London: Persephone Books, 2007, pp. 30–31. (Translation slightly modified.)

p. 105 '*as if she… tomorrow.*' Ibid., p. 101. (Translation slightly modified.)

p. 105 *'I am awfully... compels me.'* In: Christian Goeschel, *Selbstmord im Dritten Reich*, p. 252.

p. 105 *'A friend... the only one.'* Doris E., in: Lothar Steinbach, *Ein Volk, ein Reich, ein Glaube? Ehemalige Nationalsozialisten und Zeitzeugen berichten über ihr Leben im Dritten Reich*, Bonn, 1983, p. 94.

p. 106 *'A wave of suicides... they die.'* Udo von Alvensleben, *Lauter Abschiede. Tagebuch im Kriege*, Frankfurt, 1971, p. 448.

p. 106 *'Given my conduct... my shame.'* Horst Wilking, in: Walter Kempowski, *Swansong 1945*, p. 316. (Translation slightly modified.)

THE WAXWORKS OF LEIPZIG

p. 108 *'What kind... average man?'* Margaret Bourke-White, *'Dear Fatherland, Rest Quietly': A Report on the Collapse of Hitler's 'Thousand Years'*, New York: Simon and Schuster, 1946, p. 61.

p. 109 *'I know... individual terror.'* Ibid.

p. 109 *'Death seemed the only escape.'* Ibid., p. 43.

p. 109 *'During the retreat... Americans came.'* Ibid., p. 45.

p. 110 *'Making myself... ever had.'* Ibid.

p. 110 *'In its brief flare... fast enough.'* Ibid., p. 46.

p. 110 *'We didn't know! We didn't know!'* Ibid., p. 73.

p. 111 *'Hurry to the Rathaus... waxworks.'* Ibid., p. 49.

p. 111 *'Reclining... on the desk.'* Ibid., p. 50.

p. 112 *'In a nearby room... beside him.'* Ibid.

p. 113 *'beautiful landscape... by schizophrenics'.* Lee Miller, 'Germany, The War That Is Won', in: Antony Penrose (ed.), *Lee Miller's War: Photographer and Correspondent with the Allies in Europe 1944–45*, Boston: Bulfinch Press, 1992, p. 161.

p. 113 *'The love of death... themselves.'* Ibid., p. 176.

p. 114 *'A girl... waxen and dusty.'* Ibid.

p. 115 *'Our glorious idea... them myself.'* Magda Goebbels, letter to Harald Quandt, 28 April 1945.

Notes

CITY WITHOUT HOPE

p. 119 *'They should have been... indefinitely.'* Margret Boveri, *Tage des Überlebens. Berlin 1945*, Munich, 1970, p. 8.

p. 120 *'I'd had a small tin... when inhaled.'* Ibid., p. 108.

p. 120 *'In the last days... for bazookas.'* Ibid., p. 109.

p. 121–22 *'Can we really... life and death?'* Jacob Kronika, *Der Untergang Berlins*, p. 42.

p. 122 *'This paralysed nation... life and future.'* Ibid., p. 76.

p. 122 *'Not many people... no difference.'* Ibid., p. 91.

p. 123 *'Presumably a mother... never know.'* Ibid., p. 92.

p. 123 *'Death will catch... sweeping the country!'* Ibid.

p. 123 *'There are droves... right moment.'* Ibid., p. 124.

p. 123–24 *'We see something... dead Germans.'* Ibid.

p. 124 *'If you are dishonoured... but to die.'* Ruth Andreas-Friedrich, *Schauplatz Berlin. Tagebuchaufzeichnungen 1945 bis 1948*, Frankfurt am Main, 1984, p. 23.

p. 124 *'It's over... He went.'* Friederike Grensemann in: Walter Kempowski, *Swansong*, p. 70.

p. 124 *'It was so hard... my throat!'* Ibid., p. 289.

p. 126 *'It is up to us... a sin.'* Jakob Kronika, *Der Untergang Berlins*, p. 194.

p. 126 *'Who are we... unbearable.'* Ibid., p. 193.

THE DARK FIGURE

p. 131 *'In their fear... wiped out.'* Letter from municipal employee I.R. from Schönlanke, Netzekreis, Pomerania, in: *Die Vertreibung der deutschen Bevölkerung*, vol. 2, no. 196, p. 214.

THE WOUND THAT WAS GERMANY

p. 135 *'The din from... glorious mystery.'* Melita Maschmann, *Fazit. Mein Weg in der Hitler-Jugend*, Munich, 1979, p. 11. (Translator's note: the translations from this book are my own, but for the full text see Geoffrey Strachan's translation, Melita Maschmann, *Account*

Rendered: A Dossier on my Former Self, Lexington, Massachusetts: Plunkett Lake Press, 2016.)

p. 136 *'She loved... in her love.'* Ibid., p. 10.

p. 136 *'Even before... dear and vulnerable.'* Ibid.

p. 137 *'That's how wide... German society.'* Gerhard Starcke, *Mit Stenoblock und Kübelwagen. Berichte meines Lebens 1907–1972*, Deutsches Tagebucharchiv Emmendingen 1479, p. 63.

p. 137 *'One belief... for EVERYTHING.'* Ibid., p. 87.

p. 138 *'The age into which... a new world war.'* Ilse Cordes, *Erinnerungen an den Sohn 1921–1941*, Deutsches Tagebucharchiv Emmendigen 1428/II, p. 1.

p. 139 *'The pair of them... darling mother!'* Ibid.

p. 139 *'And so... of his life.'* Ibid., p. 2.

p. 140 *'Day after day... from despair.'* Ibid., p. 3.

p. 140 *'It wasn't possible... a poor country.'* Melita Maschmann, *Fazit*, p. 14.

p. 140 *'It was an awful... bitter resort.'* Gerhard Starcke, *Mit Stenoblock und Kübelwagen*, p. 78.

p. 141 *'I know I'm lonely.'* Renate Finkh, *Sie versprachen uns die Zukunft. Eine Jugend in Nationalsozialismus*, Tübingen, 2002, p. 31.

p. 141 *'But there was... more keenly.'* Ibid., p. 50.

p. 141 *'The men wore... large eyes.'* Ibid.

p. 142 *'Sex, murder... Particularly bloodshed.'* Sefton Delmer, *Trail Sinister: An Autobiography*, vol. 1, London: Secker & Warburg, 1961, p. 75.

p. 142 *'Looking back... Vesuvius eruption.'* Ibid.

p. 142–43 *'Complete liberty... compartmentalising.'* Stéphane Roussel, *Les Collines de Berlin: un regard sur l'Allemagne*, Paris: Éditions Mazarine, 1985, p. 30.

p. 143 *'It did not surprise... hungry too.'* Sebastian Haffner, *Defying Hitler: A Memoir*, tr. Oliver Pretzel, London: Phoenix, 2011, p. 48. (Translation slightly modified.)

p. 143 *'Indeed, my father... the times.'* Ibid.

p. 144 *'the uncurbed, cynical... end in itself.'* Ibid., p. 44.

p. 144 '*A generation… chaos and peril.*' Ibid., p. 57.

HUNGRY AND FANATICAL

p. 145 '*Indeed, the mood… save the world.*' Sebastian Haffner, *Defying Hitler*, p. 53.

p. 146 '*What impressed me… than ever before.*' Sefton Delmer, *Trail Sinister*, p. 97.

p. 148 '*Would-be intruders… up to anyone.*' Reiner Hamm, *Erinnerungen*, German Diaries Archive Emmendingen, 1815, p. 81.

p. 148 '*It was depressing… nothing moved.*' Ibid., p. 82.

p. 149 '*My father was moved to tears.*' Ibid., p. 85.

p. 149 '*We Germans prefer… and waiting.*' Gerhard Starcke, *Mit Steno-block und Kübelwagen*, p. 88.

p. 150 '*It was mass… a revelation.*' Ibid., p. 92.

p. 150 '*was that he… about Versailles*'. Ibid.

p. 150–51 '*When they talked… including us.*' Renate Finkh, *Sie versprachen uns die Zukunft*, p. 58.

p. 151 '*He said the… save Germany.*' Ibid., pp. 60–61.

p. 151 '*Songs are sung… going on.*' Ibid., p. 61.

p. 151 '*There is something… fire is dancing.*' Ibid., p. 62.

p. 152 '*I have become… found a saviour.*' M. Hoffmann, Der Retter (n.d.), in: Henrik Eberle (ed.), *Briefe an Hitler. Ein Volk schreibt seinem Führer. Unbekannte Dokumente aus Moskauer Archiven—zum ersten Mal veröffentlicht*, Bergisch Gladbach, 2007, p. 117.

p. 152 '*But no one… no convictions whatsoever.*' René Juvet, *Ich war dabei. 20 Jahre Nationalsozialismus 1923–1943. Ein Tatsachenbericht*, Zurich, 1944, p. 18.

p. 152 '*Brüning may not… that landslide.*' Ibid., p. 24.

TORCHES IN WINTER, VIOLETS IN MARCH

p. 153 '*I have nothing… southern Germany.*' René Juvet, *Ich war dabei*, p. 26.

p. 153–54 '*On the whole… very dejected indeed.*' Ibid., p. 31.

p. 155 '*No rallying cry… community.*' Melita Maschmann, *Fazit*, p. 8.

p. 155–56 'Her dark eyes... appealed to me.' Ibid., p. 7.

p. 156 'What was I... drift with it.' Ibid., pp. 8–9.

p. 157 'It was a matter... life and death.' Ibid., p. 9.

p. 157 'I wanted... of my contemporaries.' Ibid.

p. 157 'People shout... as possible.' Stéphane Roussel, *Les Collines de Berlin*, p. 62.

p. 158 'There are few... the theatre.' Sebastian Haffner, *Defying Hitler*, p. 86.

p. 158 'but I did... interpret it'. Ibid., p. 85. (Translation slightly modified.)

p. 159 'All this was... business as usual.' Ibid., p. 91.

p. 160 'His eyes widened... the sun.' Sefton Delmer, *Trail Sinister*, p. 149.

p. 161 'Hitler himself... German fatherland.' Ibid., p. 151.

p. 162 'In 1933... took second place.' Reiner Hamm, *Erinnerungen*, p. 93.

p. 162 'We were surrounded... in Munich.' Ibid., 97.

p. 163 'The faster you act... conviction.' René Juvet, *Ich war dabei*, pp. 31–32.

p. 165 'As my parents... sacrifice.' Melita Maschmann, *Fazit*, p. 17.

p. 165 'Because I was... hoi polloi.' Ibid., p. 19.

p. 165 'That's why... one big family.' Ibid., p. 21.

p. 166–67 'Many who had... everyone else.' Stéphane Roussel, *Les Collines de Berlin*, p. 90.

p. 167 'The next time... tailor-made suit.' Ibid., p. 92.

PART OF SOMETHING GREATER

p. 169 'The solemnity... sense of importance.' Renate Finkh, *Sie versprachen uns die Zukunft*, p. 114.

p. 169 'It is the first... to the heart.' Ibid., p. 115.

p. 169 'I am no longer... name is Germany.' Ibid., p. 116.

p. 170 'We lived like... Brandenburg!' Ilse Cordes, *Erinnerungen an den Sohn*, p. 13.

p. 170 'Just look... frighteningly pale.' Ibid., p. 20.

p. 171 'These are difficult... deep filial love.' Ibid., p. 15.

p. 171 'Like all those... always would,' Johann Radein, *Wir sind wieder einmal*, p. 14.

Notes

p. 171 'The oath of allegiance... overwhelming.' Ibid., p. 67.

p. 171-72 'It's quite an experience... as we go.' Ibid., p. 91.

p. 173 'My youth... silent majority.' Lore Walb, *Ich, die Alte—Ich, die Junge. Konfrontation mit meinen Tagebüchern 1933–1945*, Berlin, 1997, p. 24.

p. 173 'I have a clear... speaking.' Ibid., p. 72.

p. 173 'One for all... no community.' Ibid.

p. 174 'Just as, in my dream... Hitler's picture.' Ibid., p. 88.

p. 174 'We were very popular... somehow special.' Ibid., p. 108.

p. 174 'rose daily... Führer's will!' Sebastian Haffner, *Defying Hitler*, p. 159.

p. 175 'Now we were... fear of me.' Ibid., p. 210.

p. 175 'We trusted... civilian life?' Ibid., p. 231.

p. 175 'You are under... inhuman.' Ibid., p. 236. (Translation slightly modified.)

AN INNER RIFT

p. 178 'One has no right... these lines.' Melita Maschmann, *Fazit*, p. 21.

p. 178 'Our parents may have... natural.' Ibid., p. 41.

p. 178 'At the time... of life, then.' Ibid., p. 43.

p. 179 'But it went against... no harm.' Renate Finkh, *Sie versprachen uns die Zukunft*, p. 78.

p. 180 'I pushed it... stench pervaded.' Ibid., p. 80.

p. 180 'We sang the same... depression.' Johann Radein, *Wir sind wieder einmal*, p. 104.

p. 180 'fell into a... very lonely'. Ibid.

p. 181 'Strangely enough... against the horror.' Sebastian Haffner, *Defying Hitler*, p. 114.

p. 181 'The only way... of reality.' Ibid., p. 169. (Translation slightly modified.)

THE HAPPY YEARS

p. 184 'There was something... in Germany.' Marie Dabs, *Lebenserinnerungen*, p. 54.

Notes

p. 184 *'I filled... long in coming,'* Ibid., p. 55.

p. 184 *'Everyone wanted... that evening.'* Ibid., pp. 61–62.

p. 185 *'Dad was full... right.'* Renate Finkh, *Sie versprachen uns die Zukunft*, p. 76.

p. 185 *'I often sat... proud of me.'* Ibid., p. 97.

p. 186 *'The sight of him... of life.'* Lore Walb, *Ich, die Alte—Ich, die Junge*, pp. 35–36.

p. 187 *'We are living... thick and fast.'* Ibid., p. 75.

p. 187 *'If he could only... his goal.'* Ibid., p. 76.

p. 188 *'Anyone who had... with him ideologically.'* René Juvet, *Ich war dabei*, p. 40.

p. 188 *'You've grown small-minded... had a Hitler.'* Ibid., p. 43.

p. 189 *'He had conquered... satisfied.'* Ibid., 74.

IN LOVE WITH THE FÜHRER

p. 190 *'Germany... with Hitler.'* Sefton Delmer, *Trail Sinister*, p. 282.

p. 190 *'They were adoring... when to cheer.'* Ibid.

p. 191 *'[T]hey all... authority over others.'* Ibid., p. 283.

p. 192 *'Suddenly, the storm... poured in.'* Stéphane Roussel, *Les Collines de Berlin*, p. 74.

p. 192 *'Since Hitler... without reaching him.'* Ibid.

p. 192 *'[T]hey're yours... and yours.'* Ibid., p. 76.

p. 193 *'It wasn't you he was talking to.'* Ibid., p. 79.

p. 194 *'The Führer's emotive... full of energy.'* Johann Radein, *Wir sind wieder einmal*, p. 184.

p. 195 *'His blue eyes... see every flaw.'* Gerhard Starcke, *Mit Stenoblock und Kübelwagen*, p. 103.

p. 195 *'Those years... reality set in.'* Martin Sieg, *Im Schatten der Wolffschanze. Hitlerjunge auf der Suche nach dem Sinn*, Münster, 1997, p. 24.

p. 196 *'I saw Hitler... gave me his hand.'* Ibid., p. 61.

p. 197 *'I felt somehow... almost numb.'* Ibid.

THE SMELL OF FEAR

p. 199 'For a second... fait accompli.' Melita Maschmann, *Fazit*, p. 58.

p. 199 'I pushed the memory... of my life.' Ibid.

p. 199 'All this could... fast asleep?' Renate Finkh, *Sie versprachen uns die Zukunft*, p. 124.

p. 200 'But you and I... do you hear!' Ibid., p. 125.

p. 200 'I clearly recall... any of it!' Lore Walb, *Ich, die Alte—Ich, die Junge*, p. 120.

p. 201 'I ask him... clear to me.' René Juvet, *Ich war dabei*, p. 82.

p. 202 'Dear God!...nights on end.' Marie Dabs, *Lebenserinnerungen*, p. 67.

p. 202 'He couldn't... How naive I was!' Ibid.

p. 203 'Nobody joined... anthem either.' René Juvet, *Ich war dabei*, p. 95.

p. 203 'I remember... everywhere.' Melita Maschmann, *Fazit*, p. 59.

p. 204 'Anyone who has... way of life.' Ibid., p. 64.

VICTORS

p. 205 'Last great test of fate.' Gerhard Starcke, *Mit Stenoblock und Kübel-wagen*, p. 181.

p. 205 'It was only now... our fathers.' Ibid., p. 188.

p. 206 'It didn't occur... and necessary.' Ibid.

p. 206 'I said to myself... necessity.' Melita Maschmann, *Fazit*, p. 73.

p. 206 'I developed... that foreign nation.' Ibid., p. 71.

p. 207 'Our life... difficult duty.' Ibid., p. 76.

p. 208 'My dears... I've made it!' Ilse Cordes, *Erinnerungen an den Sohn*, Anhang: Feldpostbrief von Hermann-Friedrich Cordes vom 1.2.1941.

p. 208 'It is a proud... and detached.' Ibid., 4.5.1941.

p. 209 'Isn't it terrific?... you.' Lore Walb, *Ich, die Alte—Ich, die Junge*, p. 177.

p. 209 'The words and cadences... I weep...' Ibid., p. 131.

p. 209 'World history... to be German.' Ibid., p. 141.

p. 210 'It's strange to think... living in.' Ibid., p. 186.

p. 210 'For the first time... wrong.' Ibid., p. 200.

Notes

A SENSE OF FOREBODING

p. 211   'Mum's standing... for real.' Renate Finkh, *Sie versprachen uns die Zukunft*, p. 173.

p. 212   'That moment... wisely and responsibly.' Melita Maschmann, *Fazit*, p. 97.

p. 212   'The people around me... to rain.' Ibid.

p. 213   'My dears... in advance.' Ilse Cordes, *Erinnerungen an den Sohn*, Anhang: Feldpostbrief von Hermann-Friedrich Cordes vom 21.6.1941.

p. 213   'I'd like to embrace... your Reich!' Ibid., 8.7.1941.

p. 213   'Despite the hard blows... premature end.' Ibid., p. 1.

p. 214   'He didn't give... higher things.' Ibid., p. 22.

p. 215   'We received quantities... rather think not.' Marie Dabs, *Lebenserinnerungen*, p. 72.

p. 215   'By then... would end up.' Ibid.

p. 215   'They all had... suddenly all alone.' Ibid., p. 75.

p. 216   'The war had carved... untouched.' René Juvet, *Ich war dabei*, p. 121.

p. 216   'Germany, he said... point of this war.' Ibid., p. 129.

p. 217–18 'I was often... what was happening.' Johann Radein, *Wir sind wieder einmal*, p. 71.

p. 218   'Fear, pain and grief... her grief.' Ibid., p. 45.

p. 218–19 'He turned up... remained cool.' Renate Finkh, *Sie versprachen uns die Zukunft*, pp. 200–201.

p. 219   'The days ticked on... stopping.' Ibid., p. 202.

p. 219   'I remember... gave me the chills.' Ibid., p. 204.

p. 220   'A German girl... do everything.' Ibid., p. 208.

p. 220   'His hate-filled eyes... murderers, too?' Ibid. p. 209.

p. 221   'That day... without realising.' Melita Maschmann, *Fazit*, p. 113.

p. 221   'What was evil... desperate situation.' Ibid.

THE SHADOW OF OTHERS

p. 222   'For reasons... damage.' René Juvet, *Ich war dabei*, p. 128.

Notes

p. 223 'Those people… killed there.' Renate Finkh, *Sie versprachen uns die Zukunft*, p. 219.

p. 223 'From then on… hidden in shadow.' Ibid., p. 220.

p. 224 'What did the Poles do to her?' Ibid., 225.

p. 224 'We have to… will be awful.' Ibid., p. 226.

p. 225 'If the Führer… we think.' Johann Radein, *Wir sind wieder einmal*, p. 222.

p. 225 'That traumatic incident… friend and me.' Ibid.

p. 225 'But what will come after defeat?' Ibid., p. 224.

p. 226 'We have to stay… win the war.' René Juvet, *Ich war dabei*, p. 129.

p. 226 'If Germany… will be killed.' Ibid., p. 138.

FROZEN SOUL

p. 228 'I have to go… going to end?' René Juvet, *Ich war dabei*, p. 153.

p. 228 'No aspect… contradictions and extremes.' Ibid., p. 155.

p. 229 'This speechlessness… felt it myself.' Johann Radein, *Wir sind wieder einmal*, p. 214.

p. 230 'Reluctantly I take… kitchen wall.' Ibid., p. 262.

p. 230 'I was ashamed… more than ever.' Renate Finkh, *Sie versprachen uns die Zukunft*, p. 237.

p. 230 'In the chill… soul was frozen.' Ibid., p. 221.

p. 231 'I could see… I had said.' Ibid., p. 259.

p. 231 'We'd got into… allow for collapse.' Ibid., p. 259.

p. 231 'Everything I'd built… falling apart.' Ibid., p. 263.

p. 232 'Even at this stage… filled the room.' Gerhard Starcke, *Mit Stenoblock und Kübelwagen*, p. 338.

p. 233 'Those who had led… with them.' Ibid.

p. 233 'I was quite certain… go with it.' Melita Maschmann, *Fazit*, p. 175.

p. 234 'A swarming frenzy… danse macabre.' Ibid., pp. 156–157.

p. 235 'I was filled… end up surviving.' Ibid. p. 175.

p. 235 'I had no plans for the future.' Ibid. p. 180.

p. 236 'What fate… to be destroyed???' Lore Walb, *Ich, die Alte—Ich, die Junge*, p. 253.

Notes

p. 236 *'But we mustn't...end of the war?'* Ibid., p. 301.

p. 237 *'My mind alone... never again.'* Ibid., p. 344.

p. 237 *'Better dead than slaves.'* Martin Sieg, *Im Schatten der Wolfsschanze*, pp. 76–77.

p. 237 *'What possible reason... dark thoughts.'* Ibid., 168.

p. 237–38 *'Your mum said... lost you already.'* Ibid., p. 93.

CURTAINING OFF REALITY

p. 241 *'Our philosophy... than reason.'* Baldur von Schirach, *Hitler-Jugend. Idee und Gestalt*, Leipzig, 1934, p. 130.

p. 242 *'The past... illusion.'* Martin Sieg, *Im Schatten der Wolfsschanze*, p. 87.

p. 242 *'That letter... with the past.'* Ibid., pp. 95–96.

p. 243 *'Life had slammed... to yesterday.'* Ibid., p. 97.

p. 243 *'That way I... self-destruction.'* Melita Maschmann, *Fazit*, p. 195.

p. 244 *'There was only one... altogether.'* Ibid., p. 205.

p. 244 *'The destruction... didn't add up.'* Julius Posener, *In Deutschland 1945 bis 1946*, Berlin, 2001, p. 18.

p. 245 *'What was that... bottom of an abyss.'* Ibid. pp. 18–19.

p. 246 *'A lot of Germans... awful as that?'* Ibid. p. 25.

p. 246 *'Nowhere is this... evident everywhere.'* Hannah Arendt, 'The Aftermath of Nazi Rule', p. 342.

p. 247 *'Germans mail... in their midst.'* Ibid.

AN INABILITY TO FEEL

p. 248–49 *'This general lack... what really happened.'* Hannah Arendt, 'The Aftermath of Nazi Rule', p. 342.

p. 249 *'a half-conscious refusal... inability to feel.'* Ibid.

p. 250 *'He's at peace... war has destroyed.'* Lore Walb, *Ich, die Alte—Ich, die Junge*, p. 338.

p. 250 *'Hitler is dead... anymore.'* Ibid., 345.

p. 251 *'Until we awoke... struck with blindness.'* Gerhard Starcke, *Mit Stenoblock und Kübelwagen*, p. 383.

p. 252 *'Hitler was dead!... to rain.'* Melita Maschmann, *Fazit*, p. 187.

p. 252 'What had happened...loved Hitler.' Stéphane Roussel, *Les Collines de Berlin*, p. 247.

p. 253 'When I tell...elicits a reaction.' Ibid., p. 242.

p. 253 'It was best...talented authors.' Ibid., p. 248.

VICTIMS

p. 254 'For most Germans...victims of them.' Stéphane Roussel, *Les Collines de Berlin*, p. 242.

p. 255 'This is usually...cancels the other...' Hannah Arendt, 'The Aftermath of Nazi Rule', p. 342.

p. 256 'But what about...abandoned.' Lore Walb, *Ich, die Alte—Ich, die Junge*, p. 338.

p. 256 'What a course...to see this!' Ibid.

p. 257 'I despised those...necessary.' Melita Maschmann, *Fazit*, p. 205.

p. 258 'I saw my return...my release.' Gerhard Starcke, *Mit Stenoblock und Kübelwagen*, p. 380.

p. 258 'The English can't have probed very deeply.' Ibid., p. 379.

p. 258 'However bleak...turn for the better.' Ibid., p. 411.

p. 259 'Watching the Germans...against reality.' Hannah Arendt, 'The Aftermath of Nazi Rule', p. 345.

GHOSTS OF THE FORGOTTEN

p. 260 'But this is not real...no longer touch.' Hannah Arendt, 'The Aftermath of Nazi Rule', p. 345.

p. 261 'hardly recognised anyone'. Renate Finkh, *Sie versprachen uns die Zukunft*, p. 265.

p. 261 'I had to keep...upset anyone.' Ibid., p. 266.

p. 262 'Guilt and shame...loyalty evil too.' Ibid., p. 268.

p. 262 'Many had felt...youth like that?' Ibid., p. 269.

p. 263 'Sometimes I'd be...eased off.' Melita Maschmann, *Fazit*, p. 212.

p. 263 'Emotionally and psychologically...rock bottom.' Ibid., p. 213.

p. 264 'The line...without our noticing.' Ibid., p. 239.

Sources and Bibliography

DIARIES, MEMOIRS, REPORTS

Hannah Arendt, 'The Aftermath of Nazi Rule: Report from Germany', *Commentary* 10, 1950, pp. 342–353.

Margaret Bourke-White, *'Dear Fatherland, Rest Quietly': A Report on the Collapse of Hitler's 'Thousand Years'*, New York: Simon and Schuster, 1946.

Margret Boveri, *Tage des Überlebens. Berlin 1945*, Munich, 1970.

Irene Bröker, *So war's! Lebenserinnerungen 1922–1997*, Deutsches Tagebucharchiv Emmendingen, 131.

Norbert Buske, *Das Kriegsende in Demmin 1945. Berichte—Erinnerungen—Dokumente*, Schwerin, 2007.

Norbert Buske, conversation with the author, Greifswald, 16 April 2014.

Ilse Cordes, *Erinnerungen an den Sohn 1921–1941*, Deutsches Tagebucharchiv Emmendingen, 1428/II.

Marie Dabs, *Lebenserinnerungen*, Lübeck, 1984.

Wilhelm Damann, 'Die letzten Kriegstage 1945 in Demmin', Demminer Regionalmuseum, newspaper 5093.

Sefton Delmer, *Trail Sinister: An Autobiography*, Volume One, London: Secker & Warburg, 1961.

Henrik Eberle (ed.), *Letters to Hitler*, ed. Victoria Harris, tr. Steven Rendall, Cambridge: Polity Press, 2012.

Sources and Bibliography

Renate Finkh, *Sie versprachen uns die Zukunft. Eine Jugend im Nationalso-zialismus*, Tübingen, 2002.

Sebastian Haffner, *Defying Hitler: A Memoir*, tr. Oliver Pretzel, London: Phoenix, 2011.

Sebastian Haffner, *Germany: Jekyll & Hyde. 1939—Deutschland von innen betrachtet*, Berlin, 1998.

Reiner Hamm, *Erinnerungen*, German Diaries Archive Emmendingen, 1815.

Adolf Hitler, *Mein politisches Testament*, Berlin, 29 April 1945.

René Juvet, *Ich war dabei. 20 Jahre Nationalsozialismus 1923–1943. Ein Tatsachenbericht*, Zurich, 1944.

Walter Kempowski, *Swansong 1945: A Collective Diary of the Last Days of the Third Reich*, tr. Shaun Whiteside, London: Granta, 2014.

Jacob Kronika, *Der Untergang Berlins*, Flensburg, 1946.

Hans Graf von Lehndorff, *Ostpreussisches Tagebuch. Aufzeichnungen eine Arztes aus den Jahren 1945–1947*, Munich, 2005.

Oliver Lubrich (ed.), *Travels in the Reich, 1933-1945: Foreign Authors Report from Germany*, tr. Kenneth J. Northcott, Sonia Wichmann and Dean Krouk, Chicago: University of Chicago Press, 2010.

Melita Maschmann, *Account Rendered: A Dossier on my Former Self*, tr. Geoffrey Strachan, Lexington, Massachusetts: Plunkett Lake Press, 2016.

Renate Meinhof, *Das Tagebuch der Maria Meinhof. April 1945 bis März 1946 in Pommern. Eine Spurensuche*, Reinbek bei Hamburg, 2006.

Antony Penrose (ed.), *Lee Miller's War: Photographer and Correspondent with the Allies in Europe 1944–45*, Boston: Bulfinch Press, 1992.

Julius Posener, *In Deutschland 1945 bis 1946*, Berlin, 2001.

Johann Radein, *Wir sind wieder einmal davongekommen*, Deutsches Tage-bucharchiv Emmendingen, 1300.

Leopold Reitz, *Jahre im Dunkel*, Neustadt an der Weinstrasse, 1959.

Stéphane Roussel, *Les Collines de Berlin: un regard sur l'Allemagne*, Paris: Éditions Mazarine, 1985.

Karl Schlösser, conversation with the author, Demmin, 15 April 2014.

Sources and Bibliography

Martin Sieg, *Im Schatten der Wolffschanze. Hitlerjunge auf der Suche nach dem Sinn*, Münster, 1997.

Gustav Adolf Skibbe, *Kriegstagebücher 1944–1945*, Deutsches Tagebucharchiv Emmendingen, 1344.

Gerhard Starcke, *Mit Stenoblock und Kübelwagen. Berichte meines Lebens 1907–1972*, Deutsches Tagebucharchiv Emmendingen, 1479.

Sterbebücher des Standesamtes Demmin 1945 (Demmin Registry Office death registers 1945), vol. 1–3.

Ursula Strohschein, 'Rote Armee in Demmin', *Pommersche Zeitung*, 1 April 1995, 13/95.

Hildegard Theinert, 'Der letzte Eintrag', in: Hans Richard Schittny, *Erinnerungen*, Deutsches Tagebucharchiv Emmendingen, 1106.

Die Vertreibung der deutschen Bevölkerung aus den Gebieten östlich der Oder-Neisse, Munich, 2004.

Lore Walb, *Ich, die Alte—Ich, die Junge. Konfrontation mit meinen Tagebüchen 1933–1945*, Berlin, 1997.

Wareneingangsbuch der Demminer Friedhofsgärtnerei 1945, Friedhofsverwaltung Demmin (Demmin Cemetery Nursery Record of Incoming Goods 1945, Cemetery Administration, Demmin).

Mathilde Wolff-Mönckeberg, *On the Other Side: Letters to My Children from Germany 1940–1946*, tr. Ruth Evans, London: Persephone Books, 2007.

SELECT BIBLIOGRAPHY

Götz Aly, *Hitlers Volksstaat. Raub, Rassenkrieg und nationaler Sozialismus*, Frankfurt, 2005.

Antony Beevor, *Berlin: The Downfall 1945*, London: Penguin, 2002.

Richard Bessel, 'Hatred after War. Emotion and the Postwar History of East Germany', *History and Memory*, 17/2005.

Martin Broszat, 'Soziale Motivation und Führer-Bindung des Nationalsozialismus', *Vierteljahrshefte für Zeitgeschichte*, 18/1970.

Petra Clemens, *Das Kriegsende in Demmin 1945. Umgang mit einem schwierigen Thema*, Demmin, 2013.

Sources and Bibliography

Joachim Fest, *Inside Hitler's Bunker: The Last Days of the Third Reich*, tr. Margot Bettauer Dembo, New York: Farrar, Straus and Giroux, 2004.

Norbert Frei, *Der Führerstaat*, Munich, 2013.

Robert Gellately, *Backing Hitler: Consent and Coercion in Nazi Germany*, Oxford: OUP, 2002.

Christian Goeschel, *Suicide in Nazi Germany*, Oxford: OUP, 2009.

Richard Grunberger, *The 12-Year Reich: A Social History of Nazi Germany*, New York: Holt, Rinehart and Winston, 1971.

Ludolf Herbst, *Hitlers Charisma. Die Erfindung eines deutschen Messias*, Frankfurt, 2010.

Ian Kershaw, *The End: Hitler's Germany 1944–45*, London: Allen Lane, 2011.

Ian Kershaw, *The 'Hitler Myth': Image and Reality in the Third Reich*, Oxford: Clarendon Press, 1982.

Peter Longerich, *'Davon haben wir nichts gewusst!'. Die Deutschen und die Judenverfolgung 1933–1945*, Munich, 2006.

Eva-Maria Muschik, *Kollektive Selbsttötung in Deutschland 1945 am Beispiel der Stadt Neustrelitz*, Berlin, 2009.

Sönke Neitzel/Harald Welzer, *Soldaten. Protokolle vom Kämpfen, Töten und Sterben*, Frankfurt, 2011.

Hans Dieter Schäfer, *Das gespaltene Bewusstsein. Vom Dritten Reich bis zu den langen Fünfziger Jahren*, Göttingen, 2009.

Thomas Scheck, 'Echt deutsch und national—Die vorpommersche Kleinstadt Demmin im Jahr 1933', *Zeitgeschichte regional. Mitteilungen aus Mecklenburg-Vorpommern*, 4/2, December 2000.

Illustrations

DR FLORIAN HUBER is the author of several works of history, including a recent study of the dramas of German family life in the postwar period. He has also produced award-winning documentaries on contemporary subjects, such as the fall of the Berlin Wall, the mysterious end of the poet Antoine de Saint-Exupéry and the 1936 Olympic Games.

IMOGEN TAYLOR is a literary translator based in Berlin. Her translations include *Fear* and *Twins* by Dirk Kurbjuweit, Sascha Arango's *The Truth and Other Lies* and Melanie Raabe's *The Trap* and *The Stranger*.